A
0

J

PREVENTING ADOLESCENT PREGNANCY

OTHER RECENT VOLUMES IN THE
SAGE FOCUS EDITIONS

PREVENTING ADOLESCENT PREGNANCY

Model Programs and Evaluations

Brent C. Miller
Josefina J. Card
Roberta L. Paikoff
James L. Peterson
editors

SAGE PUBLICATIONS
International Educational and Professional Publisher
Newbury Park   London   New Delhi

Copyright © 1992 by Sage Publications, Inc.

For information address:

 SAGE Publications, Inc.
2455 Teller Road
Newbury Park, California 91320

SAGE Publications Ltd.
6 Bonhill Street
London EC2A 4PU
United Kingdom

SAGE Publications India Pvt. Ltd.
M-32 Market
Greater Kailash I
New Delhi 110 048 India

Printed in the United States of America

Library of Congress Cataloging-in-Publication Data

Main entry under title:

Preventing adolescent pregnancy: model programs and evaluations /
  Brent C. Miller . . . [et al.].
       p.   cm.—(Sage focus editions; 140)
   Includes bibliographical references and index.
   ISBN 0-8039-4390-3.—ISBN 0-8039-4391-1 (pb)
   1. Birth control—United States. 2. Teenage pregnancy—United
States. I. Miller, Brent C.
HQ766.8.P74 1992
363.9'6'0835—dc20   91-45070

92 93 94 95 10 9 8 7 6 5 4 3 2 1

Sage Production Editor: Diane S. Foster

Contents

Preface

Prevention efforts aim to reduce the incidence of a problem behavior, event, or disorder. In the early 1990s, research and policy interest in preventing adolescent pregnancy continues at a high level because pregnancy begins the process of family formation and because early parenthood is often problematic. Adolescents themselves, the children born to them, their parents, and frequently others of us as friends, taxpayers, and professionals are affected adversely by early unintended pregnancies. Federal agencies and private foundations have recognized the need to develop adolescent pregnancy prevention programs and, more recently, to evaluate seriously their effects.

The purpose of this book is to highlight model adolescent pregnancy prevention programs that have included rigorous evaluation designs. While many others will find this book interesting and useful, we expect that its greatest value will be for three groups of professionals. The first audience consists of professionals who design and deliver programs to prevent adolescent pregnancy. The second potential audience consists of researchers and scholars whose main concern is evaluating and estimating the effects of such programs. The third audience consists of policy makers and public and private agency officials who must consider alternative solutions to the problems of adolescent pregnancy and parenthood. It is critically important for program planners, evaluators, and agency officials to be aware of the program principles and evaluation methods that have shown the greatest promise for preventing adolescent pregnancy. Sexual intercourse and contraceptive behavior determine the risk of pregnancy and are the focus of prevention efforts. Empirical and ideological controversies about the relative merits of abstinence and contraceptive programs exist, but the basic facts are quite clear: fewer pregnancies will result if the onset of sexual intercourse among adolescents is postponed or its frequency reduced. And, fewer pregnancies will occur if adolescents use an effective contraceptive from the first time they have sex and if they consistently use contraceptives from then on. In this book we have deliberately featured programs that seek to influence both sexual and contraceptive risk behaviors, whether separately or in combination.

The introductory chapter has been written to provide a context for the more focused chapters that follow. The body of the book is a collection of chapters written by program developers and/or evaluators about programs they know well. Each chapter provides a description of the program and its evaluation, including the program elements, the evaluation design, the evaluation results, and finally, both programmatic and evaluation lessons and recommendations. The programs included are very diverse, ranging from those with a focus on delaying sexual involvement to those that emphasize effective contraceptive use. The concluding chapter integrates and synthesizes prevention models and evaluation issues across programs and takes a broader view of the program and evaluation issues involved in preventing adolescent pregnancy.

—Brent C. Miller
Utah State University

1

Adolescent Pregnancy Prevention Programs

Design, Monitoring, and Evaluation

JOSEFINA J. CARD
JAMES L. PETERSON
CATHERINE G. GREENO

Background

The United States has one of the highest rates of teenage childbearing in the developed world (Moore, 1988). Since the early 1970s, a large number of studies have been devoted to documenting the rate of teenage pregnancy and discovering which teens are at highest risk of becoming pregnant (Hayes, 1987). These investigations proved to be good examples of cumulative and converging social science research. Scientists from a variety of disciplines found that teen pregnancy is rooted in a set of clearly identifiable demographic and social factors (Miller & Moore, 1990) and that early parenthood has multiple negative consequences for the young mother, her partner, and their child.

That sexual activity is strongly influenced by biological development is clear from studies of the relationships between age, biological maturity, and hormone levels on the one hand and the incidence of sexual behavior on the other (Udry, Billy, Morris, Groff, & Raj, 1985). Gender differences are also striking; despite the earlier physical maturation of

1

girls, the sexual activity rates of boys exceed those of girls for all ages. Both differences in biology (especially testosterone levels) and differences in socialization and social norms probably account for these sex differences in behavior. That social and cultural factors play a strong role in sexual behavior is attested to by the large though somewhat diminishing differences among various religious, racial, and ethnic groups. The social influences upon sexual behavior are many, but family and peers are the primary agents. What parents believe regarding the appropriateness or inappropriateness of sexual behavior for their teen children can be influential under conditions of open parent-child communication (Moore, Peterson, & Furstenberg, 1986). A parent's own behavior is also of great importance; for example, teens living with single mothers who date are more likely to be sexually active than teens with single mothers who are not dating (Moore, Peterson, & Furstenberg, 1984). Peers are also highly influential. While teens may not accurately report the sexual activity of their peers, their perceptions of the sexual behavior of their friends are highly predictive of their own behavior (Newcomer, Gilbert, & Udry, 1980). Because schools shape the context in which peer groups develop, the composition of the student body sets the boundaries within which peer groups can form. For example, members of minority groups that collectively exhibit high rates of sexual activity will have higher rates of sexual activity themselves if they attend largely minority schools than if they attend largely integrated schools (Furstenberg, Morgan, Moore, & Peterson, 1987).

Personal traits also play a role in influencing sexual activity. Sexual activity is less likely among adolescents who have high educational or career aspirations, who have a greater confidence in their own abilities to affect their environment, and who have a lower propensity to take risks. Even personal skills come into play: high achievers in school and more assertive teens are less likely to become sexually active.

Contraceptive use and frequency of sexual activity are the primary factors determining whether the sexually active become pregnant. Many of the same factors that incline some teens to become sexually active are related to their frequency of sexual activity and to their contraceptive use. These factors, however, do not always affect behavior in the same direction or with the same strength. For example, those from very traditional home backgrounds are less likely to become sexually active than those from more permissive homes; however, once sexually active, the former are less likely to use contraception than are the latter. On the other hand, older teens are more likely to be sexually active than younger teens, but they are also more likely to use contraceptives. Contraceptive use, in addition to being influenced by the personal and social factors described in the previous paragraphs, is affected also by more immediate factors, such as knowledge of contraception; the availability of contraceptive devices; and attitudes and beliefs about the morality, side effects, and effectiveness of contraceptive use.

A large body of research literature has developed documenting these and other causes of teen sexual behavior (Miller & Moore, 1990). An equally large body of research has focused upon the consequences of pregnancy and childbearing for the mother and child (Card, 1981; Moore & Burt, 1982). Most of this research has documented a long list of negative consequences: truncated educations, lower paying jobs, greater unemployment, greater likelihood of poverty, larger families and closer spacing between children, greater likelihood of marital disruption or of out-of-wedlock childbearing, children who are slower to develop and who do more poorly in school when they begin their education.

Largely as a result of these findings regarding the consequences of teen pregnancy and parenthood, "care" programs, designed to ameliorate these negative effects, proliferated in the 1970s. These programs generally provided comprehensive prenatal and postnatal health services for the young mother and her child. Many care programs also assisted the teen mother to stay in or return to school.

In the early 1980s, program planners began to look more to prevention as an effective way to address the problems of teen pregnancy and parenthood. New programs, which were aimed at preventing early pregnancy or birth from occurring in the first place, began to emerge. A variety of approaches was tried, based upon the research literature summarized above, as well as program planners' ad hoc ideas about what would be effective in preventing pregnancy. Among the approaches tried: *"Just say no"* approaches, which teach young people the benefits of abstinence and the skills to refuse unwanted advances; *contraceptive provision* approaches, which facilitate access to contraception by the sexually active, for example, by opening school-based contraceptive clinics; *sex education* approaches, which focus upon teaching teens about the reproductive process and about contraception; and more general *life option* approaches, programs with such broader activities as academic remediation, job training, or adult mentoring, which are founded upon the premise that the belief in a compelling personal future or goal is a strong incentive to avoid a teen pregnancy.

Unfortunately, the relative effectiveness of these various approaches to pregnancy prevention remains largely untested. When new programs are developed in response to a perceived need, funders and program administrators typically draw upon their own philosophical, ideological, or moral understandings—in addition to their reading of the scientific literature—to design new programs that they believe will best meet their goals. Regardless of the theoretical or philosophical basis of a particular program, however, its effectiveness in meeting its stated goals is an empirical question subject to testing and verification.

One might expect that evaluation research aimed at assessing the effectiveness of these pregnancy prevention programs—comparable in number and quality to the basic research that led to the programs' initiation in the first place—would follow. This has not happened readily. On the whole, the effectiveness of programs designed to affect teenage pregnancy has not been well documented or tested. The lack of information about what programs are working, and for whom they work best, impedes our ability to address the critical social problem of teenage pregnancy. This book is intended to help bring together the best and most current information about what is being done to help prevent early pregnancy and childbearing in this country.

A number of serious obstacles have stood in the way of conducting successful evaluations of program effectiveness. First, are the tensions, some more real than others, between service and science. Service providers have generally been reluctant to divert program dollars to scientific endeavors whose benefits are perceived as being relatively remote. In addition, both funders and service providers are often wary about possible fallout from a negative evaluation. Beyond this, some funders have felt constrained by fact or politics to deny support to approaches not in line with their mission, or their legislative mandate. As the national debate has grown over related issues, such as abortion and providing contraception to minors, schools and other powerful institutions have become increasingly reluctant to ally themselves with controversial solutions, such as school-based clinics, or contraceptive education and provision. Tensions have surfaced also between the requirements of science and the realities of program administration. For example, science encourages the random assignment of subjects to treatment and control groups; administrators often reply that it is unacceptable to withhold treatment from those in need, especially when the funds are available to provide the service. Science demands that baseline and follow-up data be collected from the same subjects and that each subject's data be linkable across all waves of the study so that changes in individuals can be observed over time; administrators often reply that, for cost and confidentiality reasons, this kind of research is too hard to do.

In 1987, a Panel on Adolescent Pregnancy and Childbearing, organized by the National Academy of Sciences, identified the scarcity of good evaluation research as a priority problem. Indeed, the panel encouraged the conducting of scientific program evaluations as one of its four major recommendations (Hayes, 1987). Scientifically credible attempts to evaluate programs designed to reduce teenage pregnancy have been rare. A high percentage of the evaluations that have been attempted have been compromised seriously by flaws in the methods used to plan the evaluation or to gather the information. Many of these flaws could have been avoided easily, had someone trained in evaluation been available to guide the evaluation effort and had resources been sufficient to meet the task. Beyond bringing together up-to-date information on model programs and evaluations, this book is intended to facilitate and encourage good evaluations, when called for by program size, strength, and dollars.

In the next section, we discuss aspects of program design, focusing upon features that are likely to make interventions more successful. The following section deals with evaluation, including the benefits of doing an evaluation and the types of evaluation options that are available. An appendix provides a list of resources for more detailed information.

Program Design

Programs to prevent teen pregnancy usually are designed and put into effect by administrators whose primary motivation is to address a perceived social problem. Their primary goals might be to prevent or delay sexual intercourse (some programs), to increase effective contraceptive use (some programs), and to prevent pregnancy among unmarried teenagers (all programs). Starting with their perception of the problem, such administrators draw upon their understanding of the social forces in effect to design and administer programs they believe will be effective in bringing about the desired outcomes.

Needs Assessment

A *needs assessment* is the first step in any program design. This step, easily passed over as trivial or self-evident, is essential to successful program planning and must be done carefully. Three questions need thoughtful answers during the needs assessment phase: (a) What is the specific nature of the problem that needs to be addressed? (b) What is the incidence, prevalence, and scope of the problem? (c) How is the problem distributed in the population?

Problem Definition

Defining the problem may not always be straightforward. A perception that we now have an "epidemic" of teen pregnancies may lead one to focus immediately upon pregnancies as the problem. Indeed, many programs do define the problem in terms of pregnancies and focus their interventions accordingly. While this is a perfectly defensible approach, some additional thought needs to be spent before it is adopted. Is an excess of pregnancies the only problem? (What about sexual intercourse among the very young, sexually transmitted diseases, and the problem of how unmarried teens decide to resolve their pregnancies?) Are all teen pregnancies a problem, or only certain ones (such as nonmarital pregnancies, or pregnancies to very young teens, or second pregnancies)? Is it the pregnancy itself that is the problem, or is it that pregnancy leads to other problems, such as frequent resort to abortion, poor birth outcomes, single parenthood, or truncation of education and occupational plans? Is sexual behavior among unmarried teens a problem even when such behavior does not result in pregnancy?

Size and Scope of the Problem

Once the problem is defined, it is important to measure its magnitude. One kind of measure is *incidence,* the proportion of teens who experience a certain event in a given period of time, usually a year. The incidence of pregnancy is the proportion of teens becoming pregnant during the year. The incidence of initiating sexual activity is the proportion of teens who are virgins at the beginning of the year who become nonvirgins during the course of the year. A second kind of measure is *prevalence,* the proportion of teens in a given status at a particular point in time. The prevalence of parenthood is the proportion of teens who are parents at a point in time; the prevalence of sexually transmitted diseases is the proportion of teens who are infected with a disease at a point in time. To use either of these kinds of measures, one must first define the population upon which they are to be based. This usually will be the population of the community or catchment area of the anticipated program. And within this geographic area, the population usually will be restricted to a narrow band of teenage or early adult years. For some kinds of programs, the population may be further restricted to females, although a growing number of programs are recognizing that an exclusive focus upon females may limit the effectiveness of pregnancy prevention programs.

Distribution of the Problem

Along with gaining overall measures of incidence and prevalence, it is important to understand how the problem is distributed in the population by such factors as geographic residence, race, or ethnicity. Do high-risk groups exist? How does the problem vary by age? Do some teen females become pregnant repeatedly, and do some teen males cause multiple pregnancies? If so, what are the characteristics of these teens in comparison with others? To answer questions about the size and distribution of the problem, program planners need to gather relevant data. Much of this information may be obtained from the local department of health, which maintains vital statistics records and other information that may be helpful. Schools and clinics may also be of assistance. For some measures, it may be necessary to estimate by adjusting national statistics to fit the local population. Statistical consultants from a nearby college or university may be of assistance in this task. If resources permit, a local survey could be undertaken to gather data not otherwise available.

Intervention Design

Program administrators come from a variety of backgrounds: social work, nursing, education, counseling, and public administration. Though many keep up with the findings of social research, few were trained as social scientists. Nevertheless, most could anticipate a rationale for the specific activities and features of the programs they design and administer. They have, in effect, a theoretical underpinning for what they do. In forming such rationales, administrators draw upon many sources, only one of which is the scientific research literature. Also affecting their thinking are their values regarding what is right and good and their beliefs about human nature, especially in its adolescent stage of development. For example, advocates of "Just say no" approaches place a high value upon chastity and tend to believe that individuals, including teens, are generally quite capable of shaping their own lives and directing their own actions. Advocates of contraceptive provision approaches, on the other hand, are likely to place more value upon freedom of choice than upon chastity; yet within this group are many who believe that social and psychological factors may severely constrain human behavior.

While it is not the role of science to arbitrate conflicting values, science can shed light upon the validity of some of these beliefs. By estimating the relative strength of various factors that influence teen sexual activity and pregnancy, science can point the way to designing more effective programs to achieve a variety of goals. And, by direct application of the scientific method in program evaluation, specific approaches can be tested and their effectiveness measured. Scientific findings can also be useful in helping administrators identify those critical points at which intervention can be most effective. For example, research can identify those subpopulations most at risk of sexual activity and pregnancy, helping programs focus their efforts upon groups most in need of intervention. Findings that pregnancies are particularly likely to occur within a few months of the initiation of sexual activity may point programs toward interventions with the newly sexually active, to encourage them to adopt the use of contraceptives, or to return to a nonactive status. Because research shows that family and peers have such powerful influences upon the sexual behavior of teens, programs may choose to leverage their own influence by working with families and/or peers to change the social context that surrounds teens. The finding that teens with strong educational or occupational aspirations are less likely than others to become pregnant may suggest that boosting teens' motivations in these directions may be an effective intervention.

Viewed differently, however, research may make the job of designing programs harder by forcing planners to be realistic. Research has shown that for many teens several personal and social problems tend to go together. Being a school dropout, being prone to delinquency, using drugs, the early initiation of sexual behavior, and the failure to use contraception are characteristics often found together (Elliott & Morse, 1989). Attempts to address just one of these problems—teen pregnancy—may have little effect unless the entire constellation of problems is confronted jointly. Yet few programs have the resources to launch such a multifrontal attack.

1. The capacity to identify a population at risk for teen pregnancy.
2. The ability to reach an at-risk population with the program.
3. The appropriateness of the timing of the preventive intervention.
4. The duration and intensity of the program.
5. The breadth or specificity of the program.
6. Skill and training level of the program staff.
7. Program structure and integration/collaboration with other community services.
8. Simplicity/complexity of prevention messages.

Figure 1.1. The Design of Adequate Interventions: Factors Influencing the Effectiveness of Pregnancy Prevention Programs.

SOURCE: Adapted from Mueller, D. P., & Higgins, P. S. (1989). Prevention programs in human services. In J. J. Card (Ed.) *Evaluating programs aimed at preventing teenage pregnancies.* Los Altos, CA: Sociometrics Corporation.

Program Strategies

In a recent paper, Mueller and Higgins (1989) reviewed programs for the prevention of a variety of adolescent problems, including pregnancy, school dropout, child abuse, and substance use. They suggest several factors that may enhance program effectiveness; these factors are shown in Figure 1.1. Below we describe their application to teen pregnancy prevention programs.

Choose an at-risk population. To maximize cost-effectiveness, programs should be directed to a population that is known to be at risk for high incidence of early pregnancy. Poverty, family instability, minority status, and failure in school are important risk factors in adolescent pregnancy. Because many risk factors may not be readily observable to program planners (poverty or family instability, for example), characteristics highly associated with risk factors may have to be used to identify target populations. Place of residence is often a good predictor, and one that is a natural criterion for placing a program.

Consider strategies for reaching high-risk populations. Although prevention efforts are best directed at high-risk populations, such populations are often difficult to reach. School-based programs, for example, will not reach school dropouts, one high-risk group. Programs that are staffed solely with white middle-class personnel are not likely to attract clients from poor families or from minority groups. Program planners need to locate programs and intervention activities at times and places that are most likely to attract the high-risk teens they are aiming to reach.

Consider the timing of the message. For a program to be effective, it must be offered to teens at a time when the intervention is most likely to have its maximum effect. Programs directed toward teaching teens decision-making skills to handle social pressures to engage in sex should be timed so that they reach teens before their sexual activity patterns are well established; indeed, it is presumably best for them to be timed before sexual behavior is initiated. They probably should not be presented, however, before sexuality becomes an issue with teens. While it is important to provide information about contraception to sexually active teens who have never been pregnant, teens who have already become pregnant or have just delivered are especially receptive to such information because they are highly motivated at this time to prevent a second pregnancy. The more consistent the program with teens' developmental processes, the better.

Longer, more intense programs are more successful. Teen pregnancy prevention programs should be aware that quick fixes are not likely to be effective. Programs are competing for influence against forces that surround the teen daily: peers, family, advertising, the social norms of the neighborhood. Against such forces, a 1-hour class, a single film, or a brochure will have little effect.

Make the focus as specific as possible. Pregnancy prevention programs tend to be more successful when they are specifically, rather than broadly, focused. Specific objectives need to be delineated in advance. Specific activities comprising the intervention need to be designed and implemented. The specific links between intervention and objectives must be well thought out and agreed upon.

Multifaceted programs do address the multiproblem teen, and so should be considered as an alternative to the highly focused program. Multifaceted programs, however, also require many times the resources as specific programs, in keeping with differences in program scope. Without a large resource base, such multifaceted programs merely become diffuse and ineffective. A possible approach is to link one's specific program with other, related efforts in the community.

Integrate efforts with existing community services. Related, ongoing efforts to attack adolescent problem behaviors are likely to exist in any community. Sometimes a multifaceted approach can be put together from a coalition of complementary programs. Such coalitions are increasingly being tried as a way for programs to build upon, rather than compete with, the efforts of other programs. Coordination with other programs can also save valuable effort: program lessons may be learned, resources may be pooled for some efforts, and community acceptability can be more forcefully addressed. Communitywide coalitions can result in reaping the benefits of a focused program, as well as the benefits of a multifaceted program.

Make use of skilled staff. Skilled and caring program people are needed to implement a program successfully. Time and resources devoted to finding good staff and providing them with good training are well spent. The specific skills needed are determined by the intervention being used. Among the personnel often required are counselors, educators, nurses, managers, mentors, organizers, even celebrities.

Be aware that in adolescent pregnancy prevention, the message is complex. The message to be imparted in teen pregnancy programs is not a simple one. On the whole, prevention programs with a simple message, such as "It is best to never start smoking" or "never take drugs" are more effective than programs in which the message is less clear. "Just say no" approaches to teen pregnancy attempt to build upon a single, simple message. The problem with this approach is that it does not address the circumstances of those who have already said "yes" or of those who will not heed the "Just say no" message but can be influenced to adopt an effective method of contraception. Herein lies the complexity of teen pregnancy prevention programs: to urge abstinence on the one hand and to urge the adoption of effective contraceptive methods among the nonabstinent on the other is to give a complex and possibly mixed message. The more clearly and precisely this complex message can be articulated, the better. The inherent complexity of the sex-related message, coupled with hormonal development in the teen years, make pregnancy prevention a difficult area, and the duration and intensity of the programs should be adjusted accordingly.

Program Assessment

Increasingly, program administrators are recognizing that program design is an ongoing process, not just an up-front activity done once, when the program is begun. It is undoubtedly important to define the target precisely and to take careful aim; it is equally important to determine whether the target has been hit. Program assessment is the necessary tool for the ongoing readjustment of program design.

Rationale for Assessment

What Is Assessment?

Program assessment is a sequential process of documenting what a program's goals are, what activities are being undertaken to meet these goals, and what degree of success has been achieved in meeting such goals.

Assessment can be as simple as making a statement of the program's service provision goals, keeping a record of services provided, and using the information to decide how well the service provision goals are being met and what program aspects need to be changed. Or, it can involve a complex and technical study design and measurement that assesses whether desired behavioral outcomes—such as delay of sexual intercourse or prevention of unwanted pregnancy—are being achieved.

Why Conduct an Assessment?

Carefully conducted scientific assessments provide information about program performance that can be examined, debated, and largely agreed upon. It is through careful, systematic, and thorough assessment that we can come to know whether teenage pregnancy can be prevented by urging teens to abstain from sex or by providing contraceptives. Careful assessment will be required to determine whether one of these approaches is more effective than the other or if both approaches could be used in combination. Among the uses of assessments are the following:

1. *Assessment is a useful management information tool.* Many aspects of assessment provide information that will be useful to program administrators and staff. The process of stating program goals and setting out the program's approach to attaining them is a useful exercise for staff that sometimes uncovers hidden assumptions and surprising differences among staff in their conceptions of the program. As the program unfolds, knowledge of which clients are receiving which services helps staff understand whether service goals are being met, and plan corrective action if they are not.

2. *Assessment provides information that can be shared with the teen pregnancy prevention community.* When a particular approach to teen pregnancy prevention has been evaluated and documented to be successful, it can serve as an example for other programs that have the same goals and operate under similar circumstances.

STEP 1: DESCRIPTION

What are this program's short- and long-term objectives?
What will it do to meet these objectives?

STEP 2: MONITORING

What services are actually being delivered?
To whom?

STEP 3: PROCESS EVALUATION

Is the program being implemented as planned?
Are service delivery objectives being met?

STEP 4: IMPACT EVALUATION

Is this program meeting its outcome and impact objectives?
What works? For whom? Under what circumstances?

Figure 1.2. Steps in Assessing a Teen Pregnancy Prevention Program.

3. Assessment is increasingly required to obtain or maintain funding. Increasingly, funders want evidence of a program's effectiveness when they decide where to commit their dollars. This fact actually creates some reluctance to evaluate, because a negative assessment could cause an interruption in funding. Such fears, however, are probably greater than they need to be. In the current climate, any credible documentation increases the chances of receiving funding. Having credible documentation shows that the program personnel possess the technical skills to document the program, or the willingness to find a way to do so. Furthermore, it is rare that the results of an assessment are all negative. The results are more likely to illuminate some clear areas of success and some areas for improvement, either of which can be used to gain credibility with funders.

Assessment can be divided into a sequence of steps (Figure 1.2), each subsequent step adding more to the power and utility of the assessment, yet also adding to the complexity and cost. Not all programs should aspire to progress through every step, yet every program can, indeed *should,* take the first step. No matter how far in the sequence a program progresses, useful results will be obtained that will improve program design and implementation. Four basic steps to program assessment may be distinguished: (a) *Description*—a careful statement of program goals and objectives, as well as the program design or model intended to meet those objectives; (b) *Monitoring*—keeping track of how the program actually is delivered and to whom it is delivered; and (c and d) *Evaluation*—the scientific measurement of the effectiveness of the delivered program in matching the program design (process evaluation) and/or achieving the program goals (impact evaluation).

Description: The Program Model

It may seem reasonable to assume that those funding and operating teen pregnancy prevention programs will have spelled out clear goals and objectives before the programs get underway and will have then selected program activities and clients to serve such goals. Unfortunately, this is often not the case. Goals are often vague or abstract. They may not be operationalized in terms of concrete objectives. Moreover, the relationship between goals and objectives on the one hand and clients and activities on the other may be poorly thought out, if at all. Administrators and their publics are so often caught up in the need to "do something," that they are willing to "do anything." Once a program is underway, the needs of the program and the management of its day-to-day operations often take the full attention of program administrators, so that no further attention is paid to objectives.

The first step in program assessment, therefore, is a clear statement of the general goal or goals of the program; the formulation of a set of objectives that operationalize the goals in concrete and measurable terms; and a description of the program design. The program design includes a statement of the target population of the program; the kinds of interventions that will be directed at that population; and the frequency, timing, and circumstances of delivery of the program activities. Also essential is a statement of the rationale for the program activities: what is the intervention specifically expected to accomplish, and why is it believed to be capable of bringing about this effect? Finally, program administrators need to specify the special circumstances in which they believe their interventions will work, personal characteristics of clients or social circumstances in the community that may modify the program effects, and the duration over which effects are expected to emerge and be maintained.

Interventions	Population	Moderating Factors	Intermediate Goals	Long-Term Goals
LOOKOUT: A ten-session curriculum stressing reproductive knowledge, decision skills, and parent-communication*	13- to 15-year-olds	Age Grade School	Increase knowledge Increase decision skills Increase parent-child communication	Delay first intercourse Reduce teen pregnancy

Figure 1.3. Sample Model Program.
* A booklet describing each session should accompany the program model.

Taken together, this description is often referred to as a **program model.** A program model usually consists of a specification of the intervention, the population that will get the intervention, and intermediate and long-term goals for the intervention. Sometimes "moderating variables," that is, other variables expected to affect the outcome, are also considered. Without a program model, no assessment is possible because the model defines what is to be assessed. With it, the groundwork is laid for the other assessment steps. Even if this is as far as a program goes in assessment, it is an essential step that is likely to lead to better planning and administration of a program even if program effectiveness is not subsequently measured.

Making a program model helps establish what is "do-able," as well as what might be measured. Thus establishing the program model helps with program development as well as with the planning of a program evaluation. An illustrative program model is given in Figure 1.3. Program LOOKOUT is a hypothetical curriculum that consists of 10 two-hour sessions and includes education on reproduction, and skills training to help teens communicate with their parents and say "no" to sexual advances.

A program model can be expected to evolve as the program develops. For example, as experience with program LOOKOUT is gained, sessions may be dropped, added, or modified in response to client interest or early clear indications of effectiveness. When that decision is made, the change can be recorded on a revised program model. Regular staff meetings during which everyone can be brought up-to-date on progress and program changes can help ensure proper implementation of the program. The development of a program model is a step that all programs should take. An examination of the program model presented in Figure 1.3 shows that much important program information can be contained in a simple figure. It is not difficult to create a program model; nonetheless, going from the program description that exists in other program documents, such as a grant proposal, to a program model sometimes leads to surprising results. The most challenging aspect of transforming the program description into a program model usually comes in specifying the goals, especially in specifying the intermediate goals. The intermediate, or short-range, goals of a program are a crucial statement of how the intervention is expected to cause the desired long-term changes. But specifying these goals can be difficult, and many program staff do not realize that such goals have never been specified at all. The process of reaching consensus with program personnel about the intervention and its goals, and regularly updating this consensus, is a prerequisite of effective program implementation.

Monitoring

Monitoring, the next step in program assessment, means collecting and studying performance data to keep track of which clients are getting which services (or components of the intervention). Did Mary C. attend all 10 sessions that were part of the LOOKOUT program? If not, which ones did she miss? It is essential that such monitoring data measure the services or interventions *as actually delivered.*

Monitoring data relating to program clients may be measured at the level of the individual client, as in the above example, or they may pertain to all the clients in the aggregate. How many of the 50 8th graders in Mrs. Clark's room attended the first sex education lecture? How many attended the second? In addition, some monitoring data are measures of the interventions themselves rather than of the clients' behavior: the length of classes, the numbers of pamphlets distributed, the number and timing of public service announcements, and so on. Such data are, if nothing else, an essential management tool for program administrators who are generally held accountable for suitable disbursement of program dollars. Monitoring data provide the basis for such management decisions. Moreover, collecting monitoring data is an essential preliminary step on the road toward actual program evaluation. Monitoring provides measurements of one essential part of the program model: the intervention itself, that is, the program, as actually implemented in the field.

Whether designed for data collection at the individual or aggregate level, monitoring forms can be extremely simple. As a general rule, programs should strive to monitor services received at the individual client level, unless this proves too difficult or costly. In the latter event, monitoring at the aggregate level is sufficient, but a full-scale impact evaluation will be impeded, as the next section will show.

Evaluation

Evaluation, the highest level of assessment, is the only level that potentially provides answers to questions about program effectiveness. In evaluation, the program is measured against a performance standard, whether the standard is the description of services to be delivered (a process evaluation) or the goals and objectives to be met (an impact evaluation). It is through evaluation that we can learn whether the program is being delivered as planned (process evaluation) and whether the program is having its intended effect of delaying sexual intercourse, encouraging use of contraception among the sexually active, or preventing teen pregnancy (impact evaluation).

Types of Evaluations

Process Evaluations

The goal of a process evaluation is to discover whether service delivery goals are being met. The evaluation is based upon careful records of service delivery. Many process evaluations also determine who is receiving services, and clients' level of satisfaction with various aspects of the program. Process evaluations thus can be used as an important program development tool. Process evaluations are very similar to monitoring; the difference is that in a process evaluation, unlike in simple monitoring, the progress of services delivered is compared against the program's design and model. This simple step establishes a measure of objectivity in determining whether the program is meeting its process-related objectives.

Impact Evaluations

Impact evaluations are designed to test whether the program is effective: Does the program work? For whom? Under what circumstances? Only impact evaluations can provide information about whether a program is actually benefiting clients in the manner prescribed by the program's goals and objectives. Impact evaluations are the most costly and complex of all the assessment options, yet they also provide the most information. For an evaluation to be considered an impact evaluation, it must have several features, including (a) inclusion of measures of the program or intervention as delivered (similar to process evaluation); (b) inclusion of objective measures of each of the program's short-term and long-term objectives; and (c) inclusion of data from a comparison group.

To have a comparison group, it is necessary to identify and measure a group of people who did not receive the intervention but who are otherwise like the program clients in every other relevant way. Sometimes this can be done by offering a program in only one school or clinic, while giving pretests and posttests in that setting, as well as another comparable school or clinic. Indeed this is a commonly used and sometimes acceptable way of obtaining a comparison group. Its acceptability as a comparison group, however, depends upon the similarity of the schools or clinics with regard to variables that may affect program goals and interventions. If the schools differ on key variables that affect the treatment, then outcome differences between the treatment and control groups could be due to differences in these antecedent variables rather than to the treatment itself.

A better way to obtain comparison data is to randomly assign potential clients to either receive the treatment or receive no treatment and to give them a pretest and posttest regardless of whether they received the treatment. The random assignment to treatment and no-treatment groups is the gold standard of evaluation research. It is by using randomized designs that we can most confidently establish equivalent groups for comparison and thus determine whether the program is having an effect.

Deciding How Far to Go

All programs could benefit by conducting a full-fledged impact evaluation. Practical considerations, however, such as resource limitations and the size of a program, mean that only a minority of programs are likely to be in a position to go that far. Nevertheless, all programs can undertake program assessment at some level. No program should even get underway without undertaking the description step. Moreover, established programs need to review their program models from time to time in light of changing needs and circumstances. Monitoring is a step well within the resources of most programs. In the long run, monitoring may even conserve resources by providing the program administrator with management data that enable him or her to better allocate time and funds. Administrators not familiar with the collection and use of management data may initially need to obtain some consulting help to establish monitoring. Once underway, however, monitoring can proceed at little cost or disruption to the program.

When programs have the resources necessary to undertake an evaluation, someone still needs to determine what kind of evaluation the group can most realistically undertake. It could be a choice between process and impact evaluations or both, a choice that is largely a matter of determining what cost can be borne. It is possible to have a good process evaluation without even trying to do an impact evaluation; however, an impact evaluation must include the information needed for a process evaluation. Both process and impact evaluations can answer questions about whether services are being provided as specified in the program model, to whom they are being provided, and whether the clients are satisfied with services. Only an impact evaluation, however, can address additional questions about program effectiveness: whether, and to what extent, clients are actually benefiting from the services provided.

The type of evaluation to be undertaken depends upon a variety of considerations, chief among them being the number and qualifications of available staff and the dollars available for the program and its assessment. After determining what evaluation data are most needed, constraints upon resources will guide the decisions made about the type of evaluation to be undertaken. Planning from the outset is very important. If plans within the constraints of the resources are made at the inception of the program, a much more valid assessment will be achieved in a much more cost-effective manner.

In sum, evaluations based upon data may be expensive and time-consuming, depending upon the type employed, but they are the best way to measure service delivery and to determine whether efforts to solve a problem have been successful. This said, it is far better to tailor a program assessment to available resources than to attempt to do something one cannot afford to do. A less costly assessment option done well is superior to a more comprehensive evaluation done poorly. Regardless of which description, monitoring, or evaluation option a program elects, it is imperative that program staff work together from the start to obtain consensus on the program model guiding the endeavor.

Overcoming Barriers to Assessment

Today, advances in the assessment field are steadily being made. A combination of forces—centering largely upon the forging of partnerships among formerly disparate groups—are serving to overcome the barriers to evaluation.

For their part, funders and service providers are coming to realize that a good assessment serves not only science, but also the teenage clients they are so committed to serve. The very same information on service delivery needed for a good monitoring effort and a good process evaluation can be used as a management information tool to inform the funder and service provider about where the money is going: which clients are being served and the form the service is taking. The very same information on program effectiveness needed for a good outcome or impact evaluation can be used to inform the funder and service provider about where the money should go in the future: to which elements of the program should dollars be shifted?

For their part, scientists are coming to accept and work within the cost and ethical constraints that often preclude a perfect research effort. The challenge to scientists is to work within the available financial and technical resource pool to design a useful assessment effort. Often, cost constraints make it impossible to conduct a scientifically valid impact evaluation. Rather than insisting on the impossible, scientists should help funders and program administrators realize what *can* be done (a process evaluation, perhaps, or simple monitoring of service delivery?), and then design the very best possible system, given the constraints. IT IS BETTER TO DO A SMALL JOB WELL, THAN TO DO A BIG JOB POORLY.

Next Steps

Given the urgent need to improve the quality and quantity of assessments of teen pregnancy prevention programs, and recognizing the practical constraints under which such assessments are usually carried out, we recommend several steps that we feel are realistic and productive.

First, those who provide funds and other resources to programs should (a) require of all programs they support that some form of intentional program assessment be carried out, and (b) include in the support granted a reasonable amount of funds to enable the program administrator to fulfill this requirement. Step (a) is becoming more common; step (b) needs to accompany it.

Second, all program administrators should set aside a certain proportion of their funds and resources for program assessment. Something in the neighborhood of 10% is a reasonable rule of thumb for most programs. While some may argue that this automatically cuts program delivery by 10%, the counterargument is that an ill-conceived, misdirected, or ineffective program will cut the intended effect by far more. Unless assessment at some level is an ongoing part of program procedures, a program is likely to run off course before very long.

Third, the type of assessment undertaken should match the available resources and the size and complexity of the program. No reason exists why every single teen pregnancy program should undertake or even aspire to undertake a full impact evaluation. This should be left to a minority (see next recommendation). But every program without exception can undertake the descriptive phase of assessment set out above; every program can generate a program model and obtain staff consensus that "this is what our program is about." A majority of programs can go on to monitoring. A substantial minority can even undertake process evaluations without going beyond the 10% resource base.

Fourth, a full-scale impact evaluation should be undertaken only by programs fitting the following criteria: (a) adequate resources are available (this may often require much more than the 10% level, so special funding may be needed); (b) the program is innovative or promising, or programs of its type have not been adequately evaluated elsewhere; (c) the program is one that can be replicated in other communities should the evaluation prove its effectiveness; (d) the program has enough clients to make statistical analysis possible; and (e) the program has secure funding for the several years that will be required to complete the impact evaluation.

This combination of steps will serve to raise the floor of program assessment considerably above its present level, while at the same time assuring that program resources are not wasted. Better programs and increased program effectiveness should be the result. The chapters in this monograph serve to fill out the skeleton presented in this introductory chapter. They provide needed details, give concrete examples, and carry on the argument for the value of data collection and analysis for improving program policy and effectiveness.

APPENDIX

Where to Go for Additional Information and Help

Increasingly, funders are making program evaluation a requirement for programs that receive their support. Moreover, program administrators themselves are increasingly aware of the importance of good evaluation data for measuring effectiveness and making improvements in their programs. This book is an attempt to put into the hands of program administrators and evaluators some examples of good pregnancy prevention programs and evaluation studies that will assist them in meeting their program development and evaluation goals. The editors hope that the examples provided in these chapters will serve as models for future evaluation studies. The following sections provide information about other resources that may be helpful.

Information-Related Publications

Several publications that summarize the research findings on teenage sexuality and pregnancy may be of use to administrators in the early stages of program design. The first gives a broad overview in the form of easy-to-read statements organized by topic. The second and third are much more technical and in-depth treatments of the issues.

Nelson-Kilger, S., Peterson, J. L., & Card, J. J. (1990). *Just the facts.* Los Altos, CA: Sociometrics Corp.
Hayes, C. D. (Ed.). (1987). *Risking the future* (Vol. 1). Washington, DC: National Academy.
Miller, B. C., & Moore, K. A. (1990). Adolescent sexual behavior, pregnancy, & parenting: Research through the 1980s. *Journal of Marriage and the Family, 52,* 1025-1044.

Evaluation-Related Publications

A number of publications have become available in the last few years that can help program administrators and others who wish to conduct evaluations of teen

pregnancy prevention programs. The literature on evaluation research in general is very large, and much is quite technical. Sage Publications, however, has issued a series of nine small monographs written for the program administrator that give very practical advice on evaluation research in general. Issues in the series can be obtained separately, or the entire series is sold as the *Program Evaluation Kit.*
The series titles include:

1. *Evaluator's Handbook*
2. *How to Focus an Evaluation*
3. *How to Design a Program Evaluation*
4. *How to Use Qualitative Methods in Evaluation*
5. *How to Assess Program Implementation*
6. *How to Measure Attitudes*
7. *How to Measure Performance and Use Tests*
8. *How to Analyze Data*
9. *How to Communicate Evaluation Findings*

A second series of monographs on evaluation is published by the Evaluation Research Society. Monographs appear quarterly on topics pertaining to evaluation research. These issues are directed primarily at a professional research audience, yet some articles and issues may be of interest to program administrators with particular evaluation problems to solve.

New Directions for Program Evaluation. San Francisco: Jossey-Bass. (Quarterly).

Of most direct relevance to pregnancy prevention programs is a monograph that grew out of a conference of national experts in teen pregnancy research. The monograph contains chapters written by conference participants that describe the basic requirements and technical standards for evaluation research, give an overview of prevention programs in the U.S., and provide examples of actual pregnancy prevention program evaluation studies. The monograph concludes with an appendix that contains suggested data collection instruments for pregnancy prevention program evaluations.

Card, J. J. (Ed.). (1989). *Evaluating teen pregnancy prevention programs.* Los Altos, CA: Sociometrics Corp.

A second monograph, of use to evaluators in need of comparison data, draws upon a series of national statistical data bases to present national norms for fertility-related outcome variables by age, sex, and race. The monograph explains how these data can be adjusted to match the demographic characteristics of a particular program population in order to provide comparison statistics for the program.

Card, J. J., Reagan, R. T., & Ritter, P. E. (1988). *Sourcebook of comparison data for evaluating adolescent pregnancy and parenting programs.* Los Altos, CA: Sociometrics Corp.

A very thorough book on pregnancy prevention evaluation is available, although it is narrowly focused upon school-based programs. The book describes the evaluation process from data collection through analysis, illustrating points with an evaluation of a Johns Hopkins University program. The book also includes a sample questionnaire.

Zabin, L. S., & Hirsch, M. B. (1984). *Evaluation of pregnancy prevention programs in the school context.* Lexington, MA: Lexington.

A short workbook on data management and analysis is available for program administrators with no formal research background. Starting at the point of completed questionnaires or information forms, the manual describes each of the necessary steps to preparing data for analysis.

Peterson, J. L., & Card, J. J. (1991). *Data management: An introductory workbook for teen pregnancy program evaluators.* Los Altos, CA: Sociometrics Corp.

A selective bibliography of research and evaluation materials relevant to teen pregnancy programs has been prepared by the staff of NationalNet (see below) and is available from them.

NationalNet. (1990). *A basic bibliography on adolescent sexuality, pregnancy prevention and care programs and program evaluation.* Los Altos, CA: Social Research Applications.

Training Workshops

Several workshops on teen pregnancy program evaluation are now being offered across the country. Approximately twice a year (winter and summer) the staff of NationalNet (see below) present a 2-day workshop in California on teen pregnancy program evaluation. These workshops cover basic requirements for evaluation from program-model building through impact evaluation. The workshop makes great use of exercises to give participants hands-on practical learning experience. In addition, NationalNet occasionally will give the workshop to a group or organization that requests it. (Call 415-949-3487 for more information.)

Susan Philliber (Philliber Associates) frequently conducts half-day or full-day workshops throughout the East and Midwest. Her workshops focus upon the initial steps of evaluation, especially model building. Programs or organizations wishing to have one of these workshops can arrange it directly through Philliber Associates (914-626-2126).

The National Organization on Adolescent Pregnancy and Parenting Program (NOAPPP) holds an annual meeting in the fall. The meeting usually is preceded by a program evaluation workshop. (Call 301-913-0378 for more information.)

Technical Assistance

Local Evaluator List

Program administrators wishing to conduct evaluations of their pregnancy programs have frequently sought the advice of social scientists at nearby universities or other consultants adept at program evaluation. Oftentimes, however, administrators either do not know that such help is available or do not know how to evaluate the expertise of the potential evaluator. To make the search for evaluators easier, NationalNet has compiled a list of experts throughout the country who are (a) skilled in evaluation research methods, (b) familiar with teen pregnancy research, and (c) available to serve as consultants for local programs.

NationalNet. (1990). *Local evaluator network for teen pregnancy programs.* Los Altos, CA: Social Research Applications.

NationalNet

NationalNet, operated by Social Research Applications, is a technical assistance center staffed by professionals trained in, and committed to, forging partnerships with local program staff and local program evaluators. NationalNet is funded by the Charles Stewart Mott Foundation, the Henry J. Kaiser Family Foundation, the William and Flora Hewlett Foundation, and the Northwest Area Foundation, an alliance of supporters that indicates the importance foundations are beginning to place upon high-quality evaluation. The goal of the project is to assist local programs with the design and conduct of high-quality process and impact evaluations. NationalNet staff members provide reviews of proposals, program models, research design, research instruments, data collection plans, and/or data analysis plans at no cost to the requesting program. On-site technical assistance, assistance with improvement development, review of machine-readable files, and collaborative data analysis and writing are provided at a low, negotiable cost. NationalNet is a potential model for cost-effective ways to advance a field, while simultaneously empowering local staff.

Data and Technical Standards

For those interested in taking a deeper look at evaluation results by directly analyzing data pertaining to prevention evaluation studies, a valuable resource is the Data Archive on Adolescent Pregnancy and Pregnancy Prevention (DAAPPP). This archive is a collection of original data sets pertaining to the field of teen pregnancy research. Among these data sets are several evaluation studies. These may be obtained from the archive for secondary analysis; studies may be purchased individually at modest cost; or the entire set of evaluation studies (10 in all) may be purchased together at a discount. Improvements are being made also in the availability of technical guidelines to assist program administrators and evaluators. For example, the Data Archive on Adolescent Pregnancy and Pregnancy Prevention (DAAPPP) assembles and distributes to researchers the best data sets on teen pregnancy research. To guide the archive staff in their selection of data sets, a national advisory panel has developed a set of technical standards for evaluation research that define the quality that evaluation studies need to attain to be worthy of preservation for reanalysis by other researchers. As such, these standards serve as a useful guide for evaluation researchers. The principal elements of these standards for archivability include the following points. The data should be available in a machine-readable format and should preserve data at the individual client level for at least 2 years. The machine-readable data file should include follow-up data in the time frame called for by the project study design, linkable to intake data. Intake client sample sizes should be at least 50 to 75 cases per year, and retention rates equal to or greater than 70% for each follow-up period included in the archived data. The data should include an adequate coverage of variables relevant to the program's specific intervention, as well as objectives.

Our hope is that, by drawing upon these and other resources, funders, program staff, local evaluators, and outside scientists can together move the state of the art, slowly but surely, beyond its present boundaries. The end result should be better programs providing more cost-effective service to our nation's teens.

References

Card, J. J. (1981, May). Long-term consequences for children of teenage parents. *Demography, 18,* 137-156.

Elliott, D., & Morse, B. (1989). Delinquency and drug use as risk factors in teenage sexual activity. *Youth and Society, 21,* 32-60.

Furstenberg, F. F., Jr., Morgan, S. P., Moore, K. A., & Peterson, J. L. (1987, August). Race differences in the timing of adolescent intercourse. *American Sociological Review, 52*(4), 511-518.

Hayes, D. C. (Ed.). (1987). *Risking the future: Adolescent sexuality, pregnancy, and childbearing* (Vol. I). Washington, DC: National Academy.

Miller, B. C., & Moore, K. A. (1990). Adolescent sexual behavior, pregnancy, and parenting: Research through the 1980's. *Journal of Marriage and the Family, 52,* 1025-1044.

Moore, K. A. (1988). *Facts at a glance.* (Available from Child Trends, Inc., 2100 M Street, NW, Washington, DC, 20037).

Moore, K. A., & Burt, M. (1982). *Private crisis, public cost: Policy perspectives on teenage childbearing.* Washington, DC: Urban Institute.

Moore, K. A., Peterson, J. L., & Furstenberg, F. F., Jr. (1984). *Starting early: The antecedents of early premarital intercourse.* Paper presented at the 1984 annual meeting of the Population Association of America. Minneapolis, MN.

Moore, K. A., Peterson, J. L., & Furstenberg, F. F., Jr. (1986). Parental attitudes and the occurrence of early sexual activity. *Journal of Marriage and the Family, 48,* 777-782.

Mueller, D. P., & Higgins, P. S. (1989). Prevention programs in human services. In J. J. Card (Ed.), *Evaluating programs aimed at preventing teenage pregnancies* (pp. 1-24). Los Altos, CA: Sociometrics Corp.

Newcomer, S. F., Gilbert, M., & Udry, J. R. (1980). *Perceived and actual same sex peer behavior as determinants of adolescent sexual behavior.* Paper presented at the annual meeting of the American Psychological Association, Montreal, Canada.

Udry, J. E., Billy, J. O. G., Morris, N. M., Groff, T. R., & Raj, M. H. (1985, January). Serum androgenic hormones motivate sexual behavior in adolescent boys. *Fertility and Sterility, 43,* 90-94.

2

Small Group Sex Education at School

The McMaster Teen Program

B. HELEN THOMAS
ALBA MITCHELL
M. CORINNE DEVLIN
CHARLIE H. GOLDSMITH
JOEL SINGER
DEREK WATTERS

**The McMaster Teen Program and
Its Experimental Evaluation**

Among young adolescents in developed countries, sexual activity is frequent, the use of birth control is poor, and the pregnancy rates are highest in the United States, followed by those in Canada (Jones et al., 1985; Zelnik & Shah, 1983). A recent review of the Canadian evidence suggests that the adolescent pregnancy rate has not changed significantly since the early 1980s. In 1982, among those 15 to 17 years of age, the pregnancy rates were 28.3 per 1,000, as opposed to 67.4 per 1,000 for those 17 to 19 years old. By 1987, these rates had decreased to 24.9 and 64.3, respectively (Wadhera & Silins, 1990). For the past 15 years in the United States, approximately 10% of females between the ages of 15 and 19 years have become pregnant each year (Trussell, 1988).

A variety of school-based sex education programs have been developed in an effort to reduce these rates of unintended adolescent pregnancy.

Although knowledge acquisition and attitude change have been examined in many program evaluations, very few studies have evaluated the impact of programs on actual sexual behavior (Dawson, 1986; Furstenberg, Moore, & Peterson, 1985; Kirby, 1984; Marsiglio & Mott, 1986; Zelnik & Kim, 1982). In a recent review of these evaluations, Stout and Rivara (1989) concluded that the programs had little effect on sexual activity, contraceptive use, or pregnancy rates. Most studies are methodologically weak in that they are retrospective surveys or case-control studies without randomly assigned participants or control groups. Furthermore, the results are based on self-reported exposure to programs and outcomes. No consideration is given to the variation of programs to which respondents might have been exposed. In conclusion, the authors recommend prospective rigorous evaluation of school-based programs employing a randomized controlled trial design (RCT) with a large sample of adolescents and a long-term follow-up.

Schinke (1984) reported the results of an RCT with a small sample and short-term follow-up. The results of a large-scale RCT based on this work are reported in Chapter 3 of this volume. Eisen, Zellman, and McAlister (1990) reported findings of a large ($n = 1,444$ per group) RCT to evaluate the effectiveness of a sexuality education program based on elements of the Health Belief Model and Social Learning Theory, discussed in Chapter 9 of this volume. In a 1-year follow-up of participants (aged 13-19 years at baseline), they found differences based on gender and on prior sexual activity. Virgin males in the experimental group were more likely than those in the comparison group to remain so during the follow-up year. The program had no effect on continued coital abstinence for females. At 1-year follow-up, consistent use of an effective contraception method was reported more frequently among the comparison group of young women who did initiate intercourse after the intervention. Among coitally active males and females, both the experimental and comparison programs increased consistent use of effective birth control methods. Young men from the experimental programs reported significantly greater contraceptive efficiency at 1-year follow-up than those from the comparison programs. For females, the differences between the two groups were not significant. Prior exposure to sex education was associated with improved contraceptive efficiency for both genders, regardless of timing of initiation or sexual intercourse or program attended. Based on their findings, the authors concluded that although such programs can be implemented and evaluated, because of gender, ethnic, and other differences that influenced the impact of the program, target populations need to be identified and specific programs should be developed for them.

In 1980, a group of health care providers and researchers at McMaster University in Hamilton, Canada, recognized unintended teenage pregnancy within their clinic population as a common problem. An audit of regional hospital records and other available data confirmed that the teen pregnancy rate (59.7/1,000) in the Hamilton-Wentworth Region was higher than the provincial (Ontario) rate (48.5/1,000) and exceeded rates of the contiguous regions (Orton & Rosenblatt, 1981). A review of the available interventions and their proven effectiveness led to the development of an elementary school primary prevention program known as the McMaster Teen Program (MTP) and a longitudinal randomized controlled trial to evaluate its effectiveness. The purposes of this chapter are to describe the McMaster Teen Program, to present the design and results of the evaluation study, and to discuss future implications for program development.

The McMaster Teen Program

Several investigators have attempted to identify adolescents "at risk" for unintended pregnancy (Thomas, Mitchell, & Devlin, 1990). Even in these identified groups, however, many do not become sexually active at young ages, and of those who do, many actively avoid pregnancy. Other authors believe that the problem of unintended adolescent pregnancy arises because of the combination of variations in biological, cognitive, emotional, and behavioral development among this age group. In other words, it is a developmental problem that faces all adolescents and not just those thought to be disadvantaged for one reason or another (Cvetkovich, Grote, Lieberman, & Miller, 1978; Tauer, 1983). This latter perspective has led to the application of theoretical constructs that could influence the development of primary prevention programs for general populations of adolescents (Eisen, Zellman, & McAlister, 1985; Schinke, Blythe, & Gilchrist, 1981). The McMaster Teen Program is a primary prevention program for students in grades 7 and 8, based on the cognitive-behavioral model for preventing unwanted adolescent pregnancy outlined by Schinke et al. (1981). It is designed to assist students in:

1. acquiring accurate information about development, sexuality, and relationships with others;

2. improving their communication skills around sexual choices and activities;
3. developing systematic problem-solving and decision-making skills around sexual activity, and;
4. practicing and implementing responsible decisions about sexual behavior.

The format for the program is small coeducational groups (six to eight students each) led by trained tutors. Ten 1-hour sessions were held over a 6- to 8-week period. Through the use of films, group discussion, role play, and question-and-answer periods, these sessions addressed such relevant topics as normal adolescent development, the influence of peer pressure on behavior, gender roles, responsibility in relationships, stages of physical intimacy, and teenage pregnancy and childbearing (an outline of the topics and content is displayed in Table 2.1). Contraceptive methods and their use were not included because these topics were not within the Ontario Ministry of Education Guidelines for students in grades 7 and 8 at that time.

Tutor Selection and Training

The tutors included public health nurses, elementary school physical/health education teachers, and community professionals who had been practicing public health nurses (PHNs) or teachers. Because a unique aspect of this program was the use of small coeducational, tutor-led groups, the ability of the tutors to fulfill their role effectively was crucial to successful program implementation and completion. PHNs and teachers were selected as tutors because many of them already possessed a number of the skills required to facilitate small group learning. In this situation, the role of the tutor was

1. to establish a climate in which students are free to participate actively in inquiry;
2. to demonstrate respect for the experience, creativity, personal values, and behaviors that students bring to the group;
3. to facilitate the development of communication, negotiation, problem-solving, and decision-making skills within the group;
4. to guide group process through clarification and provision of resources as necessary, and;
5. to be open and honest about his or her own biases and limitations.

To ensure that all tutors were adequately prepared to perform their role, they were given a 40-hour training workshop. The workshop was

Table 2.1 Topics and Content

Topic	Content
Problem-Solving/Decision-Making	Introduction Problem-solving process Common issues in adolescence
Puberty	Physical and emotional changes at puberty Myths Self-image Peer pressure
Male/Female Roles Role of the Media	Male/female roles Roles in a relationship Double standard Values clarification Effects of the media on behavior
Relationships	Dating and relationships (e.g., communication, honesty, responsibility, peer pressure, self-esteem, breaking up)
Peer Pressure	What is it? Why do we respond to it? Ways of dealing with it
Intimacy	Relationships and roles Types of intimacy Consequences of sexual intercourse Gender roles Peer pressure Communication
Teenage Pregnancy and Parenting	Anatomy and physiology of pregnancy Myths about intercourse, contraception, and pregnancy Risks and consequences of adolescent pregnancy Parenting

a combination of didactic and experiential opportunities in three areas related to the program. The first area addressed was human sexuality. The objectives were to assist tutors in clarifying their own sexual values, in developing a tolerance for different values, in becoming desensitized to explicit aspects of human sexual behavior, and in exploring issues, attitudes, and values related to adolescents through such techniques as role play and small group discussion.

The second component of the tutor preparation focused on the role of a small-group facilitator. Following a theoretical explanation of stages of group development, roles of the group facilitator and other group members, characteristics of an effective group, and common problems experienced in small groups, the tutors had an opportunity to apply the concepts in small groups and then obtain feedback from their peers.

Problem-based learning was the third aspect of tutor preparation. Again the process was explained and then the tutors practiced applying it in small groups of peers. They used the session outlines that had been prepared for the students. In this way, they both learned the skills and also became familiar with the actual materials they would be using with the students. Finally, a half day was spent reviewing the program and the logistics of implementing it.

Program Resources

A tutor guide was developed by the investigators and the project staff. This guide provided tutors with objectives for each session and a variety of age-appropriate resources to be used to stimulate group discussion and problem solving. One successful technique used by many tutors was the question box. At the beginning of each session, students were given paper and a pencil and asked to record any question related to the topic that they would like discussed in the group. Whether or not students had a question, all were expected to place their pieces of paper in the box. The tutor removed the questions, and the group decided which ones they wanted to discuss. In this way, students got to ask relevant questions but were protected from being exposed as the inquirer.

All participating students were given a student guide that provided them with accurate knowledge about fertility and human sexuality. As well, it included readings and other activities to complete in preparation for the sessions (e.g., crossword puzzles, fill-in-the-blank scenarios). To enhance family involvement in the process, students were encouraged to share the guide with their parents.

**Student and Parent Evaluation
of the Program**

Students were asked to complete evaluations of the program at sessions three, six, and nine. The questions were designed to determine student comfort within the group and with the process, and student assessment of the tutor's performance. Parents also completed an evaluation from their perspective after the completion of the program.

One-way analysis of variance (ANOVA) of student program evaluations after sessions three, six, and nine indicated that although significant variation existed between schools ($F = 15.83$, $p = 0.00$), a significant increase ($F = 43.38$, $p = 0.00$) in comfort occurred within the groups, and learning took place over time. These increases were significantly different ($p = 0.05$) at each point in time. Student-reported effectiveness of the tutor also increased over the three points in time ($F = 6.26$, $p = 0.002$). The professional background (i.e., teacher or public health nurse) of the tutors made no significant difference in student comfort in the groups or in student perception of tutor effectiveness.

Anecdotally, students reported that the strengths of the program included feeling comfortable talking about sex within a supportive group, hearing viewpoints from those of the opposite gender, correcting erroneous information related to sexuality, and learning to make decisions more accurately. The limitations most frequently cited were that the program was not long enough and that students did not like having to miss some physical education classes to participate.

Parent evaluations indicated that most parents whose son or daughter had taken part would enroll another child in a similar program. Parents commented that they liked the commonsense approach, that they saw the coeducational student groups as improving understanding and communication between the genders, and that the program had made it much easier for them to discuss sensitive sexual issues with their adolescent.

Evaluation of the McMaster
Teen Program

The evaluation of the MTP tested three hypotheses: that the pregnancy rate among females in the experimental group would be lower than that among the control group; that responsible sexual behavior, demonstrated by an increase in use of birth control or a decrease in sexual intercourse, would occur more frequently among students in the experimental group than among those in the control group; and that the locus of control scores among the experimental students would be lower (i.e., more internally controlled) than those among the control group.

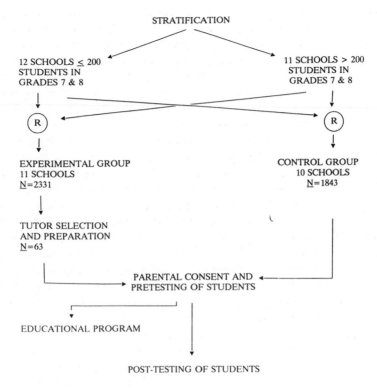

Figure 2.1. Study Design. Twenty-One Schools in the Hamilton Board of Education with Grades 7 and 8 Students.

Study Design

The MTP was evaluated using a randomized controlled trial design with a 4-year follow-up. The study design is outlined in Figure 2.1. The details of the methodology have been reported elsewhere (Mitchell et al., in press).

The unit of randomization was schools. Schools rather than students were randomized to minimize potential contamination of the comparison group through discussion of the program with classmates who might have been receiving the experimental program. Students in the schools allocated to the experimental group received the MTP. Students in the control schools received the conventional board of education sex education program offered during health class (Hamilton Board of Education,

1981). The conventional program, taught didactically to students segregated by gender, addressed individual growth patterns, secondary sex characteristics, male and female reproductive systems, and the menstrual cycle. Although this curriculum was provided for the teachers, they had considerable freedom to select specific areas on which to focus.

Description of the Sample

This study took place in Hamilton, Ontario, Canada, a medium-sized (population approximately 307,000) industrial city composed of a predominantly blue collared, multiethnic population. Because this was a primary prevention program, the target population was students between the ages of 11 and 16 years who were in grades 7 and 8 in the 21 schools comprising the public school system. Students attending private schools or schools in the Roman Catholic school system were excluded. Other exclusion criteria for students were no written parental consent, students who did not wish to be involved, students who knew they were moving out of the area within the next few weeks, those who could not write or understand English, and students who in the opinion of the school principal had severe learning disabilities or would be unable to function in a small group.

The number of schools to be assigned to experimental and control groups was determined using the data about pregnancy rates for adolescents 16 years and younger in 1982, the year the project was designed. Allowing for dropouts, a minimum sample size of 9 schools per group was established (Meinert & Tonascia, 1986). To ensure that the groups would be similar in size, the schools were stratified, prior to randomization, into those with 200 or fewer students in grades 7 and 8 and those with more than 200 students. Using a random numbers table, 11 schools were assigned randomly to the experimental group and 10 to the control group (Odeh, Owen, Birnbaum, & Fisher, 1977). Because of the level of community interest in this project, and to enhance the statistical power of the results, the Ontario Ministry of Health agreed to provide additional funds so that all 21 schools could be included.

Obtaining Parental Consent

To participate in the program, students had to have written parental consent. All parents were sent a letter and a consent form from the investigators that explained the program and outlined their son's or daughter's role in it, depending on whether they attended an experimental or control school. This letter was accompanied by a letter from the respective school principal, endorsing the program and requesting parental permission for student participation. To assist parents and students in making informed choices about participation, information nights were held at the schools. These were opportunities for prospective participants and their parents to hear an overview of the program and to ask questions. Teachers kept track of incoming consent forms. Follow-up letters were sent to all nonrespondents.

Outcome Measures

Student age and gender and the parental composition in the home were obtained from board of education registers. The remaining data were obtained from the students, using the following three paper-and-pencil self-report instruments, which took approximately 45 minutes to complete.

The Nowicki-Strickland Locus of Control measure is a 40-item scale designed for administration to students between the ages of 12 and 18 years. This scale was included to determine whether adolescents who are responsive to external pressure are more likely to become pregnant unintentionally than those who make independent decisions about their behavior. Its reliability is adequate, with an internal consistency of $r = 0.71$-0.74 and a test retest reliability coefficient of $r = 0.66$-0.71. It also has been shown to have discriminative, convergent, and construct validity (Nowicki & Strickland, 1973). Scores on the Nowicki-Strickland Locus of Control scale vary from 0-40, with higher scores representing a higher degree of responsiveness to external pressure.

The demographic questionnaire consisted of questions about individual and family variables frequently cited in the literature as correlates of unintended adolescent pregnancy. These variables included maternal and paternal occupations, educational and occupational goals of the adolescent, languages spoken in the home (a measure of ethnicity), and a 12-item subscale of the Family Assessment Device (FAD). The FAD is a 60-item measure of family function, which has seven subscales. The 12-item subscale of General Functioning (GF) used in this study has a high internal consistency with the overall FAD score (Cronbach's alpha = 0.92) (Epstein, Baldwin, & Bishop, 1983). Scores on the GF scale vary from 12 to 48, with higher scores representing a higher degree of family dysfunction.

Table 2.2 Private Ballot Questions

---

1. Are you between 11 and 16 years old?
   YES ☐   NO ☐

2. Have you ever gone around (hung around) with a special boy/girl?
   YES ☐   NO ☐

3. The following are some ways that people show affection:
   1. holding hands   4. necking
   2. hugging   5. petting
   3. kissing
   Have you ever shared your affection with a special friend in any of these ways?
   YES ☐   NO ☐

4. Sexual intercourse occurs when a boy's penis goes into a girl's vagina. Have you
   ever had sexual intercourse?
   YES ☐   NO ☐

5. The following are methods used to avoid pregnancy: the pill, the IUD (intrauterine
   device), the diaphragm, condom (safe), foam or jelly, and natural family planning.
   How often do you/your partner use any of these birth control methods? Check the
   one descriptor below which is nearest to the truth:
   ☐ Always
   ☐ Frequently
   ☐ Rarely
   ☐ Never

6. FOR FEMALES: Have you ever been pregnant?
   YES ☐   NO ☐

The private ballot was designed to collect sensitive information about sexual behavior. The ballot requested information about levels of physical intimacy in which students had engaged, frequency of use of birth control, and for female respondents, pregnancy. The specific questions included are outlined in Table 2.2. Each ballot question was hidden in a perforated pocket that was opened only if the student responded affirmatively to the previous question. The questions progressed from those least sensitive to those most sensitive. Once students responded to a question with a negative answer, they had completed the questionnaire and were instructed not to progress to the more sensitive questions. The private ballot was completed behind the privacy of a polling booth. When completed, a ballot was placed in an envelope, sealed, and deposited into a ballot box.

The format of the private ballot was developed to allay parental concerns that exposure to sensitive questions might promote sexual activity among the adolescents. The process of ballot completion maximized student privacy in answering these sensitive questions, thereby enhancing the validity of their responses (Levy, 1976).

The demographic questionnaire and the private ballot were developed by the investigators and had been pretested during a pilot study on a similar group of grade 7 and 8 students ($n = 179$) the year before the RCT began. All three questionnaires were administered before the program began, 6 weeks following the program, and then annually until each participating student reached his or her 17th birthday.

Each student was assigned a unique identification number that included information about school of origin and gender. These identification numbers were used to link data from three questionnaires within 1 year and to link data from one year to the next over the 4 years. To ensure student confidentiality, all questionnaires were identifiable by code number only. A single master list of the student names and code numbers was kept in a safe place by the project coordinator.

To validate self-reported pregnancies, these data will be compared with pregnancy data from the Ontario Health Insurance Plan (OHIP). Because of lag time for data retrieval at OHIP, these comparisons cannot be made until 1992. OHIP is a universal provincial health plan provided for virtually all Ontario residents regardless of age, health status, or financial means (Iglehart, 1986). Because the nine other provinces in Canada have similar plans and a reciprocal relationship with each other regarding reimbursement, all study respondents who seek health care services in Canada for miscarriages, abortions, prenatal care, or deliveries will be recorded in the OHIP files. These data will not include those who have spontaneous miscarriages for which they do not seek health care, those who go outside the country for abortions or deliveries, or those who attend private abortion clinics within the country.

Student Tracking

The testing over a 4- to 5-year period necessitated tracking of students as they moved from elementary to secondary school, as well as when they left the region. Student registers from the board of education were reviewed annually to locate the students who moved from one school to another within the city. Testing of students occurred in the school they attended at the time of testing. If the student was absent at the time of testing, up to three additional visits were made to the school at later dates to administer the questionnaires. Failing this, the questionnaires and a self-addressed stamped return envelope were mailed to the student's home. Preceding this mail-out, a letter was sent to the student's parents to alert them to the arrival of the questionnaires and to request that they encourage their son or daughter to complete the questionnaires, and to provide an environment as private as that created in the schools. Nonrespondents were sent a follow-up letter, and then a reminder telephone call was made. Additional questionnaires were sent on request.

For cases in which students had moved out of the Hamilton-Wentworth Region, public health nurses across the province administered the questionnaires in the students' new schools. Those students who were not found in their new schools or who had moved out of the province or country were sent the questionnaires by mail with a self-addressed stamped envelope preceded by a letter to their parents. Nonrespondents were sent a follow-up letter.

Various strategies were used to locate students lost to follow-up. Staff at schools where students completed their most recent set of posttests were asked for forwarding information. Where necessary, telephone directories and directory assistance for the city to which they had moved were used to locate the students. In an effort to minimize those lost to follow-up, students were asked at the time of testing, both in the schools and through home mailings, for future changes of address, if known.

Few students were lost to follow-up from pretest over the four posttests. Over 90% of eligible students in both the experimental and control groups completed questionnaires at first and second posttests. For third and fourth posttests, completion rates varied from 80% to 88%. No difference was seen in numbers lost to follow-up between the two groups.

Data Management and Analysis

Total scores for Family Functioning and Nowicki-Strickland Scales with missing items were calculated in the following way. If 30% or fewer items were missing, total scores were prorated by dividing the raw total score by the number of completed items and multiplying this by the total number of items on the scale. Scores were not calculated for questionnaires with more than 30% of the items missing.

Students made primarily two types of errors in completing the private ballot. For those who failed to answer the subsequent question following an affirmative response, data provided to that point were used in the analysis. For those who answered a subsequent question following a negative response, data after the first negative response were excluded.

Intraobserver variation in accuracy of computer data entry was examined by having the person who originally entered the pretest data reenter 5% of it. The number of keystroke errors was tabulated by summing the number of discrepancies with the data originally entered. The error rate was less than 0.5% for all questionnaires, over all years.

To test the baseline equivalence between the experimental and control groups, pretest data were analyzed using the SPSS/PC+ computer package (SPSS Inc., 1986). Students' t tests were used to compare differences in age, family functioning scores, and locus of control scores. All other variables were analyzed using the chi-square test. For both tests, the level of significance was set at 0.05. No adjustment was made for multiple testing.

Reported frequency rates of the primary outcomes (i.e., sexual intercourse, consistent use of birth control, and pregnancy) for pretest and the fourth posttest were calculated for the control and experimental groups by gender. Total pregnancies reported within each group over the 4 years also were calculated.

Logistic regressions were carried out separately for each gender to determine which independent variables were related at a statistically significant level to the primary outcomes of sexual intercourse, "always" using birth control, and for females, pregnancy reported at the fourth posttest. Only students who did *not* report each outcome at pretest were included in the analyses for the respective outcome. In the first regressions, a stepwise procedure was used that allowed all variables that independently contributed to the outcome of interest at the 0.05 level to enter the model.

A statistically significant pretest difference was noted between the two groups in rates of sexual intercourse among males. On closer examination, it became evident that this difference was school dependent. Therefore, in the second set of regressions, pretest rate of sexual intercourse by school and gender, as well as school size and any other independent variables that had entered the first model, were forced into the model. Treatment group was then added to the model to test its incremental effect.

Results

In the 11 experimental schools, 2,331 students were eligible for entry into the study. Consent rates in these schools varied from 87.6% to 96.2% with a mean of 90.0% (n = 2,111 students). The number of ineligible students was 109 (4.5%). In the 10 control schools, 1,843 students were eligible for entry, and the consent rates varied from 48.3% to 89.5% with a mean of 68.5% (n = 1,263). The lower parental consent rate among parents of students in the control schools probably reflects the facts that their children would have to answer intrusive questions but receive no benefit from the program, and that this was their way of publicly indicating their displeasure that their son's or daughter's school had not been selected to receive the program. To determine whether any differences existed between the consenters and nonconsenters in the control group, which might influence the outcomes of the study, the socioeconomic status of the families of the two subgroups were compared using 1981 census tract data and the proportion of single parent families in each subgroup were compared using the Hamilton Board of Education data base. No statistically significant differences were found between the subgroups on either variable. Withdrawals were very infrequent: 9 (0.4%) in the experimental group, and 2 (0.2%) in the control group.

Comparisons of the sociodemographic characteristics of the experimental and control groups at pretest are outlined in Table 2.3. Maternal and paternal occupation are not included because, in many instances, students were unable to be specific enough for the data to be categorized using any of the standard occupational classifications. Because these questions had been included to assess family socioeconomic status (SES), another strategy was used to compare the SES of the two groups. A review of census tract data for the catchment areas of the experimental and control schools indicated that the annual family income was similar for both groups.

Two significant (p = 0.01) differences were found between the groups: students in the control group were 0.1 years younger than those in the experimental group, and a higher proportion (76.8% vs. 73.0%) of students in the control group reported speaking English as a first language in their homes. Neither of these differences was clinically important. Because school principals had used the inability of students to speak or write English as a criterion for exclusion, all participating students could understand the content of the program and the questionnaires. The two groups were comparable on all other sociodemographic variables.

Table 2.3 Pretest Characteristics of Experimental and Control Groups

Variable	Experimental Group (11 schools) n = 2062*	Control Group (10 schools) n = 1228*	Difference Between Groups Test Value	P Value
Gender:				
Male n (%)	1013 (49.1)	576 (46.9)	$x^2 = 1.52$	0.22
Female n (%)	1049 (50.9)	652 (53.1)		
Occupational Goal of Student:				
Present n (%)	1845 (89.5)	1112 (90.5)	$x^2 = 0.89$	0.35
Absent n (%)	214 (10.4)	115 (.94)		
No response	0	1 (0.1)		
Language Spoken in Home:				
English n (%)	1504 (73.0)	943 (76.8)	$x^2 = 5.95$	0.01[+]
Other n (%)	554 (26.9)	283 (23.0)		
No response	1 (0.1)	2 (0.2)		
Grade:				
7 n (%)	1018 (49.4)	611 (49.8)	$x^2 = 0.95$	0.62
8 n (%)	1011 (49.0)	592 (48.2)		
Other n (%)	33 (1.6)	25 (2.0)		
Adults in Home:				
Both parents n (%)	1529 (74.2)	919 (74.8)	$x^2 = 0.39$	0.53
Other n (%)	409 (19.8)	232 (18.9)		
Data not available	124 (6.0)	77 (6.3)		
Age:				
(n,m,s; years)[@]	2044, 12.7, 0.9	1218, 12.6, 0.9	$t = 2.52$	0.01[+]
Data not available	18	10		
Family Functioning:				
(n,m,s; units)	2029, 22.8, 5.2	1210, 22.5, 5.5	$t = 1.62$	0.11
Incomplete	33	18		
Locus of Control:				
(n,m,s; units)	2022, 13.8, 4.8	1216, 14.0, 4.8	$t = -1.48$	0.14
Incomplete	40	12		

NOTE: *where n for a variable is less than total n, data were not available or questionnaires were incomplete
@ (n,m,s; units) = number, mean, standard deviation; units
+ statistically significant

The self-reported sexual behavior of the experimental and control students at pretest is displayed in Table 2.4. One difference ($p = 0.03$) was found between the two groups: a higher proportion of males in the experimental group (32.7% vs. 26.8%) reported having had sexual intercourse.

Table 2.4 Sexual Behavior at Pretest of Experimental and Control Groups

Variable	Experimental Group (11 schools) Males = 1013 Females = 1049 n (%)*	Control Group (10 schools) Males = 576 Females = 652 n (%)*	Difference Between Groups x^2	P Value
Special Friend:				
Male	928 (91.9)	514 (91.1)	0.17	0.68
Female	943 (90.2)	591 (90.8)	0.08	0.78
Shared Affection:				
Male	856 (92.3)	483 (94.5)	2.11	0.15
Female	823 (87.8)	526 (89.3)	0.63	0.43
Coitus:				
Male	275 (32.7)	127 (26.8)	4.67	0.03$^+$
Female	135 (16.7)	84 (16.2)	0.01	0.89
Use Birth Control Always:				
Male	59 (22.3)	29 (22.8)	0.02	0.90
Female	21 (16.3)	15 (18.1)	0.02	0.73
At Least One Pregnancy	3 (2.3)	2 (2.7)	0.03	0.86

NOTE: *% represents proportion responding positively out of all those who responded to the question
+ statistically significant

The changes in reported frequencies of the primary outcomes from pretest to fourth posttest are outlined in Table 2.5. Males in the experimental group reported significantly ($p < 0.05$) higher rates of sexual intercourse at both pretest and posttest four for the experimental and control groups. Also found were a steadily increasing frequency rate of reported sexual intercourse, consistent use of birth control, and pregnancy for all students in the control and experimental groups from pretest to posttest four.

Over the course of the project (i.e., summing reported pregnancies at each of the four posttests), 166 pregnancies were reported. Of these, 161 were first pregnancies. Within the experimental group, 104 (9.9%) first pregnancies were reported. Within the control group, 57 (9.9%) were reported.

The results of the logistic regressions on the three dependent variables are outlined in Table 2.6. Different variables account for the outcomes for the two genders. Results of the stepwise regression indicate that, for females, coming from an ethnic family, having educational

Table 2.5 Sexual Intercourse, Use of Birth Control, and Pregnancy Rates, Over Time, By Group

	Pretest 1		Posttest 4	
	Experimental Group	Control Group	Experimental Group	Control Group
	Females = 1049	Females = 652	Females = 831	Females = 524
	Males = 1013	Males = 576	Males = 762	Males = 453
Variable	n (%)	n (%)	n (%)	n (%)
Sexual Intercourse				
Females	135 (12.9)	83 (12.7)	399 (48.0)	246 (50.0)
Males	270 (26.7)	126 (21.9)*	412 (54.1)	200 (44.0)*
Consistent Use of Birth Control				
Females	21 (2.0)	15 (2.3)	253 (30.5)	151 (28.8)
Males	59 (5.8)	29 (5.0)	219 (28.7)	103 (22.7)
Pregnancy	3 (0.29)	2 (0.31)	38 (4.6)	15 (2.9)

NOTE: $*p < .05$ for comparison between experimental and control group

$$\% = \frac{\text{positive responses to question}}{\text{number of participants}} \times 100$$

goals beyond high school completion, age, living with both parents, and having a low N-S score (i.e., internally controlled) decrease the likelihood of having sexual intercourse before 17 years of age. For males, the only variable that delays the age of first sexual intercourse is having educational goals beyond high school completion (Table 2.6, Model 1). Among sexually active females, consistent use of birth control was influenced by ethnicity, having educational goals beyond high school completion, and by low N-S scores; whereas for males the significant variables were age, having educational goals beyond high school completion, coming from a small elementary school (i.e., fewer than 200 students), and being a member of the control group of schools. Only one variable significantly contributed to pregnancy before age 17: having a high externality score on the N-S scale.

When school size and coital rate at school of origin were forced into the models, the results on all the outcomes for females remained the same, with one exception: living with both parents no longer significantly contributed to first intercourse. Neither variable contributed to the models. Furthermore, being a student in the experimental group had no incremental effect. For males the results were different. Adding school size and coital rate at school of origin resulted in a model for

46 Small Group Sex Education at School

Table 2.6 Results of Logistic Regression on Dependent Variables By Gender

Variable	Females Model 1* p	Females Model 2** p	Males Model 1* p	Males Model 2** p
First Intercourse				
English spoken in the home	0.00	0.00	—	—
Educational objectives	0.00	0.00	0.05	0.07
Age	0.02	0.03	—	—
Parental composition	0.04	0.08	—	—
Externality score	0.04	0.05	—	—
School size	—	0.70	—	0.82
School base rate of coitus	—	0.50	—	0.54
Treatment group	—	0.53	0.06	0.18
Consistent Use of Birth Control				
Age	—	—	0.03	0.01
English spoken in the home	0.00	0.00	—	—
Student educational objective	0.00	0.01	0.03	0.06
Externality score	0.00	0.00	—	—
School size	—	0.10	0.05	0.10
School base rate of coitus	—	0.11	—	0.12
Treatment group	—	0.35	0.02	0.10
Pregnancy				
Externality score	0.03	0.03		
School size	—	0.18		
School base rate of coitus	—	0.84		
Treatment group	—	0.46		

NOTE: *variables allowed to enter stepwise
**school size, school base rate of coitus, and significant variables from Model 1 forced in, then treatment group forced in
p = probability

first intercourse that had no statistically significant independent variables. For consistent use of birth control, the only variable that made an independent contribution was age: as males got older, they used birth control more consistently. Treatment group had no incremental influence on either outcome.

Discussion

The randomization of schools resulted in equivalent groups at pretest on most important variables. Neither the statistically significant difference in age (0.1 years) nor in language spoken in the home between the two groups is clinically important. These differences probably reached statistical significance because of the large size of the sample. The finding that significantly more males in the experimental group reported experience with sexual intercourse alerted us to investigate the differences among schools in both groups and to control for this in subsequent analyses.

Although schools were the unit of randomization to minimize contamination, this strategy may only have been effective for the 1 or 2 years while students remained in the elementary school setting. Once students moved into secondary school, the combination of elementary schools may have resulted in bringing together those from the experimental and control groups.

This study corroborates several findings reported by others. Significantly more young males than young females report having experienced sexual intercourse. Two questions immediately come to mind: with whom are these youths engaging in this activity, and how valid are the data. The results indicate that by 17 years of age approximately 50% of males and females have engaged in sexual intercourse. It is imperative to remember that 50% have not had this experience. A thorough study of the attributes of those who are not sexually active could provide important information for future prevention program planning. Among those who are sexually active, consistent use of reliable birth control measures is infrequent. The rate of consistent use increases with age: by age 17, slightly over 50% of coitally active males and females report this behavior.

Our findings differ from those of others in two areas. We found neither an improvement in use of birth control nor an increased abstinence from sexual intercourse within our experimental group compared with the control group (Eisen et al., 1990; Schinke, 1984). Because this result could have been attributed to the longer period between the program and follow-up, we compared the reported data for both variables at posttest one (3 months postprogram) and at posttest two (12 months following the program). No between group differences were noted on either variable at either point in time. The fact that Eisen and his colleagues (1990) demonstrated differences in behavior of adolescents exposed to the experimental program as opposed to members of the comparison group may be a result of sample differences or program differences. Their sample was older at the time of the program (i.e., over 30% were 15-17 years of age vs. mean age of 12.7 years in our work), and therefore the information was more relevant. As well, 80% of their sample were adolescents from low-income and/or inner-city families, whereas our sample included adolescents from families of a medium-sized industrial city where the unemployment rate is relatively low. Finally, their program included sessions about the benefits and barriers to fertility control, and ours did not.

The results are interesting in that the multiple regressions show that different variables affect the behavior of the two genders. In fact, each of the three outcome variables has different models. A gender-related effect on sexual behavior was also found by Eisen and his colleagues (1990). This may account, in part, for the lack of results of this intensive, although brief, program and other reported evidence that sexual education programs to date have not consistently reduced rates of sexual intercourse, use of contraception, or pregnancy rates (Dawson, 1986; Kirby, 1984; Zelnik & Kim, 1982).

Strengths of the project include random assignment of a community sample to the intervention, high consent rates among the experimental group, acceptable consent rates among the control group, virtually no withdrawals during the program, long-term follow-up of over 80% of the study participants, and self-reported measurement of the program impact on actual behavior through the use of an innovative private ballot. The sample size of the study was large enough to ensure more than adequate statistical power to detect any differences that were present.

Implications for Future Programs

It is encouraging to have empirical evidence that large numbers of parents in a general community population will consent to having their young sons and daughters take part in such a program. Parents in Hamilton appear to value education about sexuality for their children. The lower parental consent rate among parents of students in the control schools probably reflects the facts that their children would have to answer intrusive questions but receive no benefit from the program and that this was their way of publicly indicating their displeasure that their son's or daughter's school had not been selected to receive the program.

The fact that virtually no students withdrew during the program is an indication of the value they place on this sort of education. Attendance rate at the sessions was very high; 92.5% of eligible student attended 8 or more of the 10 sessions. Anecdotal evaluation from both students and parents reinforces the importance of both the format and the content of the program for adolescents.

Mounting a prevention program involving 11 schools, 272 small groups of students, and 63 tutors was a logistical challenge. Its successful completion was largely due to the commitment of the Hamilton Board of Education and the Hamilton-Wentworth Department of Public Health Services.

Two positive outcomes of the collaboration of teachers and PHNs in their role as tutors can be stated. First, because they got to know each other better during this project, they showed much more collaboration around student health education after its completion. Second, as a result of the training workshops, teachers gained skills in facilitating problem solving and decision making that were applied in subsequent sex education and other health curricula.

Professional background of tutors made no difference in student satisfaction. It is quite likely that personal attributes of tutors are as important as professional qualifications in fulfilling the role. This is an important finding if others wish to design programs that are more long term and include "booster" sessions over time. It could dramatically affect the cost of mounting such programs and the overall cost-effectiveness of interventions. Given the considerable evidence that adolescents most frequently use peers as a source of information and support, using older students to lead groups may be an acceptable option (Chapter 4, this volume).

Although the OHIP pregnancy records have not yet been analyzed, it is discouraging to realize that the program had no effect on rates of self-reported sexual intercourse, consistent use of birth control, or pregnancy. We present a number of possible explanations for this. Treating all grade 7 and 8 students as a homogeneous group is probably an oversimplification. Because of normal developmental differences among the students, for a substantial number the material was irrelevant at the time. This program was somewhat dependent on student motivation and ability to prepare for the sessions. Most students were enthusiastic about the program, but preparation certainly varied. Although the student materials were developed to be read by grade 7 and 8 students, they were too difficult for many of the students. Every effort was made to make the suggested activities for the sessions relevant to the students' life experiences; however, some students found them irrelevant. These issues are important in development of future programs and emphasize the importance of "fitting" the program to the target population.

The results of the multiple regressions indicate that the gender of the target population and the outcome of interest should be considered when developing programs. Because absence of an educational goal and external locus of control are independent variables related to early sexual intercourse and inconsistent use of birth control among females, and because these independent variables may be amenable to change, they need to be addressed in concurrent programming for young female adolescents. Changing these behaviors is a complex social process requiring much more than a sex education program. Conversely, because females with these attributes are most likely to engage in risky sexual behavior, they should become a target population for future programs. For males the picture is not as clear. Absence of an educational goal appears to be the strongest (although statistically insignificant) variable related to engaging in early sexual intercourse. As males get older, their use of birth control becomes more consistent. Future programs could target young males (about 12 years of age) without an educational goal. One emphasis of programs for such males and females should be the effects of early childbearing on limiting future employment and the resultant instability in which many of these families live. Dryfoos (1984) suggests a similar approach.

Another shortcoming of the intervention program is that its duration was relatively brief and no "booster" sessions were provided. Additional sessions for original groups were impossible to provide because students were no longer in the same courses or even the same schools. This impossibility will be a continuing problem for school-based pregnancy prevention programs beyond the elementary school years. Interventions that are a combination of school-based and ongoing community-based programs could alleviate this problem. Another advantage of such broad-based programs is that encouraging virgins to postpone sexual activity and encouraging responsible use of birth control among the sexually active could be reinforced by the schools, parents, and the community. This might offset the strong pressure of the media, music, advertising, peers, and other adult role models.

The fact that comprehensive information about contraception could not be included in the program may have significantly diluted its effect. Clinical evidence indicates that for adolescents to use contraception, they need not only accurate information about birth control measures and how to use them appropriately, but also pragmatic assistance in understanding what to buy, how to ask for it, where it can be found, and the approximate cost. Including this information in future programs is imperative. This knowledge is of limited value if access to contraception is unavailable. Therefore, program planners and implementers must be prepared to advocate for adolescent access to contraception. This is a complex problem beyond the scope of this chapter.

The problem of unintended adolescent pregnancy continues to be a serious one for which solutions to date have been elusive. Careful planning, building on our work and that of others, along with rigorous evaluation of future programs may lead to more effective, feasible solutions.

References

Boyle, M. H., Offord, D. R., Hofman, H. G., Catlin, G. P., Byles, J. A., Cadman, D. T., Crawford, J. W., Links, P. S., Rae-Grant, N. I., & Szatmari, P. (1986). Ontario child health study: I. Methodology. *Archives of General Psychiatry, 44,* 826-831.

Byles, J., Byrne, C., Boyle, M. H., & Offord, D. R. (1988). Ontario child health study: Reliability and validity of the general functioning subscale of the McMaster family assessment device. *Family Process, 27,* 97-104.

Card, J. J. (Ed.). (1989). *Evaluating programs aimed at preventing teenage pregnancies* (Vol. 12). Los Altos, CA: Sociometrics Corp.

Cvetkovich, G., Grote, G., Lieberman, E., & Miller, W. (1978). Sex role development and teenage fertility-related behavior. *Adolescence, 50*(13), 231-236.

Dawson, D. A. (1986). The effects of sex education on adolescent behavior. *Family Planning Perspectives, 18,* 162-170.

Dryfoos, J. G. (1984). A new strategy for preventing unintended teenage childbearing. *Family Planning Perspectives, 16,* 193-195.

Eisen, M., Zellman, G. L., & McAlister, A. L. (1990). Impact evaluation of a theory-based sex and contraception education intervention model. *Family Planning Perspectives, 22*(6), 261-271.

Eisen, M., Zellman, G. L., & McAlister, A. L. (1985). A health belief model approach to adolescents' fertility control: Some pilot program findings. *Health Education Quarterly, 12*(22), 185-210.

Epstein, N. B., Baldwin, L. M., & Bishop, D. S. (1983). The McMaster family assessment device. *Journal of Marital and Family Therapy, 9,* 171-180.

Furstenberg, F. F., Moore, K. A., & Peterson, J. L. (1985). Sex education and sexual experience among adolescents. *American Journal of Public Health, 75,* 1331-1332.

Hamilton Board of Education. (1981). *Intermediate health curriculum: Grades 7 and 8.* Hamilton, Ontario, Canada: Author.

Iglehart, J. K. (1986). Canada's health care system (Part 2). *New England Journal of Medicine, 315,* 778-784.

Jones, E. F., Forrest, J. D., Goldman, W., Henshaw, S. K., Lincoln, R., et al. (1985). Teenage pregnancy in developed countries: Determinants and policy implications. *Family Planning Perspectives, 17*(2), 53-63.

Kirby, D. (1984). *Sexuality education: An evaluation of programs and their effects.* Santa Cruz, CA: Network.

Levy, K. J. (1976). Reducing the occurrence of omitted or untruthful responses when testing hypotheses concerning proportions. *Psychological Bulletin, 83,* 759-761.

Marsiglio, W., & Mott, F. L. (1986). The impact of sex education on sexual activity, contraceptive use and premarital pregnancy among American teenagers. *Family Planning Perspectives, 18,* 151-162.

Meinert, C., & Tonascia, S. (1986). *Clinical trials: Design, conduct and analysis.* New York: Oxford University Press.

Mitchell, A., Thomas, B. H., Devlin, M. C., Goldsmith, C. H., Singer, J., Walters, D., & Marks, S. (1991). *Evaluation of an educational program to prevent adolescent pregnancy.* Manuscript submitted for publication.

Nowicki, S., & Strickland, B. R. (1973). A locus of control scale for children. *Journal of Consulting and Clinical Psychology, 40,* 148-154.

Odeh, R. E., Owen, D. B., Birnbaum, Z. W., & Fisher, L. (1977). *Pocket book of statistical tables.* New York: Marcel Dekker.

Orton, M. J., & Rosenblatt, E. (1981). *Adolescent birth planning needs—Ontario in the eighties.* Ontario, Canada: Planned Parenthood.

Schinke, S. P. (1984). Preventing teenage pregnancy. *Progress in Behavior Modification, 16,* 31-63.

Schinke, S. P., Blythe, B. J., & Gilchrist, L. D. (1981). Cognitive behavioral prevention of adolescent pregnancy. *Journal of Counseling Psychology, 28,* 451-454.

SPSS Incorporated. (1986). *SPSS/PC+: Statistical packages for the social sciences for the IBM PC/XT/AT.* Chicago: Author.

Stout, J. W., & Rivara, F. P. (1989). Schools and sex education: Does it work? *Pediatrics, 83,* 375-379.

Tauer, K. M. (1983). Promoting effective decision-making in sexually active adolescents. *Nursing Clinics of North America, 18,* 275-292.

Thomas, H., Mitchell, A., & Devlin, M. C. (1990). Adolescent pregnancy: Issues in prevention. *Journal of Preventive Psychiatry and Allied Disciplines, 4*(23), 101-124.

Trussell, J. (1988). Teenage pregnancy in the United States. *Family Planning Perspectives, 20,* 262-272.

Wadhera, S., & Silins, J. (1990). Teenage pregnancy in Canada, 1975-1987. *Family Planning Perspectives, 22*(1), 27-30.

Zelnik, M., & Shah, F. K. (1983). First intercourse among young Americans. *Family Planning Perspectives, 15,* 64-70.

Zelnik, M., & Kim, Y. J. (1982). Sex education and its association with teenage sexual activity, pregnancy and contraceptive use. *Family Planning Perspectives, 14,* 117-119, 123-126.

3

Enhancing Social and Cognitive Skills

RICHARD P. BARTH
NANCY LELAND
DOUGLAS KIRBY
JOYCE V. FETRO

Concern about the level of sexual activity, pregnancies, and abortions among teenagers has been accompanied by growing public support in favor of offering sex education in the schools (Harris, 1988; Kenney & Orr, 1984). Educators consider adolescent pregnancy one of our nation's most important problems (Education Research Council, 1987; Harris, 1988), and sexuality education is more often than not viewed as a partial solution to this problem. The debate among researchers and other citizens increasingly focuses upon "how to," not "whether to," deliver family life education to prevent pregnancy and STDs among adolescents.

Adolescents in nearly every school receive some sexuality education (Kenney, Guardado, & Brown, 1989) although this normally lasts only 6-10 hours annually. These programs commonly intend to prevent pregnancy and STDs by increasing rational and informed decision making about sexuality. Emphasizing clear norms about avoiding unprotected intercourse and teaching practical skills are less common strategies.

Research on the effects of most past programs demonstrates that they are typically not sufficiently powerful to have substantial positive

AUTHORS' NOTE: We are grateful for funding from the Stuart Foundation, the William and Flora Hewlett Foundation, and the Biomedical Research Support Grant #507-RR07006-22 from the Division of Research Resources, National Institutes of Health.

impact upon sexual intercourse, contraceptive use, and pregnancy (Dawson, 1986; Kirby, 1984; Marsiglio & Mott, 1986). Studies typically indicate that sex education courses significantly increase student knowledge about sexuality, but that increased knowledge does not translate into behavioral change (Kirby, 1984; Stout & Rivera, 1989).

Emerging now is a new generation of sexuality education programs and evaluations of those programs. This new generation of programs is based upon specific theoretical models of behavior that have been effective in reducing other risk-taking behaviors; the evaluations of these new programs tend to include better evaluation designs (such as experimental designs), larger sample sizes, and longer follow-up. One of these new programs was based upon the health belief model (Eisen, Zellman, & McAlister, 1990); it had mixed effects that depended upon the gender and sexual experience of the participant before the program was implemented. A second program, Postponing Sexual Involvement, is discussed in Chapter 4 of this volume. It employed a social influences approach and clearly focused upon the norm that the junior high school students should delay having intercourse. Notably, this program was taught by rather charismatic high school peer educators. It significantly delayed the onset of intercourse but did not affect the frequency of intercourse among those who had already had sex, nor did it affect the use of contraceptives among those who had had sex. This chapter describes a third curriculum and evaluation study in this new generation of programs. Like Postponing Sexual Involvement (PSI), the Reducing the Risk curriculum is based partially upon a social influences approach and has results similar to that of PSI.

A Social and Cognitive Approach

Many factors contribute to pregnancy risk-taking. Although access to accurate information about pregnancy prevention and to methods of birth control are necessary, they are not sufficient. For knowledge about birth control and actual birth control methods to be used, youth must personalize this information, and they must have clear personal norms and also social and cognitive skills for avoiding unprotected intercourse. This is most simply illustrated by the all-too-common adolescent who has a condom in his pocket but cannot bring himself to use it.

The Reducing the Risk (RTR) curriculum evaluated in this chapter is based upon several somewhat interrelated theoretical approaches: social influence theory, social inoculation theory, social learning theory, and cognitive behavior theory.

The social influence model has two theoretical underpinnings, McGuire's social inoculation theory (McGuire, 1964) and Bandura's social learning theory (Bandura, 1977, 1986). Social inoculation theory postulates that a process of social inoculation exists that is analogous to physiological inoculation. In particular, it postulates that people develop a resistance to social pressure when they can recognize the various forms of pressure, become motivated to resist that pressure, and then practice resisting weak forms of that pressure. This theory is applied in this curriculum by discussing the various social pressures to have sex, providing youth in the classroom with common "lines" that youth give for having sex, and then helping them develop and practice effective strategies and skills for resisting those pressures. The students practice talking to other students about abstinence and birth control in situations that, over the course of the curriculum, increase in the level of difficulty. Over time, the students are expected to role play with less scripting and assistance.

Bandura's social learning theory provided a second underpinning for the social influence model. Social learning theory posits that the likelihood of a person engaging in some action such as using a birth control method is determined by (a) that person's understanding of what must be done to avoid pregnancy, (b) his or her belief that he or she will be able to use the method, (c) his or her belief that the method will be successful at preventing pregnancy, and (d) his or her anticipated benefit from accomplishing the behavior (Bandura, 1986). According to social learning theory, people learn or estimate these important factors partly by observing the behavior of others, observing the rewards and punishments their behavior elicits, and then, through practice, developing the necessary skills required for that behavior. Thus this curriculum provides modeling of socially desirable behaviors by the teacher or peers, practice of those behaviors through role playing, and illustrations of successfully avoiding unprotected intercourse without loss of a close relationship. It thereby demonstrates the benefits of these risk-avoidance behaviors.

The social and cognitive skills prevention model contains many of the same elements as social influence theory. It asserts that for behavior to change, the students need specific cognitive and social skills to resist pressures and to negotiate interpersonal encounters successfully. Based upon the work of Gilchrist and Schinke (1983), the cognitive-behavioral model has three components: activities to personalize information about sexuality, reproduction, and contraception; training in decision making and assertive communication skills; and practice in applying those skills in personally difficult settings or situations. The Reducing the Risk curriculum provides instruction and practice using social skills needed to implement knowledge about preventing pregnancy and to reduce unsafe behavior in future high-risk situations. The curriculum also includes opportunities to practice obtaining birth control information from stores and clinics.

The Reducing the Risk (RTR) curriculum gives considerable emphasis to norms; it explicitly emphasizes that the students should avoid unprotected intercourse, either by not having sex or by using contraception if they do have sex. Nearly every activity supports or reinforces this norm. For example, when the students in the classroom practice avoiding unprotected sex, they not only reinforce those skills, they also develop and reinforce the norm against unprotected intercourse.

Finally, the curriculum seeks to ensure that some discussion occurs between parent and child and requires that youth ask their parent(s) about their views on abstinence and birth control.

Evaluation

Research Design

A quasi-experimental design was used to measure the impact of the curriculum. Classes of students were assigned to the treatment and comparison groups, and questionnaires were administered to both treatment and comparison groups before the intervention, immediately after the intervention, about 6 months later and 18 months later.

Assignment to treatment and comparison groups was made by classroom. Whenever feasible, the class that was to be given the treatment was decided randomly. In some schools, when classes were of unequal size, larger classes were assigned to the treatment group to maximize the power of analyses on the treatment group. About half of comparison group classes received a different curriculum taught by the treatment teacher and half received a curriculum taught by a separate teacher. The former approach has the advantage of controlling for the teacher's experience and general teaching style but has the possible disadvantage of contamination of the experimental material into the control class-

room. This possibility was mitigated by carefully and repeatedly in-
structing the teachers that they could not—for this year—incorporate
any of their newly learned techniques in their other classes. Having
different comparison group teachers has the advantage of preventing
possible contamination but creates some threats to the validity of
findings as these teachers may have been markedly more or less effective than treatment teachers. We have no reason to believe, however,
that this is so.

In all, a total of 46 classes from 13 high schools representing 10
school districts participated in the project. The pregnancy prevention
program was taught by 18 teachers to 23 classes of students; 23 classes
were also in the comparison group. In 8 schools, the same teacher taught
the pregnancy prevention curriculum and the control program—which
was their prior curriculum; this approach included 11 teachers and 22
classes. In the remaining 5 schools, 8 additional teachers taught the
control classes; this configuration accounted for 24 classes.

The students were tested before the 3-week intervention, just after
the intervention, at 6 months, and 18 months post intervention. (Because we would not expect significant changes in behavior to have had
time to evince themselves in the 3 weeks between pretest and posttest,
we are not including posttest results in this chapter; for a report of
posttest and 6-month outcomes, see Barth, Fetro, Leland, & Volkan, in
press.)

The 6-month and 18-month efforts to recontact the students were
two-pronged. Some students were recruited by their teachers to complete the questionnaire at the school site, and the remainder were sent
questionnaires at home and then recontacted by telephone to encourage
their return of the questionnaires. At the 6-month follow-up, about 25%
were contacted at home, whereas at the 18-month follow-up this percentage had increased to more than 50%. Some youth were called more
than a dozen times by research staff before responding. All pretest,
6-month posttest, and 18-month posttest questionnaires were matched
so that nonrandom dropout rates would not bias the results.

Measures

Measures were adapted from those developed during related investigations and created anew as needed. Items were asked in a way consistent with the recommendations of the Adolescent Family Life Core Data
Working Group (Card & Reagan, 1989). Items addressed conventional

child and family demographics, allied risk factors (e.g., alcohol use), and communication with parents. The majority of the items measured contraceptive knowledge, intentions to avoid unprotected sex in high-risk situations, and sexual and contraceptive practices.

Contraceptive knowledge. The students responded to 20 items with a True, False, Don't Know format. Items were chosen because of their salience to the curriculum and do not represent the universe of all questions on contraception (e.g., knowledge questions on IUDs or diaphragms were not included because those methods were not covered in the curriculum due to their limited use by the students in our pretest sample).

Intentions to avoid unprotected intercourse. Eleven items described social situations that youth might encounter and asked the respondents about their likely course of action. The items were of three types. The first type (5 items) had varied vignettes and responses. The second set (2 items) employed a consistent format that only varied in the length of time the couple had been dating and how well they knew each other; the responses for each were identical and included (a) definitely not have sex; (b) probably not have sex; (c) probably have sex; and (d) definitely have sex. The third format (4 items) had a response format of (a) have sex, without birth control; (b) not have sex, not ready; (c) not have sex, get prepared; and (d) have sex, use birth control. The alpha coefficient for the 11 responses was .76, indicating a satisfactory covariation.

Sexual and contraceptive practices. Youth were asked whether they had had sexual intercourse and, if so, about their age at first intercourse and the frequency of sexual intercourse in the last 30 days. Measures of adolescents' use of contraception included determining whether any method had ever been used, the type(s) of method(s) used, the frequency of use, whether a method was used at first intercourse, whether effective methods were used, the kind of method used, and whether an adolescent knew how to use methods correctly. Youth were also queried about all pregnancies, pregnancy scares, and current pregnancies.

Program Implementation

School selection. Schools were recruited for the study by sending letters of inquiry to 252 high schools in 140 California school districts with existing sexuality education programs. These letters asked about the schools' interest in participating in this study.

Initially, 32 eligible school districts indicated a strong interest in participation. School districts had to have a high school with at least two classes of sexuality education so that a within-school comparison group could be selected. Letters of agreement to participate were finally received from 16 high schools. Subsequently, because of pressure on the school board or staff from interest groups concerned about the discussion of birth control in the curriculum, two school districts (with their three high schools) withdrew from the project. Several school districts indicated approval of the curriculum but were unwilling to participate because the evaluation questionnaire was only confidential and not anonymous and included questions about sexual intercourse and pregnancy.

Training of teachers. Teachers in the treatment group were self-selected and attended a 3-day training session prior to implementation. The training focused primarily upon giving teachers the opportunity to practice the exercises; in addition, 3 hours of the training addressed the proper mechanics of obtaining parental and student consent and administering the survey.

Student recruitment. The students were recruited following human subjects approval. The study was described to the students by their teachers and via written materials. Participation in the study required active student and parent permission. Sessions for parents were scheduled at night in each school to allow discussion of the curriculum and evaluation—project staff attended them if required by the teachers. Fewer than 1% of the students were excluded from the class because they did not get parental permission.

Curriculum implementation. Project staff observed all the teachers implementing the RTR curriculum during the 1988-1989 school year. Project staff were first trained in standardized protocols for observation; they then observed all treatment classes at least once and most classes two or more times.

Observers used classroom observation instruments to assess the implementation of the curriculum. These instruments consisted of a 5-point Likert-type format ranging from 1 = "none of the time" to 5 = "all of the time" and covered whether (a) the lesson plan was followed, (b) the time allotment was adequate, (c) the teacher seemed comfortable presenting the lesson, (d) the students participated in role plays, and (e) the teacher appeared to be adequately trained to implement the curriculum.

Results indicated that most of the teachers scored very well on these measures. More specifically, as rated on a 5-point scale, observers indicated that 95% of the teachers followed the lesson plan (M = 4.55), completed the activities (M = 4.49), and gave accurate answers to the students' questions "most of the time" or "all of the time." Over 85% of the teachers seemed comfortable teaching the curriculum (X = 4.50) and seemed adequately prepared to teach the curriculum (X = 4.46).

Results

Sample

At pretest, 1,033 students completed the assessment, with 586 in the treatment group and 447 in the comparison group. The smaller comparison group arose from choosing larger classes to receive the treatment when classes were discrepant in size. Of these students, 722 completed the 6-month follow-up questionnaire and 758 completed the 18-month follow-up questionnaire. The 6-month number was smaller because some questionnaires could not be matched with their pretest counterparts due to an administrative error. Thus the overall pretest/18-month attrition rate was 26.6%; for males, attrition was 31.9%; for females, 21.1%; for treatment group members, 26.8%; for the comparison group members, 26.4%.

The greatest percentage of students (55%) were in the 10th grade at pretest and were white (61%). Latinos comprised 21% of the sample; Asians, 9%; other, 6%; and blacks, 2%—the latter were underrepresented due to our inability to engage large, metropolitan school districts. The students in the sample were not highly religious, with only 23% indicating that they went to religious services once a week or more, and 28% indicating that they had no religion and never went to services; 38% of the students identified themselves as Catholic. About one quarter of the respondents indicated that their mothers had less than a high school education, and 49% indicated their mothers had not attended college. Of those with sisters, 17% indicated that their sister had been pregnant before age 19. About one third of the students lived with one parent or in another arrangement (e.g., with grandparents or foster parents). No significant differences were shown between the treatment and comparison groups on any of the demographic indicators.

The group of youth lost to attrition differed from the students who remained in the study on several dimensions. The attrition group was older (p < .001) and had significantly poorer course grades than the group that stayed in the study. They were more likely to live with a single parent, in foster care, or in some other living arrangement than with both parents. At pretest, the attrition group was no less knowledgeable about contraception than the nonattrition group but did have significantly less positive behavioral intentions. The attrition group was significantly more likely to perceive that all their peers were having sex, more likely to have had sex, more likely to have failed to use birth control because sex was not planned, and less likely to have talked to their parents about abstinence. The attrition group drank significantly more frequently but did not start drinking any earlier. No significant differences were shown between the groups on ethnicity or any other demographic variables except that more males than females were in the attrition group.

For the analysis reported in this chapter, we first matched the pretest and 18-month samples; those youth that matched constitute the primary sample analyzed here. We also analyzed the 6-month data, when those data were available for this sample. This appropriately places the emphasis upon the long-range effects of the program but also offers some indication of the directions of change over time. The aforementioned demographic data are contained in Table 3.1.

In the analyses described below, data are presented both for all the study participants and for various subpopulations based upon gender, ethnicity, risk status, and sexual experience prior to the intervention. All of these are self-explanatory except for risk status. All students were classified as either lower risk or higher risk youth. Higher risk youth (n = 396) include all youth who did not live with both parents, whose mother did not finish high school, who received grades in high school that were mostly D's or lower, or who both drank alcohol one or more times during the last month and normally drank five or more drinks on each occasion. Each of these characteristics was significantly correlated with whether the respondent had ever had intercourse, frequency of use of birth control and/or use of birth control during the last act of intercourse. Lower risk youth include all remaining youth (n = 362).

Knowledge

The students knew relatively little about the proper use of contraception at pretest (see Table 3.2). The average item received only 56% correct with a range from 20% (regarding correct use of contraceptive sponges) to 93% (a girl will get pregnant if she has sex many times

Table 3.1 Demographics of Pretest Study Sample (in Percentages)

Item	Overall (N = 1033)	Treatment (N = 586)	Comparison (N = 447)
Age (mean years)	15.4	15.4	15.4
Gender			
Males	51	50	52
Females	49	50	48
Grade			
9th	24	25	23
10th	55	53	58
11th	11	11	12
12th	9	11	7
Ethnicity			
White	61	60	62
Latino	21	20	23
Asian	9	10	7
Black	2	2	2
Native-American	2	2	2
Other	6	6	5
Lives with			
Both parents	66	66	66
Single parent	26	27	26
Foster parent/guardian	*	1	*
Other	7	7	7
Religion			
Catholic	38	36	39
Protestant	18	19	18
Born Again Christian	8	9	7
Jewish	1	1	2
Other	8	9	7
No religion	27	28	27
Religious services			
Never	28	28	29
1 or 2×s/year	30	32	27
1×/month	9	9	9
2 or 3×/month	10	10	10
Once a week	16	15	18
More than once/week	7	7	8
Mother's education			
Completed high school	72	73	71
Less than high school	23	22	25
Don't know	5	5	4
Mother attended college			
Yes	45	46	44
No	49	49	49
Don't know	6	5	7

Table 3.1 Continued

Item	Overall (N = 1033)	Treatment (N = 586)	Comparison (N = 447)
Have sisters/stepsisters			
Yes	74	74	73
No	26	26	27
If sisters, pregnant before age 19	*(n = 742)*	*(n = 423)*	*(n = 315)*
Yes	17	15	19
No	77	80	75
Don't know	6	5	7
Mean age first had sex	13.7	13.7	13.6
Mean age at first drink in years	12.6	12.6	12.5

NOTE: No between group differences are significant.
Some percentages do not sum to 100% because of rounding.
*Indicates less than 1%.

without birth control). Substantial gains in knowledge were found in both the treatment and comparison groups, reflecting, in part, the fact that members of the comparison group also participated in a sexuality education class. From pretest to 6-month follow-up, the average treatment group student increased the percentage correct from 57% to 75% (+18%) and the average comparison group student increased from 56% to 65% (+9%). By 18 months, the gain from pretest remained at 19% for treatment and increased to 11% for control. The increases in knowledge on the part of the treatment group, however, were significantly greater than the increases for the comparison group at the $p < .001$ level.

For all the important subpopulations analyzed, namely, males, females, whites, Latinos, high-risk youth, and low-risk youth, differences were approximately equal and statistically significant between the treatment and comparison groups in knowledge gain (data not shown).

Peer Norms

The students were asked what proportion of the students their age in their school had ever had sex. At pretest, no significant differences were found between the treatment and comparison groups, and both the modal and median responses were that about half their peers were having sex (see Table 3.3). By the 6-month posttest, however, the

Table 3.2 Knowledge of Pregnancy Prevention (Percentage Correct)

		Treatment (n = 429)			Comparison (n = 329)		
		Pre	6-mos	18-mos	Pre	6-mos	18-mos
1.	A girl can't get pregnant first time she has sex.	88	90	91	85	88	89
2.	Use of withdrawal to prevent pregnancy.	77	95	94	73	87	91
3.	Birth control is as effective as abstinence.	71	76	81	62	69	75
4.	Latex condoms are better than skin condoms to prevent STD.	46	65	59	39	58	49
5.	Best to leave space at end of condom.	64	94**	94*	64	79	84
6.	Girls will get pregnant if they have sex many times without birth control.	94	97	96*	92	94	92
7.	Correct way to use a contraceptive sponge.	25	71***	68***	30	51	53
8.	Correct use of condom while pulling out of vagina.	38	79***	80***	46	67	71
9.	Contraceptive sponge will not work if you have sex more than once.	19	44***	38**	20	28	28
10.	Prevent pregnancy by douching after sex.	66	88***	90***	70	70	79
11.	Use of condom with someone with STD can protect from getting disease.	73	83	81	66	78	76
12.	Legal to buy contraceptive foam, etc., without a prescription.	74	86	87	72	80	81
13.	Teenage girl can get pregnant anytime during month.	58	69	69	57	59	61
14.	Teenage girl can get birth control pills from clinics without parent knowledge.	73	89	91*	66	79	81
15.	Contraceptive foam, etc., can be put in vagina many hours before sex.	19	38**	39**	27	31	34
16.	Use of condoms most effective way to prevent pregnancy and STD.	25	35*	35	22	23	27
17.	Forgetting to take pill for 3 days will still prevent pregnancy.	59	79	79	59	69	74

Table 3.2 Knowledge of Pregnancy Prevention (Percentage Correct)

	Treatment (n = 429)			Comparison (n = 329)		
	Pre	6-mos	18-mos	Pre	6-mos	18-mos
18. Contraceptive foams, etc., provide some protection against STDs.	31	66***	53***	36	44	37
19. Girls protected from pregnancy as soon as start pill.	67	83*	89***	64	72	73
20. Condom more effective than contraceptive sponge at preventing STDs.	67	83	86*	71	79	81
Total Knowledge Score	57	76*	75*	56	65	67

NOTE: Response options were: True; False; and Don't Know. Don't Know responses were *not* tallied as correct.
*Difference in the 6-month or 18-month changes of the treatment and comparison groups is significant at .05 level.
**Difference in the 6-month or 18-month changes of the treatment and comparison groups is significant at .01 level.
***Difference in the 6-month or 18-month changes of the treatment and comparison groups is significant at .001 level.

comparison group had changed appreciably, whereas the treatment group had not. That is, more of the students in the comparison group at 6 months believed that more of their peers were having sex than did members of the comparison group at pretest; among the treatment group students, no such change was found. The difference in the change scores was significant at the $p = .01$ level. By 18 months, a difference still existed in the change in perceptions of peer sexual behavior, but the difference was smaller and no longer significant ($p < .10$). Differences between the treatment and comparison groups were also significant at either 6 months or 18 months for some of the subpopulations, including both whites and Latinos (data not shown).

Intentions

At pretest, the students reported a wide range of intentions regarding sexual and contraceptive practices. Each item presented 4 possible choices, and all received some endorsement by the students. Among the 4 choices per item, no choice was chosen by more than 66% of the students, and only 4 responses were chosen by 50% or more of the students. Only 12 of the 44 choices were chosen by as few as 10% of

text contiued on page 69

Table 3.3 Sexual Beliefs and Behaviors[1]

Outcome	Sample	Treatment Group (RTR)			Change Score		Comparison Group			Change Score	
		Pre	6 mos	18 mos	6 mos Pre	18 mos Pre	Pre	6 mos	18 mos	6 mos Pre	18 mos Pre
Perception of whether peers had ever had sex	All	3.1	3.1	3.4	.05**	.31	3.1	3.3	3.5	.26**	.45
		421	407	428	399	420	322	267	326	260	320
Total score for intentions to avoid unprotected intercourse	All	.81	.82	.81	.008	-.007	.82	.81	.80	-.011	-.018
		427	409	429	407	427	324	268	329	263	324
Ever had sex	All	37%	44%	55%	8%	18%	38%	45%	61%	9%	23%
		394	379	401	373	394	295	243	303	237	295
	Sexually inexperienced at pretest	0%	12%	29%	12%	29%*	0%	14%	38%*	14%	38%*
		250	242	250	242	250	183	151	183	151	183
Frequency of intercourse	Had sex before pretest	3.1	3.9	5.6	.9	2.4	2.2	3.5	4.6	1.3	2.2
		142	130	144	128	142	108	83	109	81	106
	Initiated sex after pretest	0.0	3.1	3.0	3.1	3.1	0.0	3.0	3.2	3.0	3.2
		71	30	71	30	71	68	21	68	21	68
Use of birth control at first sex	Initiated sex after pretest	NA[4]	100%**	51%	NA	NA	NA	53%**	54%	NA	NA
			12	71				19	68		
Use of birth control at last sex	Had sex before pretest	49%	52%	57%	3%	7%	50%	57%	52%	4%	3%
		138	132	141	127	135	108	86	112	83	108

Initiated sex[3] after pretest	NA	NA 100%** 15	68% 72	NA	NA	NA	55%** 20	61% 66	NA	NA
Use of birth control most or all of the time										
Had sex before pretest	58% 140	64% 132	60% 143	7% 128	3% 139	63% 109	63% 84	68% 112	1% 83	5% 109
Initiated sex[3] after pretest	NA	NA 100%** 21	75% 72	NA	NA	NA	70%** 20	64% 67	NA	NA
All	18% 390	21% 378	22% 399	3% 369	4% 388	19% 292	20% 243	28% 303	3% 234	9% 292
Had unprotected sex (based upon abstinence and birth control use at last sex)										
Did not have sex before pretest	0% 250	6% 241	9% 250	6% 241	9%* 250	0% 183	7% 151	16% 183	7% 151	16%* 183
All	15% 392	15% 378	19% 400	0% 370	4% 391	14% 292	15% 243	20% 301	2% 234	6% 290
Had unprotected sex (based upon abstinence and frequency birth control use)										
Initiated sex[3] after pretest	0% 250	3% 241	7% 250	3% 241	7%* 250	0% 183	4% 151	13% 181	4% 151	13%* 181
All	5.9% 389	7.7% 379	12.5% 399	1.6% 368	5.9% 387	4.4% 294	7.0% 244	10.3% 302	2.1% 236	5.8% 293
Ever pregnant										
Had sex before pretest	16.8% 137	22.0% 132	29.4% 143	4.8% 126	11.0% 136	12.0% 108	17.4% 86	24.3% 111	3.6% 83	13.1% 107
Initiated sex after pretest	0.0% 250	0.0% 240	3.2% 249	0.0% 240	3.2% 249	0.0% 183	0.1% 151	1.6% 183	1.3% 151	1.6% 183

Continued

67

Table 3.3 Continued

Outcome	Sample	Treatment Group (RTR)			Change Score		Comparison Group			Change Score	
		Pre	6 mos	18 mos	6 mos Pre	18 mos Pre	Pre	6 mos	18 mos	6 mos Pre	18 mos Pre
Talked with parents about abstinence	All	54% 417	66% 407	67% 425	13%** 396	13%* 415	60% 321	61% 266	65% 322	1%** 261	4%* 317
Talked with parents about birth control	All	39% 419	53% 399	54% 424	15%** 391	15% 415	38% 321	41% 261	45% 328	2%** 255	8% 320
Talked with parents about pregnancy	All	62% 425	70% 409	71% 428	8% 406	9% 424	64% 325	71% 267	70% 329	5% 263	6% 325
Talked with parents about STD	All	49% 427	52% 409	59% 428	4% 407	10% 426	49% 324	52% 268	56% 329	1% 264	7% 324

NOTE: *$p \le .05$ for difference between RTR and comparison group change scores at 6 months or 18 months.
**$p \le .01$ for difference between RTR and comparison group change scores at 6 month or 18 months.
[1]In each cell, the upper number is a mean or percentage; the lower number is the sample size.
[2]Chi-squared tests of significance were calculated for dichotomous outcome variables; t-tests compared interval variables.
[3]Because no pretest data exists, change scores are not appropriate, and tests of significance are based upon treatment versus comparison scores at either 6 months or 18 months.
[4]NA = Not Appropriate.

the students. Thus this distribution provides ample room for change, following participation in the program. Scores were coded as *1* if they indicated intent to use skills to prevent pregnancy and *0* if not. The treatment and comparison groups did not differ significantly at pretest, 6-month posttest, or 18-month posttest on the proportion of those who indicated an intent to use appropriate skills to avoid pregnancy. Furthermore, no significant differences were found in the change scores over time (data not shown).

Behavior

Ever had sex. About 37% of all the students had ever had sex at pretest. Logically, the sexual status of those who had already had sex could not be affected by the curriculum; thus we examined the impact of the program upon sexual experience only for those students who had never had intercourse at pretest. The results indicate that after 6 months, 14% of the comparison group and 12% of the treatment group initiated intercourse; this difference was not significant. After 18 months, however, 38% of the comparison group initiated intercourse, but only 29% of the treatment group did so; this difference was significant ($p = .05$). This represents a 24% reduction in the initiation of intercourse.

When those students who were sexually inexperienced at pretest are further subdivided into other groups (such as males, Latinos, or high-risk youth), the sample sizes become quite small. An analysis of the differences between the treatment and comparison groups for these subgroups indicates that the program had less of an impact upon whites and more of an impact upon other groups. For example, the percentage reduction in the initiation of intercourse by 18 months was only 10% (42.6% vs. 38.4%) for whites but was 36% (33.3% vs. 21.2%) for Latinos; 18% (43.4% vs. 35.6%) for high-risk youth; 27% (33.0% vs. 24.0%) for low-risk youth; and 27% (39.0% vs. 28.3%) for males but 20% (36.6% vs. 29.2%) for females. Because of the smaller sample sizes, the exact percentage reductions should not be given undue emphasis. Instead, it should be recognized that the impact of the curriculum was not limited to any particular group, but instead extended to many groups, including both minority youth and high-risk youth.

It should also be recognized that the results were smaller and not significant at 6 months and were larger and significant at 18 months, partially because time was needed for a sufficiently large percentage of the comparison group to engage in sex and for the difference between the groups to become large enough to be significant.

Frequency of sexual intercourse. No statistically significant differences were found between the treatment and comparison groups in terms of their frequency of sexual intercourse. This was true both for those students who had initiated intercourse prior to intervention and for those students who initiated intercourse after the intervention.

Use of birth control. Use of birth control was measured in three ways: use at first sex, use at last sex, and frequency of birth control use. Logically, the intervention could not have affected the use of birth control at first sex among those students who had sex prior to the intervention; thus this impact is examined only for those students who initiated sex after the intervention. All 12 members (100%) of the treatment group who both initiated sex after the intervention and who answered the questions about use of birth control used birth control the first time they had sex; in contrast, only 10 of the 19 comparison group members (53%) who initiated sex after the intervention used birth control. This difference was not statistically significant. The lack of significance should be viewed cautiously because the very limited sample size reduces the power of the test. By 18 months, group difference had entirely disappeared; approximately half of each group who initiated sex after the intervention used birth control the first time they had sex (See Figure 3.1).

During all three administrations of the survey, about 60% of the sexually experienced students used birth control the last time they had sex. Among the students who initiated sex before the pretest, this percentage increased slightly over time, but no significant differences were found between the increases in the treatment and comparison groups. As above, among those students who initiated intercourse after the intervention, at 6 months all of the treatment group students used birth control the last time they had sex, whereas only 55% of the comparison group did so. This was statistically significant ($p < .01$), but the small sample size begs for caution. By 18 months, this difference was no longer significant (See Figure 3.2).

About two thirds of all sexually experienced students reported that they used contraception either most of the time or all of the time. Among all students who had ever had sex, this proportion also increased slightly over time, but no significant differences were found in the improvements between the treatment and comparison groups. Treatment group students who initiated intercourse after the intervention, however, were

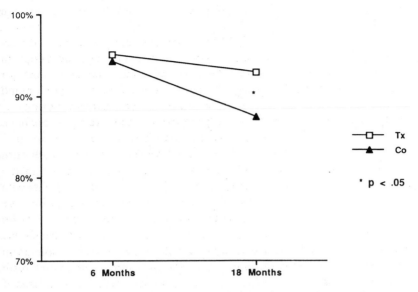

Figure 3.1. Percentage of Students Who Became Sexually Active After Pretest Who Use Contraception Regularly.

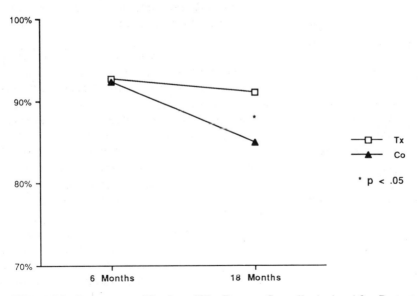

Figure 3.2. Percentage of Students Who Became Sexually Active After Pretest Who Used Contraception During Their Last Sexual Encounter.

more likely at 6 months to report using contraception most or all of the time than were their comparison group counterparts (100% vs. 70%); this was significant ($p = .01$), but the sample size was small. By 18 months, more students had initiated intercourse ($n = 139$); 75% of the treatment group and only 64% of the comparison group used contraception most or all of the time, but this effect was no longer significant ($p = .17$).

Unprotected sexual intercourse. The primary goal of the curriculum was to reduce unprotected intercourse either through the delay or reduction of intercourse or through the increased use of contraception. Thus to measure unprotected sex, two measures were created. The first measure divided the students into two groups, those who engaged in unprotected sex—they had sex and did not use birth control the last time they had sex—versus those who did not engage in unprotected sex—either they never had sex or they had sex but used birth control the last time they had sex.

The second measure of unprotected intercourse is similar to the first; it differs only in that it is based upon regularity of contraceptive use, not upon use at last intercourse. The students were defined as engaging in unprotected intercourse if they had ever had sex and did not use contraception most or all of the time. They were defined as not engaging in unprotected intercourse if they had never engaged in intercourse or used contraception most or all the time.

Among the students sexually experienced at pretest, no significant differences were found between the treatment and comparison groups at either 6 months or 18 months on either measure of unprotected sex. Differences were found, however, among important subgroups that were both programmatically and statistically significant. Among all lower risk youth, regardless of their sexual experience at pretest, there were significant differences in unprotected intercourse. At pretest, 10.8% of the comparison group and 11.3% of the treatment group engaged in unprotected intercourse at last sex; 18 months later, 22.8% of the comparison group, but only 13.1% of the treatment group, engaged in unprotected intercourse ($p < .05$). Furthermore, among all sexually inexperienced students at pretest, both lower risk and higher risk, differences on both measures were statistically significant at 18 months. On the first measure (based upon birth control at last sex), 15.1% of the comparison group engaged in unprotected sex, but only 9.0% of the treatment group did so. This represents a 40% reduction in unprotected intercourse and is significant ($p < .05$). On the second measure (based upon use of birth control most or all of the time), 12.6% of the comparison group engaged in unprotected intercourse, but only 7.1% of the treatment had unprotected intercourse, a reduction of 44% ($p < .05$).

Some of the increases among subpopulations were even more dramatic. For example, among females who were sexually inexperienced at pretest, 16.2% of the comparison group regularly had unprotected intercourse, but only 3.6% of the treatment group did so ($p < .001$).

Pregnancy. At the time of the pretest, 5.9% of the students reported ever having been pregnant (or having gotten someone pregnant). During the elapsed 18 months, no statistically significant difference occurred between the treatment and comparison groups in the proportion of students that became pregnant after the pretest. This finding partly reflects the fact that the curriculum did not have a significant impact upon unprotected intercourse among all students; rather, it affected those that had not initiated intercourse prior to the program. Among this latter group, the pregnancy rates for the treatment and comparison groups were too small to be statistically meaningful.

Communication with Parents

The questionnaire asked the students whether they had ever talked with their parents about abstinence, birth control, pregnancy, and STDs.

Prior to participation in the program, only about half of students reported having participated in discussions with their parents about abstinence or STDs. Nearly 6 of 10 youth reported discussing pregnancy with their parents, but only 37% had discussed birth control.

Two curriculum activities called for the students to talk with their parents about both abstinence and birth control. Thus the curriculum would be expected to have a direct impact upon that communication but might not affect communication about pregnancy or STDs.

The percentage of students in the treatment group who had ever discussed abstinence with their parents increased 13 percentage points (from 54% at pretest to 66% at 6 months and 67% at 18 months), while the percentage of students in the comparison group who had discussed abstinence increased only 5 percentage points (from 60% to 61% to 65%). The differences between these increases were significant ($p < .005$ at 6 months and $p < .05$ at 18 months).

Similarly, the percentage of students in the treatment group who had discussed birth control with their parents increased from 39% at pretest to 53% at the 6-month posttest and 54% at the 18-month posttest. In contrast, the percentage of students in the comparison group who

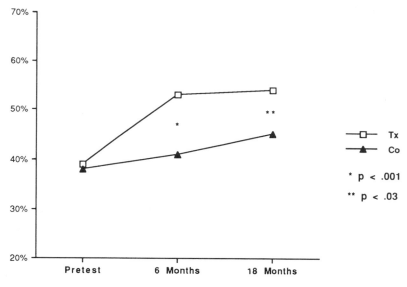

Figure 3.3. Percentage of Students Communicating With Parents About Birth Control.

discussed birth control with their parents increased from 38% at pretest to 41% at 6 months to 45% at 18 months. The differences in these increases were significant at 6 months ($p < .001$), but not quite at 18 months ($p = .03$) (See Figure 3.3).

The data indicate that the curriculum did not significantly increase communication about either pregnancy or STDs among all students and parents. A few significant differences were found, however, in the increase in communication for selected subpopulations. For example, the percentage of female students in the treatment group who had ever discussed pregnancy with their parents increased significantly more than did the percentage for the comparison group females. The increase in discussions between parents and Latino youth in the treatment group was particularly large—27 percentage point increase by 18 months—(data not shown).

Student, Teacher, and Parent Satisfaction

Student satisfaction. Immediately after completing the curriculum, treatment group students reported a positive reaction. They generally agreed or strongly agreed that they found the role-play situations useful (83%) and, to a lesser extent, that the role plays were realistic (61%). About half the youth (52%) completed the visit to a retail store to gather information about nonprescription birth control; somewhat fewer students (25%) visited a clinic or physician to learn about prescription contraceptives. Still, treatment group youth made more than 400 trips to gather information about contraception. Of all students, 28% reported using skills learned during the 3-week course period, 80% agreed or strongly agreed that they could more easily talk to their boyfriends or girlfriends about sexuality as a result of this course, and about 50% agreed or strongly agreed that they could more easily talk with their parents—a reasonably high percentage, given that only 60% completed the exercise involving talking with parents.

Teacher satisfaction. Teachers also endorsed the curriculum. Almost all teachers strongly agreed that the curriculum was clearly written and that the organization and format were easy to follow—even the first time through the curriculum. Almost 90% agreed that the role-play situations were realistic, and 75% disagreed or strongly disagreed that they had difficulty getting students to role play. Just two teachers were uncomfortable presenting the curriculum—the remaining 16 strongly disagreed that they had been uncomfortable. Teachers were almost unanimous in their agreement that most students participated in class discussions and that the amount of content on abstinence was appropriate. All agreed that the birth control content was relevant to the students. Teachers did report that only 33% of the students completed the visit to a clinic assignment, 50% visited a retailer that sold birth control, and 75% talked with their parents as assigned (teachers reported completion of the exercise more often than students did).

Parent satisfaction survey. In addition to using an experimental design to measure the impact of the program, we mailed parent surveys to the homes of all students who participated in the experimental curriculum and provided a usable address ($n = 551$). Roughly 20% of the parents ($n = 110$) returned questionnaires. They responded to items about the homework activities they participated in with their son or daughter. (For example, being interviewed by their child about their views on love, intimacy, sexuality, and birth control.) Of the parent respondents, more than 60% included additional written comments.

Parents who completed surveys were generally pleased with the program. About one fourth of the parents indicated that this was the first time they had discussed these pregnancy prevention topics with their children. The median length of the parent-youth discussions was 30 minutes. Almost all parents (91%) indicated that the class assignments made their communication with their children somewhat or a lot easier, and three fourths had discussed these topics again since the time of the class. Almost half of the parents reported that the class made their youth somewhat or much less likely to have sex—only 75 believed that it made them more likely to have sex. Almost 72% thought the course made their children more likely to use birth control when they ultimately did have sex. Finally, 90% of respondents thought the school was a good place to teach about abstinence, obtaining and using birth control, and STDs.

Discussion

The Reducing the Risk curriculum and this study were at one time controversial. In several communities, vocal minorities of parents strongly opposed the implementation of the curriculum in their children's schools; other parents opposed the implementation of the study, and three schools dropped out of the study because of the controversial nature of either the curriculum or the study. Nevertheless, the survey of parents whose children actually participated in the curriculum demonstrated broad support for the curriculum, and a large percentage of parents believed it had positive effects upon their children or upon their communication with their children.

Furthermore the study was completed without changes that threatened the validity of the design or the study more generally. This is important, because no previous studies have measured the impact of sex education by randomly assigning classes of students in high schools and then tracking those students for 18 months. This study demonstrates that it is feasible to use this evaluation methodology in schools even with politically sensitive issues such as sexuality.

But the most exciting findings of this study are those that measure the impact of the program. Because an experimental design was used and because the impact of the curriculum was assessed by comparing the change over time in the treatment group against that of the comparison group, it is appropriate to attribute statistically significant differences to the effect of the program.

The data presented above indicate that the Reducing the Risk curriculum produced a variety of programmatically and statistically significant effects. Among all students, it increased communication with parents about abstinence and birth control. Because the curriculum dictated that students discuss these topics with their parents, the effect was immediate. In fact, the greatest effect appeared on the immediate posttest. Over time, an increasing percentage of the students in the comparison group discussed the topics of abstinence and birth control with their parents, but a significantly greater percentage of students in the treatment group had discussed these topics with their parents 18 months after the intervention.

In general, greater parent-child communication about these topics did not lead to significantly greater communication about other sexual topics, such as pregnancy and STDs. Significantly greater communication did occur, however, for some subpopulations, such as females. This finding suggests that additional assignments for other topic areas may need to be included in the curriculum if the goal is to increase communication in these other areas.

The curriculum also significantly increased knowledge among all students. This is not terribly surprising; nearly all previous evaluations of sex education have shown increases in knowledge. This finding, however, should be viewed in the light of three factors: the curriculum did not focus upon knowledge acquisition but upon role playing, many members of the comparison groups also received sex education, and the impact upon knowledge lasted for 18 months. These factors make this result much more impressive and suggest that when a cognitive-behavioral approach is used, knowledge gain may be greater and may be retained for a longer period of time.

One of the goals of this norm- and skills-based curriculum was to change norms about unprotected sex and to change the students' perceptions that "everyone is doing it." The RTR curriculum apparently did not diminish the perceived proportions of students their age in their schools that had ever had sex, but the curriculum apparently did prevent those perceptions from becoming worse over time. That is, over time, the students in the comparison group thought ever-increasing proportions of students their age had ever had sex, but in the treatment group this did not happen as much, especially until the 6-month posttest. By the 18-month posttest, a difference still existed, but it was no longer significant. Possibly the curriculum had this effect for 6 months or more by reducing the "bragging" about sexual exploits or by reducing other more moderate claims about engaging in sex. Given that the students in the treatment group represented only small proportions of the entire student bodies, and given that they interacted with other students in the school, this effect might be enhanced substantially if the curriculum were implemented schoolwide.

It is very difficult to measure social skills even if demonstrations of those skills are videotaped during spontaneous scenarios. This was not possible for a sample size this large or for skills involved in the most intimate of settings. Originally, we hoped the questions that provided scenarios and asked students what they would do would, in fact, provide some measure of skills. But it became clear over time that these scenarios really did not measure skills; at best, they measured behavioral intent. The overall score for behavioral intent and the scores for each individual behavioral intent item (data not shown) indicated that the curriculum did not change intent to refrain from intercourse or to insist upon use of contraception.

The curriculum apparently delayed the initiation of intercourse. Within 6 months of curriculum implementation, only small percentages of students in the treatment and comparison groups had initiated intercourse, and the difference between these two groups was too small to be statistically significant. By 18 months, however, larger percentages of students in each group had initiated intercourse, making it easier to detect program effects. The data suggest that the curriculum may have reduced the initiation of sex by about 24%. This exact percentage should be viewed cautiously because of the large confidence interval.

The data indicate that the RTR curriculum did not affect the frequency of intercourse among the students who already had initiated intercourse. The curriculum did not increase sexual activity, as some opponents feared, but it did not decrease sexual activity either.

Similarly, the data indicate that among all sexually experienced students the RTR curriculum did not affect the use of birth control during either first intercourse or last intercourse, nor did it affect the frequency of contraceptive use during intercourse. Similarly, according to all three measures of birth control, the curriculum did not appear to have increased the use of contraception among those students who initiated intercourse after receiving the curriculum. This null finding should be viewed cautiously because of the small sample size.

The measures of unprotected intercourse, which combined measures of sexual initiation with measures of contraceptive use, also indicated that the RTR curriculum did reduce unprotected intercourse among lower risk students and those students who had not yet initiated intercourse. The percentage reduction was about 40%; this appears to be both programmatically and statistically significant. The results were not limited to any particular group of students. The sample did not include a large percentage of African-American students but did include a large percentage of Latino students and approximately equal percentages of lower and higher risk youth. The data indicated that many effects of the program extended to all these groups. Because of the large Latino population in California and the relatively high frequency of adolescent pregnancy among Latinos, this was a particularly important subgroup. The percentage of Latino students in the treatment group who talked with their parents about types of birth control more than doubled by follow-up, whereas comparison group students showed no real increase. Parent-child discussions about how girls become pregnant also increased twice as much for Latinos in the treatment group than for Latinos in the comparison group. Similarly, discussions of abstinence increased sharply for treatment students but not for controls.

These results—not just for Latinos, but for all youth—are particularly impressive, given that about half of the students in the comparison group received a more traditional sex education course of the same length. Thus these data suggest that a sex education curriculum based upon this theoretical model and employing these activities is more effective at producing these desired changes than are more traditional curricula.

The curriculum apparently produced changes in the students' behaviors but did not produce changes in behavioral intent. This may be a measurement problem; the scenarios may not have been a valid method of measuring intent or skill. Or alternatively, the curriculum may simply have provided the skills to those youth who needed skills to behave effectively and assertively in a manner consistent with their intent. That is, the comparison group may have engaged in unprotected intercourse when that was not their intent, but the treatment group did not do so (or did so to a lesser extent).

The combination of findings reported here—that the curriculum delayed the onset of intercourse but did not affect the frequency of intercourse among those who had already initiated intercourse—are strikingly similar to the results of Postponing Sexual Involvement. Like RTR, PSI is also based upon a social influence approach, emphasizes norms and skills, and was shown to delay the onset of intercourse. These two studies in combination provide stronger evidence that this theoretical approach is an effective one. They also strongly indicate that it is important to reach youth before they initiate intercourse. Furthermore, the RTR curriculum (but not the PSI curriculum) was designed to increase the use of contraception, but the failure of both this curriculum and PSI to increase the use of contraception suggests that it may actually be more feasible to delay the onset of intercourse than to increase the use of contraception among those who had already initiated intercourse. Certainly, additional studies are needed to substantiate this. This study also has implications for other sexuality education research, both past and future. With the exception of the two other recent studies, previous evaluations of specific sex education programs collected follow-up data for up to 3 or at most 6 months. In this study, if the 18-month data had not been collected, important behavioral effects would not have been measured. It took 18 months for the sexually inexperienced youth in the comparison group to initiate sufficiently greater risk-taking behavior in order for the difference between the treatment and comparison groups to be significantly different. This finding means that previous evaluations may have simply not measured the delayed effects of sexuality education programs.

Similarly, if the initial sample size had been any smaller, important behavioral effects would not have been identified because the sample size of important subpopulations (e.g., the sexually inexperienced at pretest) would have been too small to detect programmatically significant effects. These two findings suggest that, in the future, evaluations must have large sample sizes and must track youth for at least 18 months in order to detect important effects.

This research was strong but not definitive. Although the overall sample size was relatively large, power analysis of the findings indicates that a 20% probability exists of incorrectly failing to reject the null hypothesis of a difference between two groups with alpha set at .05 for effect sizes of .10. For subsamples, the power is less. The positive findings on the transition to protected sex or delayed onset of sexual activity occurred despite worse odds. With our sample of 433 nonsexually experienced youth, the probability of detecting a small difference ($ES = .10$) is only 56%. This probability is important because numerous differences existed between the treatment and comparison groups that were in the desired direction but not statistically significant. If the effect size had not been diminished by sample attrition, some of these effects may have been significant. This suggests the need for a still larger sample size.

These data indicate that although the RTR curriculum was effective, it is by no means a complete solution to unprotected intercourse; many youth in the treatment group continued to have unprotected intercourse.

Many professionals working with youth recognize that more complete solutions require more comprehensive programs involving the school, parents, and the community (Dryfoos, 1990; Schorr & Schorr, 1988; Kamerman & Kahn, 1990; Zabin, this volume). Such programs undoubtedly will need to improve the life and career opportunities for youth. Comprehensive programs require effective components, however, and this research suggests that the RTR curriculum may be one such component. In addition, this curriculum has an important virtue that more comprehensive programs do not have—it can be incorporated into the existing family life education programs in schools.

References

Bandura, A. (1977). *Social learning theory.* Englewood Cliffs, NJ: Prentice-Hall.

Bandura, A. (1986). *Social foundations of thought and action.* Englewood Cliffs, NJ: Prentice-Hall.

Barth, R. P., Fetro, J., Leland, N. L., & Volkan, K. (in press). Preventing adolescent pregnancy with social and cognitive skills. *Journal of Adolescent Research.*

Card, J. J., & Reagan, R. T. (1989). Strategies for evaluating adolescent pregnancy programs. *Family Planning Perspectives, 21,* 27-32.

Dawson, D. A. (1986). The effects of sex education on adolescent behavior. *Family Planning Perspectives, 18,* 162-167.

Dryfoos, J. (1990). *Adolescents at risk.* New York: Oxford University Press.

Eisen, M., Zellman, G. L., & McAlister, A. L. (1990). Evaluating the impact of a theory-based sexuality and contraceptive education program. *Family Planning Perspectives, 22(6),* 262.

Education Research Council. (1987). *Teen pregnancy: Impact on the schools.* Alexandria, VA: Capitol.

Gilchrist, L. D., & Schinke, S. P. (1983). Coping with contraception: Cognitive and behavioral methods with adolescents. *Cognitive Therapy and Research, 7,* 379-388.

Harris, L. (1988). *Public attitudes toward teenage pregnancy, sex education, and birth control.* New York: Planned Parenthood of America.

Kamerman, S. B., & Kahn, A. J. (1990). Social services for children, youth, and families in the United States. *Children and Youth Services Review, 12,* 1-184.

Kenney, A. M., Guardado, S., & Brown, L. (1989). Sex education and AIDS education in the schools: What states and large school districts are doing. *Family Planning Perspectives, 21,* 56-64.

Kenney, A., & Orr, T. (1984). Sex education: An overview of current programs, policies, and research. *Phi Delta Kappan, 65,* 492-501.

Kirby, D. (1984). *Sexuality education: An evaluation of programs and their effects.* Santa Cruz, CA: Network.

Marsiglio, W., & Mott, F. L. (1986). The impact of sex education on sexual activity, contraceptive use and premarital pregnancy among American teenagers. *Family Planning Perspectives, 18,* 151-162.

82   Enhancing Social and Cognitive Skills

McGuire, W. (1964). Inducing resistance to persuasion. In L. Berkowitz (Ed.), *Advances in experimental social psychology* (pp. 191-229). New York: Academic Press.
Schorr, E. B. & Schorr, D. (1988). *Within our reach: Breaking the cycle of disadvantage.* New York: Doubleday.
Sonenstein, F., & Pittman, K. (1984). The availability of sex education in large city school districts. *Family Planning Perspectives, 16,* 19-25.
Stout, J. W., & Rivera, S. P. (1989). Schools and sex education: Does it work? *Pediatrics, 83,* 375-379.

4

An Information and Skills Approach for Younger Teens

Postponing Sexual Involvement Program

MARION HOWARD
JUDITH A. McCABE

This chapter discusses the evaluation of a hospital-based outreach educational program that has been successful in helping youth from low-income families postpone sexual involvement. The program's two components, entitled Human Sexuality, and Postponing Sexual Involvement: An Educational Series for Young Teens, have been implemented in a local public school system since 1983 by the Henry W. Grady Memorial Hospital in Atlanta, Georgia. The initial funding used to present the two components and to evaluate their effect on sexual behaviors of the hospital's adolescent population was granted by the Ford Foundation. The positive findings from the evaluation led to permanent adoption of the program by the hospital and the school system. The Postponing Sexual Involvement Educational Series is now being disseminated throughout the United States as an abstinence model for young teens.

The Henry W. Grady Memorial Hospital serves the indigent population in the two most populous counties in Georgia. Beginning in 1977, through an agreement with the largest of the area's four school systems, the hospital began giving a five-class-period outreach education program entitled Human Sexuality to all eighth-grade youth in that system. This program was designed to provide youth with basic factual information and decision-making skills related to reproductive health, including knowledge about contraceptives and how to use them effectively. An evaluation carried out in the early 1980s (Howard, 1988), however, indicated that such a program by itself was not effective in reducing the rate of sexual involvement or teen pregnancy. Therefore, in 1983 a five-class-period experientially oriented Postponing Sexual Involvement component was added. The purpose was to give youth more skills in using the information provided through the previously developed knowledge-based program. In particular, the Postponing component was designed to improve the ability of youth to deal with social and peer pressures that lead them into early sexual involvement.

The Postponing Sexual Involvement component was based on the social influence model, which holds that youth are more likely to engage in negative health behaviors because of social and peer pressures rather than lack of knowledge about the harmful effects of such behaviors (McAlister, 1980). For example, when asked why many teenagers do not wait to have sexual intercourse until they are older, 61% of the 1,000 teenagers interviewed by Harris pollsters cited social pressures. A higher proportion of girls (73%) than boys (50%) indicated that they thought social pressures were the main reasons why teenagers do not wait to have sex (Harris & Associates, 1986). Indeed, the fact that knowledge alone does not change behavior is nowhere more clearly evident than in the fact that millions of Americans still smoke over 20 years after the Surgeon General's report on its harmfulness.

At the heart of the social influence model is the adaptation of the public health concept of immunization as a strategy for combating social and peer pressures toward negative health behaviors. By exposing young people in small doses to the "noxious" social influences, while at the same time enabling them to examine those influences and develop skills to deal with them, this strategy helps young people build up an immunity to them. The model thus utilizes a social immunization (inoculation) approach, as it were. To achieve the immunity, programs based on this model rely on specific activities that (a) help youth identify where pressures to use drugs, smoke, drink, or have sex come from; (b) help them examine motivations behind those pressures; (c) assist them in developing ways to respond to the pressures; and (d) help them learn skills that they can use to say no to pressure situations. This social inoculation model has yielded encouraging results. For example, programs in the area of preventing or reducing smoking behavior based on this model have reported differences in rates of cigarette use among young people exposed to the program compared with those who were not, ranging from 25% to 66% (Ellickson & Robyn, 1987).

Another important aspect of the social inoculation model is that it utilizes role models—teens slightly older than those being given the program—to present the factual information, identify pressures, role model responses to pressures, teach assertiveness skills to use in refusing to participate in the behavior, and demonstrate ways to handle problem situations. Teen leaders have been shown to produce greater and more lasting effects than do adults (Luepker, Johnson, Murray, & Pechacek, 1983). Young people want to be and act older than they are. Besides imparting attitudes and skills, slightly older teens illustrate that those saying no to the pressured behavior can be admired and liked by other teens and be successful in the teen world. In the case of the Postponing Sexual Involvement Educational Series, they also clearly demonstrate to the younger teens that having sex is not the way to attain such status.

The revised educational program also took into consideration the fact that adolescent growth and development under age 16 is very uneven. Indeed, during that period most young people have not completed some of the most important phases of their growth and development. For example, cognitive growth and development is such that despite their earlier physical maturation, young people under age 16 often still are using concrete thinking skills. As a result, they are much less likely to conceive of the impact of their choices on their future and much less likely to see the consequences of their actions beyond the immediate.

Programs such as the original outreach program designed by the hospital, which rely on youth being able to use a decision-making process, are bound to be somewhat thwarted by young people's inability to apply more adult, sophisticated thinking skills. Decision making involves conceptualizing alternatives and long-range impacts, something very difficult for those youth with concrete thinking focused on the immediate. Adolescents in a concrete stage of thinking are concerned with their world as it is today, not what it might be like in the future. It is much more difficult for them to engage in planning, which requires not only the ability to think about tomorrow but the ways in which today's actions could lead to consequences tomorrow. Hence, an educational program must be very specific and teach adolescents attitudes and skills that they can use until such time as they become capable of using more adult attributes in managing their sexuality.

As a basic guide for developing the new age-appropriate five-part educational series, hospital staff used the social influence-based Smoking Prevention Curriculum developed by Alfred McAlister (McAlister, 1980). The adaptation developed by the hospital's Emory/Grady Teen Services Program was the first in the country to apply the social influence model as a way of delaying beginning sexual intercourse. Further impetus to the development of the program was the result of a 1982 sample survey of the over 1,200 female adolescents annually seen in the Emory/Grady Teen Services Program family planning clinic. When asked what they would most like more information on, 84% checked the item: How to say no without hurting the other person's feelings. This item turned out to be the single most frequently checked in a long list of items covering information of interest to young teens.

The philosophy of the added component, Postponing Sexual Involvement Educational Series for Young Teens, is as follows: (a) Young people under age 16 are not yet able to understand fully the implications of their actions. (b) Young people under age 16 generally are not mature enough to handle the consequences of their actions. Such consequences are most often negative for that age group—premature pregnancy, for example. Further, the needs that young people often identify that they are trying to meet through sexual intercourse (e.g., being popular, becoming a man, satisfying curiosity, keeping a boyfriend) could best be met in other ways. (c) Young people under age 16 are often pressured into engaging in behaviors that they really do not want to engage in. Such pressure comes from the glamorous images of sexual involvement presented by the media, as well as pressures from peers. (d) Young people need to be given the tools and skills to be able to resist pressures to become sexually involved. They do not naturally know how to do this, and they need to be supported and given practice in such learning.

It is important to note that the Postponing Sexual Involvement Educational Series differs from other sex education programs in several major ways: The Postponing Sexual Involvement Educational Series is not value free (although few things are). It starts with a given value that young people ought not to be having sexual intercourse. Everything in the series is designed to support the value of not beginning sexual intercourse at a young age. Further, the Postponing Sexual Involvement Educational Series for Young Teens is experiential. Through activities in which young teens constantly interact, the series helps young people develop and practice skills that enable them to carry out the desired goal of postponing sexual intercourse. The Postponing Sexual Involvement

Educational Series also differs in that youth are seen as the primary communicators of messages rather than adults. Because the series is aimed equally at young males as well as young females, two teen leaders—one male and one female—slightly older than the youth to whom the series is given usually present the series together.

Thus the revised outreach education program consists of the original Human Sexuality component and the added skill building component. The Human Sexuality part takes five class periods and is implemented by nurses and counselors from the hospital's Emory/Grady Teen Services Program. Material covered is to be found in the *Discussion Guide on Human Sexuality* published by the Teen Services Program. The skill-building component of the program also takes five class periods but is taught by 11th- and 12th-grade youth under the supervision of the nurses and counselors of the Emory/Grady Teen Services Program. Material covered is to be found in *Postponing Sexual Involvement: An Educational Series for Young Teens* published by the Emory/Grady Teen Services Program at Grady Memorial Hospital.

Much controversy has arisen regarding telling young people about contraceptives and also urging them to postpone sexual involvement. Many critics of sex education programs feel it is too mixed a message when a program does both. The Emory/Grady Teen Services Program experience, however, is that young people already think they know about birth control, albeit much of the information they have is erroneous. Combining sound factual information about reproductive health, including information about birth control and how to use it, as in the original Human Sexuality program, with strong rationale and support for postponing sexual involvement, as in the added skill-building program, is necessary for young teens in today's society.

Indeed, results of the program's evaluation showed that young people who were given the combined program of five class periods on human sexuality, including contraceptive information, and five class periods on postponing sexual involvement not only were significantly more likely to postpone sexual involvement than those who did not have the program, but also were more likely to use contraceptives if they did have sex. Indeed, of youth who used birth control, twice as many youth who had the program said they used birth control because of what they learned in school than did those who did not have the program. These data strongly suggest that the two messages are not incompatible. Moreover, the Teen Services Program feels the two messages are essential. This is so because only promoting birth control use leaves young people who wish to postpone without explicit adult and peer support and, therefore, unnecessarily vulnerable. On the other hand, providing abstinence information to youth who have decided to have or are already are having sexual intercourse without also giving them the information they need to protect themselves, is unconscionable.

Evaluation Design

The hospital was interested in learning to what extent the combined Postponing Sexual Involvement and Human Sexuality education program components influenced the sexual behaviors of low-income young people—those male and female youth most likely to utilize the hospital's services when they need health care. Therefore it was decided to study all youth who were born at the hospital in 1971-1972 whose families had received services at the hospital since 1981, thus assuring that the young people in the study group not only had been born in poverty but had remained in poverty. In the Atlanta community, such youth generally are considered to be those at highest risk for early sexual involvement and subsequent premature pregnancy, and also the most difficult to serve. In addition to being born at the hospital, the youth had to be entering the eighth grade in the fall of 1985, because that was the grade in which the combined Postponing Sexual Involvement and Human Sexuality education program components would be given. Criteria for those participating in the evaluation, therefore, were (a) born at Grady Memorial Hospital sometime during 1971-1972, (b) entering the eighth grade in the fall of 1985, (c) resident of an Atlanta area county, (d) mother or child active at Grady Hospital sometime since 1981, and (e) parental/guardian permission to participate. Exclusion from participating in the evaluation resulted from (a) inability to locate mother and/or child by phone, (b) child no longer living in the Atlanta area, (c) child not entering the eighth grade in the fall of 1985, and (d) parental/guardian permission for participation not granted.

Although the program was given to close to 5,000 young people during the 1985-1986 school year, no attempt was made to evaluate the impact on any young people other than those poverty youth described above. Further, no attempt was made to assign randomly the poverty youth to program or no-program groups. Whether a poverty youth received the program was determined solely by whether he or she happened to be enrolled in one of the schools where the program was given. Where the program was given was determined by the hospital's choice of an educational system in which to offer the program. The hospital gave the program in only one of the four educational systems in the Atlanta area served by the hospital and thus in only one of the four school systems attended by poverty youth. All eighth-grade young people in the school system chosen by the hospital, however, were scheduled to be given the program regardless of poverty status. The groups of poverty program and no-program study youth were located in 53 separate schools. The poverty youth in the program group were distributed throughout each of the 24 schools in which the Postponing Sexual Involvement and Human Sexuality components were given. The highest number of study subjects in any one school of the 24 schools where all eighth-grade youth were given the program was 20. The lowest number of study subjects in any one school where all eighth-grade youth were given the program was 1. The no-program poverty youth were scattered among 29 schools. The highest number of these study subjects in any one school of the 29 schools where the program was not given to eighth-grade youth was 10. The lowest number of no-program youth in any one school where the program was not given to eighth-grade youth was 1. Subsequent postprogram data analysis increased confidence that differences in outcomes were due to the program and not to differences among schools. This was so because youth in program schools who, for one reason or another, missed the program had outcomes similar to those in no-program schools.

Basing the evaluation on the hospital population circumvented several problems encountered by those trying to evaluate sex education programs. One problem is that although many sex education programs are given in schools, even school systems that are willing to implement sex education programs often balk at allowing youth to be asked about their actual sexual behaviors, particularly over time. Fear of parental disapproval and/or community sensitivity are the main reasons given. On the other hand, parents who had been long-time patients at the hospital (having been seen minimally for over a decade and sometimes for their whole lives) were likely to give consent for the child's participation in the health study. Indeed, 99% of the parents whose children were eligible for participation in the study initially agreed to let them participate.

A second common problem is that of finding a comparison group of youth similar to those who are being given the program and arranging for their participation in a study. Because it chose as a study population

Table 4.1 Program and No-Program Youth Comparisons Prior to Intervention (*n* = 536)

Characteristics	% Youth in Program Schools	% Youth in No-Program Schools
Is black	99	99
Lowest income categories[a]	56	45*
Lives with two parents	36	57*
Gets mostly A or B grades in school	71	65
Plans more education after high school	86	87
Is involved in club, team, or activities	53	52
Is leader in club, team, or activity	20	16
Never says no when asked to do something doesn't want to do	13	8*
Has boyfriend/girlfriend	46	38
Thinks most/several friends have had sex	45	45
Thinks almost everybody/a lot of 8th graders have sex	41	40
Thinks best friend has sex	44	50
Thinks friends would disapprove if had sex	44	36
Thinks parents would be very upset if had sex	73	73
Alone with someone who wanted sex last month	41	47
Thinks will have sex in next 6 months	21	23
Would find it hard to say no to sex with someone care about	46	49
Has had sex	25	23
Has drunk	21	23
Has smoked	9	6
Gets 8 hours sleep each school night	81	83
Exercises strenuously 1/2 hour three times/week	92	92
In good health	92	97
Eats fruits/vegetables everyday	78	78

NOTE: [a]paid less than standard low-income fee at last hospital visit
*$p < 0.05$

only youth who were born at Grady Memorial Hospital and who had remained in poverty, the hospital felt that the life circumstances of the young people would contribute strongly to common characteristics. Indeed, when treatment and comparison group responses given prior to the intervention were compared, the youth proved to be remarkably similar (see Table 4.1). No statistically significant initial background differences were found that would bias any outcomes in favor of those who were to receive the program.

Low-income youth often have poor reading skills, which can make use of written questionnaires difficult and responses suspect. The hospital dealt with this issue by using telephone interviews to gather the data, thus avoiding problems due to misreading. So that anyone within listening distance would not understand the responses the youth were giving to questions being asked, the answers either were structured to be nonrevealing, or verbal codes were given to the youth for use in responding.

A third problem is whether data collection at the same site where the program is given, often carried out by those giving the program, may influence youth responses. To deal with this issue, the data gathering was carried out on evenings and weekends through a subcontract with the Center for Public and Urban Research of Georgia State University. Further, youth actually participated in a broader study of the health habits of eighth-grade youth. Although the primary purpose of the data collection was to evaluate the hospital's outreach education program, information useful to the hospital concerning a wide variety of youth health habits was collected during the study. By using this broader interview approach, the hospital was able to place questions about eating habits, exercise and sleep habits, smoking, drinking, and drug use around the questions relating to sexual behavior so that the sexual behavior questions did not stand out. Indeed, many similar questions were asked about smoking, drinking, and sexual behaviors. The telephone interviewers who called the youth were employed by the Center for Public and Urban Research. They identified themselves as calling from Georgia State University on behalf of Grady Memorial Hospital, thus further separating the Postponing outreach education program and the interviews.

Finally, a fourth problem is that studies of outcomes of sex education programs mostly rely on self-reports regarding sexual intercourse or generalized birth/abortion rates in the area served by the program. The hospital was in a unique position to corroborate the telephone interview data about sexual involvement among the girls. In only 1% of the cases was information in the medical records judged to be contradictory to statements made by the girls in telephone interviews. Thus the record review greatly increased confidence in the interview data.

What Did the Hospital Hope to Learn?

The key questions to be answered by the evaluation were (a) How would youth react to the Postponing Sexual Involvement program?

(b) Would youth who had not had sexual intercourse before they were given the program postpone sexual involvement in the eighth grade? (c) Would youth who had not had sexual intercourse before they were given the program continue to postpone sexual involvement in the ninth grade? (d) Would both boys and girls who had not had sexual intercourse before they were given the program postpone sexual involvement? (e) Would youth who began sexual intercourse after having had the program report less sexual involvement? (f) Would girls who had the program have fewer pregnancies? (g) Would youth who had sexual intercourse before the program change behaviors as a result of the program?

The Evaluation Population

Over the summer of 1985, the Grady Hospital Birth Logs from the years 1971 and 1972 were used to identify youth who would be age 13-14 in the fall of 1985. The logs contained data on over 5,500 babies. All names of babies weighing greater than 500 grams were pulled from the September to December 1971 and the January to December 1972 birth logs. Then an attempt was made to match hospital record numbers of the babies and their mothers with those in the Grady Hospital Patient Master File to see whether either one was still an active patient at Grady Hospital. Active patients were defined as having been to Grady (ambulatory care or inpatient) since 1981. An attempt then was made to reach all active families to ascertain whether the child found in the birth logs was entering the eighth grade and, if so, whether a parent or guardian would give permission for participation in the study. A change in school admission policies at the time the selected birth cohort was scheduled to enter school reduced the size of the eligible group. Nevertheless, 1,114 young people were determined to meet the criteria for the study; less than 1% of their parents refused to let them participate. The 1,005 consenting parents then were sent a letter further explaining the study and confirming in writing their verbal permission to allow their child to be contacted by telephone.

Interview Procedures

During the 1985-1986 school year, preprogram and postprogram data and comparison data were gathered on 665 young people who were in the eighth grade (two thirds of the 1,005 youth whose parents initially

Table 4.2 Reasons for Youth Not Completing Pre- and Postprogram Interviews

End of Eighth Grade Interview Status	Program Group n = 734	No-program Group n = 271	Total Youth n = 1,005
Completed interviews	487 (66%)	178 (66%)	665 (66%)
Disconnected phones	109 (15%)	29 (11%)	138 (14%)
Youth unreachable[a]	119 (16%)	52 (19%)	171 (17%)
Parent/child refusal	19 (3%)	12 (4%)	31 (3%)

NOTE: [a]Primarily Not Home or No Answer at time of 10 calls, but also Moved, Juvenile Detention Center, etc.

had given permission for participation in the study). All young people were sent a letter prior to their interview, encouraging their participation and enclosing a $2 bill. This procedure was followed for all five waves of interviews that were carried out in the eighth and ninth grades. Youth with connected, listed telephones received up to 10 call-backs in an attempt to complete data-gathering interviews. Those with unlisted numbers were sent letters asking for their unlisted number and, if supplied, also received up to 10 call-backs. A breakdown of completed interviews and reasons for 340 youth not completing the required number of preprogram and postprogram interviews by the end of the eighth grade are shown in Table 4.2.

No significant differences were found in the composition of the final study group of 665 and the initially identified group of 1,005 youth in terms of sex, school system, and income classification according to hospital criteria (either paying full public hospital fees or less than full public hospital fees). Nor were differences based on race (99% of the original group were black and 99% of the final group were black).

The next year, attempts were made to conduct follow-up telephone interviews with the 665 youth who, by completing interviews at the beginning, middle, and end of the eighth grade, had participated in both a pretest and a posttest and thus were considered participants in the formal evaluation. The midyear interview the first year was necessary because program youth could receive the intervention either the first semester or the second semester and the evaluators wished to have as tight a preprogram and postprogram assessment as possible. Follow-up telephone interviews, however, were conducted with youth only at the beginning and end of the ninth grade (the 1986-1987 school year).

These interviews were used to determine the longer term effects of the hospital's education program.

Six hundred eight (608) youth completed the interview at the beginning of the ninth grade. The beginning-of-ninth-grade interviews constituted a follow-up anywhere from approximately 6-12 months following program intervention. At the end of the ninth grade, interviews were completed with 560 youth. The end-of-ninth-grade interviews constituted a follow-up anywhere from 12-18 months following program intervention. Of these end-of-year youth, however, 21 did not complete the beginning-of-ninth-grade interview. At the end of the ninth grade, the study retention rate of the 665 youth who had complete preinterviews and postinterviews in the eighth grade was 84%. No significant differences were found in the retention rates between program and no-program group youth. Nor were significant differences found in the rate of retention based on the sex of youth in each group. Slightly more girls than boys in both the program and no-program groups, however, completed all five interviews. As with the initial groups, the youth who completed all five interviews were scattered throughout the many schools attended by low-income youth in the Atlanta area. In total, the youth were located in 53 separate schools.

Although data are available on 560 youth at the end of the ninth grade, for the purposes of presenting the richest and most complete data set, the information used in the analysis is presented only on the 536 youth who completed all five telephone interviews. The major outcomes of these 536 youth did not differ significantly from the 560 youth who were still participating in the follow-up study at the end of the ninth grade. By using the group with five completed interviews (a drop of 4% of the youth), the numbers of youth in the study remain consistent throughout and, therefore, comparisons are made easier.

Issues in Analyzing the Data

A number of problems emerged in trying to analyze the data. The most critical decision to be made was who had sexual intercourse and when. How this was decided was central to the key evaluative question—the Human Sexuality and Postponing Sexual Involvement program's effect on youth sexual behaviors.

Those studies that ask young people only once about sexual intercourse can accept that one answer as valid. Because they never ask again, they gather no contradictory data. Data analysis thus is fairly easy. For those studies that ask youth the same question several times over a period of years, however, the analytical problems become more difficult. This is so because not all individuals when asked the same question over a period of several years will give the same answer each time. Because the study described here was a longitudinal study (young people were followed throughout their high school careers), problems with inconsistency of responses are inevitable and bothersome but require the most thoughtful attention possible. To evaluate the program's influence on young people's sexual behavior in the eighth and ninth grades, the first and most difficult analytical task was to ascertain which youth had had sexual intercourse before they had the program and which had not. Sexual intercourse was defined for youth each time they participated in a wave of the study. Youth were asked: People refer to sexual intercourse in many ways—making love, having sex, or going all the way. Have you ever had sex?

Because the program was designed to help youth who had not yet had sex postpone sexual involvement, making this determination was essential to understanding the effect of the program on youth outcomes. In some ways, this task was made easier by the fact that, regardless of the approach the evaluative staff used to make this determination, the Postponing Sexual Involvement Educational Series' effect on beginning sexual involvement remained fairly strong and consistent. Other outcomes were dependent on this categorization, however, so the issue was explored as thoroughly as possible. (See the appendix for a thorough discussion of the data organization alternatives.)

Results of the Postponing Program on Sexual Behaviors

The differences between program and no-program groups 12-18 months following the program are shown in Table 4.3. It is clear that the program did have an impact on the youth in terms of postponing beginning sexual intercourse both immediately and over time. Group differences in sexual intercourse experience, depending on how the data were organized, would appear to be in the range of 8% to 15% with an average of 12%.

All of the comparisons shown in Table 4.3, except the method of using youngest age ever given for having begun sexual intercourse as the primary determinate, show a statistically significant difference ($p <$ .05 or greater) based on tests of significance for the difference between

Table 4.3 Percent Who Reported Having Had Sexual Intercourse at
12-18 Months Postprogram, by Group

Program	No Program	Multiple Response Organization
22%*	33%	All "yes/no" inconsistent cases removed
23%**	36%	"Yes/no" inconsistent cases left in
27%*	42%	Age 13 and over as the primary determinate
20%	28%	Youngest age as the primary determinate
24%*	39%	Multiple prospective criteria
28%*	39%	Multiple prospective criteria and unknowns conservatively distributed

NOTE: $*p < 0.05$, $**p < 0.01$

proportions using a one-side normal curve test applied to the arcsine transformations of the proportions (Cohen, 1988).

Indeed, even if the data (all inconsistent cases left in) are presented in their entirety just as given by all youth with no preprogram/postprogram differentiation made for either program or no-program group, the program still had a noticeable impact on sexual behaviors. As shown in Table 4.4, even though a greater proportion of the program youth stated they had had sex at the first interview at the beginning of the eighth grade than did the no-program youth, by the last interview at the end of the ninth grade the situation was reversed. By the end of ninth grade, a greater proportion of the no-program group stated they had had sex than did the program group. (This is represented by a first-to-last interview increase of 18% for the program group and a same-period increase of 25% for the no-program group.) Also shown is the 23% increase for young people who should have had the program because they were in the same schools as those who were given the program, but who missed being given the program.

**Validation of Interview Data and
Handling of Inconsistencies**

The hospital was in a unique position to corroborate the telephone interview data about sexual involvement among the girls. Because these were hospital patients, the medical records of the girls in the study could be checked by research staff. Ten months following the final interview

Table 4.4 Sexual Intercourse Experience Over Time, By Group ($n = 536$)

Group	Beginning 8th Grade		End 8th Grade[a]		Beginning 9th Grade		End 9th Grade	
	Had Sex	No Sex	Had Sex	No Sex	Had Sex	No Sex	Had Sex	No Sex
Program[b]	92	277	110	259	125	244	159	210
$n = 369$	25%	75%	30%	70%	34%	66%	43%	57%
No program[c]	32	109	44	97	53	88	67	74
$n = 141$	23%	77%	31%	69%	38%	62%	48%	52%
Missed program[d]	4	22	9	17	10	16	10	16
$n = 26$	15%	85%	35%	65%	38%	62%	38%	62%

NOTE: [a]The End 8th Grade category includes three boys under Had Sex who began having sex preprogram.
[b]First-to-last interview sexual involvement increase of 18%
[c]First-to-last interview sexual involvement increase of 25%
[d]First-to-last interview sexual involvement increase of 23%

wave, the records on hospital visits were examined for notations with respect to sexual involvement, pregnancy tests, pregnancies, births, abortions, treatment of sexually transmitted diseases, and family planning counseling and/or family planning services. The interview and hospital data turned out to be remarkably consistent. In other words, if a girl in her interviews said she had not been sexually involved, usually no contraindication in the medical record and sometimes a notation of "not sexually active" was found. On the other hand, for girls who said they had had intercourse, the medical record often showed some indication of sexual involvement and/or it was noted that the girl stated at the time of the hospital visit that she was sexually involved.

The medical record review also was helpful in other respects. For example, in her end-of-ninth-grade telephone interview, one girl who reported that she was pregnant actually was not. Hospital records showed that when the patient came for a pregnancy test 1 month later, the results were negative. Thus the hospital record information was useful in verifying accurate pregnancy, abortion, and birth data. In only 1% of the cases was information in the medical records judged to be contradictory to statements made by the girls in telephone interviews. Thus the record review greatly increased confidence in the interview data. It also increased confidence in the method of organizing data to deal with inconsistencies.

**Youth Who Started to Have Sex During
the Semester the Program Was Given**

One problem still remained, however, that was particularly relevant to determining the main program outcome. It concerned the unknowns—18 program youth (14 boys and 4 girls) who appeared to have begun having sex during the same semester in which the program started. These youth said they had not had sex when they were first interviewed but indicated that they had had sex at the end of the same semester in which they were given the Postponing Sexual Involvement program. Unfortunately, the ages given by some of these youth over the five waves of data collection as to when they first had sexual intercourse also were inconsistent. Thus it was impossible to determine whether these youth had sex before they started the program, during the time they were being given the program, or following the program. It was assumed, however, to be most unlikely that all youth would fall into either the preprogram (preprogram completion) group or postprogram with respect to beginning sexual involvement. If they followed the pattern of their fellow program youth, the outcome data would not vary; on the other hand, it was important to consider what the data might look like if the sexual behaviors of the 18 youth were not the same as that of their peers who also had the program.

As a conservative approach to handling these "unknowns," the data were analyzed also as if these 18 program youth followed the same sexual behavior patterns as those youth who were not given the program. To do this, the 18 youth were distributed by sex in the program group between the preprogram sexually involved group and the postprogram sexually involved group in the same proportions as the sexually involved youth in the no-program group. When this was done, a statistically significant difference still remained between the program and no-program groups. Table 4.5 shows the final organization of the data that are used as the basis for the evaluation of the Postponing Sexual Involvement Educational Series. Added into the table are the youth who missed the program and the unknowns. The full table shows the outcomes of program youth following participation in the Human Sexuality and Postponing Sexual Involvement program in contrast with a comparison group of young people who did not have the program (the no-program group). Significant differences are found between the program group and the no-program group. The outcomes of the program youth also are contrasted with a group of youth who were in the same schools as the young people who received the program but for some reason missed being given the program. Significant differences are found between the program group and the missed program group as well. Although the numbers are small, this latter finding supports the conclusion that the difference between the program and no-program groups is not due to the differences between the two kinds of schools attended but to the impact of the program. Although not without problems, this final categorization seemed the best way to try to include youth with inconsistent responses in the program evaluation. It is on this data division that the rest of the analyses were performed.

**Examining Explanations
for Evaluation Outcomes**

Once the data were organized to show sexual behavior status at various points and the differences between the outcomes of the program and no-program groups were verified, it became important to ascertain further that the reduction in sexual involvement was due to program impact as opposed to other differences between groups. To do this, the evaluation looked at a number of key factors, including (a) similarities and differences between program and no-program groups prior to intervention, (b) relationship status throughout the study period—that is, having a boyfriend or girlfriend, (c) situational opportunity status throughout the study period—that is, being alone with someone who wanted to have sexual intercourse, and (d) perceived helpfulness of the program to program participants.

Similarities and differences between program and no-program groups prior to the intervention were first examined. No statistically significant initial background differences were found that would bias any outcomes in favor of those who were to receive the program (see Table 4.1).

In order to explain program outcomes, it also was important to see whether youth who had the Postponing Sexual Involvement program were less likely to have boyfriends or girlfriends and, therefore, some of the difference in rates of sexual involvement could be attributed to less interpersonal involvement. That did not turn out to be true, however. Overall, those who had not had sex and who were given the Postponing Sexual Involvement program had just as many, if not more, boyfriends and girlfriends than did those in the no-program group (boys and girls combined—End 8th Grade: 47% vs. 45%; End 9th Grade: 50% vs. 43%). Thus having a boyfriend or girlfriend does not seem to account for differences in the outcomes observed between groups.

Table 4.5 Sexual Intercourse Experience and Timing, by Group (n = 536)

Group	Began Sex Before Program (n = 131) Had Sex	Did Not Begin Sex Before Program (n = 405)								
		Status End 8th Grade			Status Beginning 9th Grade			Status End 9th Grade		
		Had Sex	No Sex	UK Sex	Had Sex	No Sex	UK Sex	Had Sex	No Sex	UK Sex
Program										
Received[a] with unknowns	101 27%	21 8%	247 92%	0 —	42 16%	226 84%	0 —	74 28%	194 72%	0 —
Received without unknowns	95 27%	9 4%*	247 96%	18 —	30 12%**	226 88%	18 —	62 24%**	194 76%	18 —
Missed	4 15%	4 18%	18 82%	0 —	6 27%	16 73%	0 —	8 36%	14 64%	0 —
No Program										
	32 23%	22 20%	87 80%	0 —	29 27%	80 73%	0 —	42 39%	67 61%	0 —

NOTE: [a]The Received Program Group appears with and without the 18 unknowns (UK Sex) distributed within it following the same preprogram and postprogram pattern of sexual involvement (by sex) as the No-Program Group.
*p < 0.01 when contrasted with the No-Program Group, **p < 0.05 when contrasted with the No-Program Group.

Another way of measuring opportunity for sexual involvement was by whether the youth were ever alone with someone who wanted to have sexual intercourse with them. The problem with using this measure for the program group is that the Postponing Sexual Involvement program taught that one way to avoid sexual involvement is to avoid being alone with someone where sexual intercourse would be possible. Nevertheless, if young people in the program group were more likely to never be alone with someone who wanted to have sex with them, it might offer a partial explanation for the differences in sexual behavior.

In each group of young people who had not had sex, however, at least a fifth of the youth said at each interview that they were alone in the last month with someone who wanted to have sex with them. Overall, no discernible pattern was found that would place one group who did not have sex at greater risk than the other. Over 2 years, on the average 30% of the no-program group youth who never had sex were alone in the last month with someone who wanted to have sex with them, and 27% of the program group were alone with someone under the same circumstances. Thus young people in the program group who had not had sex were just about as likely to be alone with someone who wanted to have sex with them as youth in the other groups. Thus it does not seem as if opportunity for sexual involvement can account for behavioral differences among those who did and did not have the Postponing Sexual Involvement program.

**Helpfulness of the Postponing Sexual Involvement
Program to Program Participants**

In order to explain outcomes, it was important to learn whether the youth perceived the Postponing Sexual Involvement program as enabling them to have more control over their sexual behavior. To obtain such information, the evaluation asked youth postprogram: With respect to the information the teen leaders or person from Grady Hospital taught, how helpful will that information be to you personally in saying no to sex? Youth reacted extremely favorably to the Postponing Sexual Involvement program. Of the young people who had not had sex before the program, 95% said the Postponing Sexual Involvement program would be helpful personally to them in saying no to sex. Indeed, well over three quarters felt the program would be extremely helpful or very helpful. Overall, girls and boys were almost equally likely to say they thought the program would be helpful personally (92% of boys said so as did 96% of girls). Girls, however, were more likely to rate the program as extremely helpful or very helpful. Based on their positive attitude toward the information given them through the teen-led Postponing Sexual Involvement program and the fact that young people who had the program had reduced rates of sexual involvement, it seems apparent that the Postponing program did affect the behaviors of young people.

Major Findings

The program helped youth postpone sexual involvement. Youth who had not had sexual intercourse before they participated in the Postponing Sexual Involvement program were significantly more likely to postpone sexual involvement. By the end of the eighth grade, youth who were not given the program were as much as five times more likely to have begun having sex than were young people who were given the program (see Table 4.5, second column). Youth who had not had sexual intercourse before they were given the Postponing Sexual Involvement program also were much more likely to continue to postpone sexual involvement. By the end of the ninth grade, one third fewer of the youth who were given the program had begun having sex than had young people who were not given the program.

The program was of assistance to both boys and girls. Boys who had not had sexual intercourse before they participated in the Postponing Sexual Involvement program were significantly more likely to postpone sexual involvement. By the end of the ninth grade, one third fewer of the boys who were given the program in the eighth grade had begun having sex than had the boys who were not given the program. Girls who had not had sexual intercourse before they were given the Postponing Sexual Involvement program also were significantly more likely to postpone sexual involvement. By the end of the ninth grade, one third fewer of the girls who were given the program in the eighth grade had begun having sex than had the girls who were not given the program.

Youth who had sex were less likely to continue. Youth who began sexual intercourse after having had the Postponing Sexual Involvement program were more likely to report less sexual involvement at the end of the ninth grade than were similar youth who did not have the program. They were much more likely to report "I tried sex once or twice," (28% vs. 43%) as opposed to youth who did not have the program who more often reported that they had sex "sometimes" or "often" (table not shown). Youth who began sexual intercourse after having had the Postponing Sexual Involvement program, at the end of the ninth grade also were more likely to report that they did not expect to have sex in the next 6 months (53% vs. 72%) than were similar youth who did not have the program (table not shown).

Fewer pregnancies occurred. Among the youth who were given the Postponing Sexual Involvement program, fewer girls were sexually involved. Because of this, one third fewer pregnancies occurred than would have occurred if the girls who were given the program had followed the sexual involvement patterns of the girls who did not have the program (table not shown).

The program did not have an impact on those who had had sex prior to being given the program. Youth who had had sexual intercourse prior to being given the Postponing Sexual Involvement program did not change their sexual involvement, nor were they more likely to have fewer pregnancies than similar youth who were not given the program (tables not shown).

Summary and Conclusions

The major goal of Grady Memorial Hospital's outreach Postponing Sexual Involvement educational program given in the eighth grade was to assist young people in postponing sexual intercourse. The evaluation focused on behavioral outcomes of low-income, hospital-affiliated youth, and the findings are based on information collected from 536 such youth who completed telephone interviews at the beginning, middle, and end of the eighth grade and the beginning and end of the ninth grade.

Overall, nearly three quarters of the study youth who were given the Postponing Sexual Involvement program had not yet had sexual intercourse. Significant differences were found in the rates of beginning sexual intercourse among youth who had not had sexual intercourse and who were given the program, in contrast with a comparison group who were not given the program. Differences in rates of continuation of sexual involvement among the two groups further indicated that the program had an important effect on sexual behaviors. Moreover, the program's impact lasted at least 12-18 months. A follow-up study is now underway to evaluate the program's impact on youth for a longer period. Youth are being followed through ages 17-18 (the usual time of graduation from high school).

The longitudinal study with repeated rounds of data collection presented challenges for the evaluative staff. Nevertheless, the time-consuming and intensive effort expended in establishing the evaluative population, the careful structuring of the data-collection mechanism, and the lengthy process of data organization and analysis all helped show that the program outcomes were meaningful and significant for this high-risk, low-income population. Corroborating medical records research on participating female youth was uniquely helpful in increasing confidence that the self-reported behavior of the females in the study was accurate.

The authors hope such a description highlights the importance of careful evaluation. Without sound evaluations, the hospital's Emory/Grady Teen Services Program would not have known that its first knowledge-based educational outreach program was not having the desired effect. Nor would they have known that the addition of the skill-building component could contribute significantly to the desired outcome of helping young people gain more control over their sexual behavior.

Further, it is important to note that the manner in which the study was designed and carried out permitted those involved in the Emory/Grady Teen Services Program to learn from the evaluation in ways that already have spawned further innovative program efforts. For example, by collecting data on multiple health behaviors, it became clear that young people who became sexually involved also were more likely to experiment with smoking and drinking, thus establishing patterns that could harm reproductive health throughout life, in addition to affecting immediate pregnancy outcomes. Therefore, funds have been secured to develop innovative ways of helping young people better understand the interrelationship of substance use and reproductive health. Such concepts will be integrated into the hospital's outreach education program.

Additionally, it was clear from the data that once sexually involved, young people were a great risk for pregnancy despite increased use of birth control. Many young people who became pregnant previously had used birth control at one time or another. Hence, new ways of improving contraceptive use are being devised and will be integrated into both the hospital's Emory/Grady Teen Services Program outreach education effort and its family planning clinic for young teens.

Finally, the data emphasized that young people entering the eighth grade already had a number of misperceptions—for example, they greatly overestimated the number of their peers who were sexually involved. Along with related findings and the fact that a number of young people already had become sexually involved before the eighth grade, the hospital made two important decisions. One, the hospital should recommend implementation of the Postponing Sexual Involvement for Young Teens program as being appropriate at both the seventh- and eighth-grade levels. Two, an age-appropriate postponing sexual involvement curriculum for fifth and sixth graders (10-12-year-olds) should be developed. Indeed, such an educational program, Postponing Sexual Involvement: An Educational Series for Preteens, already has been developed and field tested. The preteen program now is being disseminated throughout the state of Georgia.

The program authors and evaluative staff recognize that, despite the initial positive findings and the richness and breadth of the information learned from the evaluative study described in this chapter, issues surrounding the original Postponing Sexual Involvement Educational Series remain for further investigation. These issues are particularly important for program implementation elsewhere. For example, it is not known whether the Postponing Sexual Involvement Educational Series is as effective with other population groups as it is with low-income, high-risk youth. Nor is it known if the series is as effective with adults leading the program as opposed to the teen leaders the hospital uses to present the program. It also is not known if the series, given by itself without a complementary human sexuality education program, would be as effective. Some clues about these questions can be found in the research that has been done on the social influence model as it is applied to other fields. Definitive answers, however, will have to come from research on the application of the social influence model in the human sexuality area. Replication studies and further research on the Postponing Sexual Involvement Educational Series and related outreach education programs are needed.

APPENDIX

A fuller description about the handling of inconsistencies is included here because they are assumed to present issues that other evaluators must face, particularly those who collect data from young people over a period of time in an effort to learn at what age youth begin certain behaviors.

Deciding About Inconsistencies

It was decided that it would be best to report on all the youth who had completed each of the five interviews in the study. Eliminating some youth, it was felt, might unnecessarily bias the results. Of particular concern in keeping all youth in the study, however, were inconsistent responses made by youth. A major task, therefore, was deciding how to present the data from all youth—in particular the data from youth who sometimes gave inconsistent responses—in a way that preserved the integrity of the evaluation.

Over the 2-year interview period, the evaluative staff had anticipated some inconsistencies would occur, if for no reason other than lapse of time and dimming of memory. As a whole, the young people who were in the program group were slightly more likely to give consistent yes/no responses about sexual behavior (89% vs. 84%) than were those in the no-program group. By consistent yes/no responses, it is meant that if a young person ever said yes to the question asking about sexual intercourse, he or she subsequently never said no. With respect to questions about intercourse, however, the sex of the respondent seemed to be the major determinate of consistency and/or inconsistency. The boys in both the program and no-program groups were more than twice as likely to give inconsistent yes/no responses about their sexual behavior as were girls in those groups (19% vs. 7%).

Prospective Approach to Analyzing
Preprogram Sexual Involvement

As part of trying to determine whether young people had had sex before being given the Postponing Sexual Involvement program, the evaluative staff ended up analyzing the data in several different ways. One way was to use the yes/no responses given to the question "People refer to sexual intercourse in many ways—making love, having sex, or going all the way. Have you ever had sex?" while ignoring the context formed by responses to other questions. Two approaches using the yes/no responses alone were tried: one was to leave all the yes/no inconsistencies in; another was to remove them all. The problem with these methods was that, in the first case, the Had Sex and Not Had Sex categories each included different youth at each interview point, some dropping in and some dropping out. Further, it did not accurately reflect the total number of youth who had or had not had sex at any given point. In the second instance, the problem with limiting the study to only those youth who gave consistent answers was a possible biasing of the study toward those youth who indicated that they never had sex. In other words, all of the youth who said no at each of the interviews were included. Among youth who at some point said yes they did have sex, however, a number were eliminated from the study when at some later point they said no they did not have sex.

Using some of the other information gathered through the questionnaire, therefore, seemed appropriate. Because young people who said yes to the sex question were also asked at what age they first had sex, yet another approach tried was to use the yes/no answers combined with ages given for first intercourse. Because the birthdates of the youth were known, it was clear that all youth were 13 years of age or older at the beginning of the study. Under this combined data method, if youth at any time over the five waves indicated (even if it was the last wave and contradicted previous information) that they had had sex before age 13, they were put into the Began Sex Before Program category. In another combined data approach, only if they indicated that they had had sex before age 13 when first asked, were they put into the Began Sex Before Program category. In both instances, each youth's status was held constant once sexual involvement was determined.

Using age as a primary determinant of when young people had sex, however, also appeared to have some biasing effect. The evaluative staff felt that using the youngest age given to determine placement of the youth in the Began Sex Before Program pool unnecessarily reduced the postprogram sexually involved pool, as well as the postprogram sexually uninvolved pool. In particular, because the purpose of the study was to look at sex postprogram, this seemed to have the possibility of skewing data results. The evaluative staff also felt that it may have given inappropriate weight to one piece of conflicting information over another; that is, favoring past ages over present ages, particularly when the purpose was to evaluate postprogram sexual involvement (age 13 and older).

The principal problem with using age alone as the main arbiter of when young people became sexually involved, however, was that young people had great difficulty in giving consistent ages for when they began having sexual intercourse. Because some youth did not begin having sex until later in the study, they did not have as many chances to be inconsistent (for example, those who at the end of the ninth grade first reported beginning sex and gave an age did not have a chance to be inconsistent, while those who at the beginning of the eighth grade reported having sex and gave an age had four chances to be inconsistent). Over the five interviews, only 15% of the youth who answered the age question more than once gave the same age each time for beginning sexual involvement. (This fell to 8% for young people who each time said they had had sex and, therefore, gave an age at all five interviews.) Even allowing for a 1-year difference among ages given, less than half (45%) of the young people gave a consistent answer. (Among young people who gave an age at all five interviews, the proportion of those giving consistent ages with a 1-year difference fell to 32%.) It also was apparent that boys had much more difficulty giving consistent ages than did girls. Only about a third of the boys gave consistent ages—allowing for a 1-year difference in the ages given—as opposed to two thirds of the girls. (Among the boys who gave ages within a 1-year difference at all five interviews, only a quarter of them did so consistently, as opposed to nearly two thirds of the girls.)

Finally, it was decided that at time of first interview, what the youth said about their preprogram sexual intercourse status should be accepted regardless of ages given then or later. This appeared to subject the youth's initial response to less interpretation and to be more respectful of the data as collected. Relying on the youth's self-perceptions of their preprogram status also seemed appropriate to the prospective nature of the study.

Prospective Approach to Analyzing
Postprogram Sexual Involvement

A number of difficult questions arose about how to look at postprogram sexual involvement. Because inconsistent ages given by some youth varied widely and the evaluation centered on sexual involvement postprogram at age 13 and above, ultimately the data were organized to look prospectively at postprogram sexual involvement as well. It was decided that youth who said at the first interview that they had had sex should be placed into the Began Sex Before Program category regardless of later inconsistencies. The only exceptions made to this were the three program youth (three boys) who did not have the Postponing series until the second semester but started having sex the first semester. It also was decided that youth who said at the first interview that they had not had sex should be placed into the Did Not Begin Sex Before Program category regardless of later inconsistencies. Given this division of the data, postprogram sexual involvement then was determined by multiple factors. Postprogram sexual involvement took into account responses to four questions: (a) Have you ever had sex? (b) How old were you when you first had sex? (c) On how many days did you have sex in the last month? (d) Which of these statements best describes you now? I have sex often, I tried sex once or twice, I used to have sex but I don't anymore.

Using this information, a young person who said he or she had not had sex at the preprogram interview was determined to have had sex postprogram if he or she gave any indication of current or ongoing sexual involvement following the program. Thus young people who said no to the question, Have you ever had sex? at the first interview were adjudged to be sexually involved postprogram if, at any subsequent interview, they (a) said yes (had sex) and gave a starting age 13 or above, and/or (b) gave the number of days they had sex in the last month, regardless of age given for first sexual experience, and/or (c) described themselves currently as having sex often or sometimes, regardless of age given for first sexual experience. The youth's sexual involvement status was held constant thereafter.

References

Cohen, J. (1988). *Statistical power analysis for the behavioral sciences* (2nd ed.). Hillsdale, NJ: Lawrence Erlbaum.

Ellickson, P., & Robyn, A. (1977, October). Toward more effective drug prevention programs. *A Rand Note.*

Louis Harris & Associates, Inc. (1986). *American teens speak: Sex, myths, TV and birth control.* The Planned Parenthood Poll. New York: Author.

Howard, M. (1988). Helping youth postpone sexual involvement. In D. Bennett & M. Williams (Eds.). *New universals, adolescent health in a time of change.* Australia: Brolga Press.

Luepker, R. V., Johnson, C. A., Murray, D. M., & Pechacek, T. F. (1983). Prevention of cigarette smoking: Three-year follow-up of an education program for youth. *Journal of Behavioral Medicine, 6,* 53-62.

McAlister, A. (1980). Adolescent smoking: Onset and prevention. *Creative Curricula.*

5

A Comprehensive
Age-Phased Approach

Girls Incorporated

HEATHER JOHNSTON NICHOLSON
LETICIA T. POSTRADO

By the early 1980s teenage pregnancy and parenthood were widely considered to be significant social problems (Alan Guttmacher Institute, 1981; Chilman, 1980; Furstenberg, Lincoln, & Menkin, 1981; Ooms, 1981). By the mid 1980s analysts had written about the likely causes of these problems, and schools and other organizations were developing and testing programs to intervene (for a review of these, see

AUTHORS' NOTE: Major support for *Preventing Adolescent Pregnancy* has been contributed by Carnegie Corporation of New York, William T. Grant Foundation, The William and Flora Hewlett Foundation, The Henry J. Kaiser Family Foundation, The David and Lucile Packard Foundation, The Prudential Foundation, and DeWitt Wallace-Reader's Digest Fund, Inc. Additional support has been contributed by foundations, corporations, and individuals at the national level and at participating sites.

The authors wish to acknowledge the significant contributions of Jane Quinn, currently with the Carnegie Council on Adolescent Development, Catherine H. Smith, Julie K. Hamm, and Ellen Wahl of the Girls Incorporated national staff; curriculum developer and advisor, Pamela M. Wilson; and other members of the Advisory Panel, Joy G. Dryfoos, Irma R. Hilton, Frank F. Furstenberg, Jr., and Douglas Kirby to the Preventing Adolescent Pregnancy project. Special thanks are also due the staff, board, and members of the eight Girls Incorporated affiliates that made the project possible. The authors are solely responsible for the findings and interpretations.

110

Hofferth, 1987, and Nicholson, 1988). Girls Incorporated, then Girls
Clubs of America, was already well situated to be one of the organizations
taking action to help young women get through their teen years without
becoming pregnant or parents. In 1981 the council, the organization's
largest governing body, had adopted a policy statement endorsing
sexuality education by schools and affiliates in support of parents' role
as the primary sex educators of their children. With training and technical assistance from the national organization, 83% of affiliates reported in 1983 that they delivered sexuality education for at least some
age groups.

The Girls Incorporated Initiative

Girls Incorporated is a national youth organization serving girls and
young women ages 6-18. Its purpose is to offer a balanced program of
informal education to enable girls to become confident, competent, and
economically independent women, overcoming the barriers they con-
front in an inequitable world. Girls Incorporated has a service population of 250,000, and its affiliates operate more than 200 professionally
staffed centers in 120 cities in 33 states. Of the girls and young women
served, more than two thirds are from low-income families, more than
half are from single-parent families, and about half are girls and young
women of color. It seemed especially appropriate for Girls Incorporated
to address teen pregnancy and parenthood because these were issues
already being confronted by affiliates, many members were at relatively
high risk of becoming teen parents, and both research and practice
indicated that pregnancy and parenthood were experienced as problems
by the young women themselves. An estimated 80% of adolescent
pregnancies are not intended at the time of conception (Hayes, 1987).

By 1985 Girls Incorporated had enlisted a distinguished advisory
panel, worked with them to outline a comprehensive four-component
model of pregnancy prevention and to design a longitudinal and quasi-
experimental evaluation, secured initial funding from pioneering private foundations, and selected four experimental and four control sites
from among the 20 affiliates applying to be part of the project. First
drafts of the curricula were written by experienced consultant Pamela
M. Wilson, professional staff at the experimental sites were trained to
deliver the programs, and pencil-and-paper survey instruments were
developed and pretested so that by October 1985 the girls and young

women ages 12-17 in those eight affiliates were completing the first of four annual surveys. This report is based on program groups and comparison groups in each of the four experimental sites: Dallas, TX; Memphis, TN; Omaha, NE; and Wilmington, DE. An explanation for using data only for experimental sites is given in the section "Data Collection and Measurement." For the remainder of this chapter the word *site* refers to these four Girls Incorporated affiliates.

The Comprehensive Model

At the time the program was designed, the evidence already seemed strong that teen pregnancy and childbearing are intractable problems requiring comprehensive and sustained efforts if intervention is to be successful. Thus rather than try one program in each of four sites and compare the results, the project was designed to offer all four components of the comprehensive program in each of the four sites. Overall, the model focuses on four approaches thought in 1985 to be promising strategies for preventing pregnancy: family communication about sexuality, and skills in resisting pressure to be sexually active, for girls ages 12-14; and motivation and resources to postpone pregnancy, and overcoming barriers to effective contraception for sexually active teens, for young women ages 15-17. A specific hypothesis was that participation in two or more components would be more effective in preventing pregnancy than participation in only one component of the program. This is the hypothesis addressed in this chapter.

Growing Together

In 1985 the literature on parent-daughter, especially mother-daughter, communication about sexuality suggested this strategy as an important aspect of comprehensive pregnancy prevention. Early studies had suggested that daughters who communicated with their mothers about sex were less likely to be sexually active (see McAnarney, 1982, and Fox & Inazu, 1980, for reviews) and more likely to practice birth control if they were having intercourse (Coles & Stokes, 1985). Yet few parents did communicate about sexual information and values, and the overwhelming majority said they needed help in talking about these issues (Alan Guttmacher Institute, 1981). It was on this basis that Growing Together was designed, though later studies are more mixed and some report no significant relationship between family communication and either delayed initiation of sexual intercourse or more regular contraceptive use (Furstenberg, Herceg-Baron, Shea, & Webb, 1986; Treboux & Busch-Rossnagel, 1990).

As conducted during this study, Growing Together was five 2-hour sessions, the first for parents only, and the remainder for parent-daughter pairs. As noted above, the girls were ages 12-14. The focus of the program, both as initially delivered and in its final form, is on comfort and skill in communicating within the family about sexual information and values. The goal is to delay the initiation of sexual intercourse among young participants, thus preventing pregnancy. All the sessions are interactive and playful, with a trained sexuality educator facilitating a series of role-playing and discussion exercises.

The first session is designed to establish rapport of the facilitator with the parents and the parents among themselves, and especially to assure the parents that they have what it takes to talk to their daughters about such subjects as sexuality, dating, and sexual behavior. Subsequent sessions focus on physical and emotional changes at puberty, the anatomy of reproduction, myths and facts about sexuality and getting pregnant, values about when and under what circumstances girls and boys should be together in dating situations, and many other topics on which parents and adolescent daughters often disagree. The groupings for the exercises intentionally vary to show that not all disagreements are parent-daughter conflicts. In some exercises individuals speak for themselves without prior consultation; in others parents form one group and daughters another, and toward the end of the series the participants work as parent-daughter pairs or family groups (a parent and two daughters). Always the focus is on giving both parents and daughters practice in talking about issues that most families say they have difficulty discussing.

Most of the participants in Growing Together were mother-daughter pairs, though several fathers participated. Girls needed an adult in order to enroll in the program but were encouraged to enlist another trusted adult if a parent was not available, though this did not occur frequently. Once the program began, both parents and daughters could continue to participate even if the partner could not attend a session. More daughters than parents attended every session. Recruitment of parent-daughter pairs to participate in the program was a challenge at every site.

Will Power/Won't Power

By 1985 experts had concluded that sexuality education should begin early and go beyond knowledge and attitudes to give practice in the recommended behaviors—that is, should build skills (Kirby, 1984). McAnarney (1982) among others was noting that adolescents younger than age 16 have not yet reached the cognitive stage of formal operations that enables them to think about the future and to think abstractly. Thus they argued, pregnancy prevention efforts should be more directive for early adolescents, emphasizing the inappropriateness of sexual intercourse for young teens and providing skills in recognizing and resisting the pressure to become sexually involved. Though the impetus was cognitive, social learning theory was the basis for much program development.

The subsequent research lends support to this approach focused on skill building, and social learning. For example, Howard and McCabe (1990) found that eighth-grade students who had participated in the Postponing Sexual Involvement program were less likely to report being sexually active at the end of the eighth and ninth grades than those who had not participated. Similar results have been reported for a program targeting resistance to the use of harmful substances by early adolescents (Ellickson & Bell, 1990).

As conducted during this study, Will Power/Won't Power consisted of six 2-hour sessions for a total of 12 hours for the participants aged 12-14. The goal of Will Power/Won't Power is to delay the initiation of sexual intercourse among participants, thus preventing pregnancy. The program is interactive and uses humor and a light touch to convey its important messages. The program begins with group-building exercises, an introduction to relationships, and basic assertiveness skills. Exercises and films address recognizing pressure to have sex that emanates from the media and other societal sources, peers, and certain dating situations. Levels of physical affection, reasons to abstain from sexual intercourse, recognizing and resisting pressure "lines," and the consequences of early sexual involvement are explored through exercises, including assertiveness role-plays directly related to resisting the pressure to have sexual intercourse.

Will Power/Won't Power had the highest enrollment of any of the components of the Preventing Adolescent Pregnancy model. Staff used posters, flyers, and inexpensive incentives to encourage enrollment, but word-of-mouth advertising from participants was effective, and often

11-year-olds were eager to turn 12 so that they could participate. The original design of the study had three levels of Will Power/Won't Power, with graduates from one year being encouraged to sign up for level two in the following year of the study as long as they were still in the 12-14 age range. Though some girls did participate in the second and even third levels, recruitment to a second year of the program by the same name proved taxing for staff. Consequently, the refined version being implemented by affiliates is one program with eight 90-minute sessions.

Taking Care of Business

By the early 1980s analysts were linking the prevention of adolescent pregnancy with the educational expectations and career plans of teen women. Catherine Chilman (1980) concluded from her review of studies that across cultural groups, young women with clear goals and high aspirations were less likely to experience pregnancy and childbirth than their peers who had lower aspirations and less clear life goals. Joy Dryfoos (1983) argued that programs needed to go beyond the "capacity" to prevent pregnancy to address the "motivation" to postpone pregnancy and childbearing until later in life.

Various versions of what has come to be called the life options model are being used in schools and agencies across the country. They have in common a focus on decision making and often assertiveness skills, career exploration, and sometimes assistance in making connections to job and educational opportunities, attention to the obstacles confronted by teen parents, and information and resources for responsible sexual decision making. Some also have components for improving basic skills (STEP), addressing sex role stereotyping (Choices), or developing leadership skills (Teen Outreach Program). Among the early versions were Life Planning Education of the Center for Population Options (Hunter-Geboy, Peterson, Casey, Hardy, & Renner, 1985) and Choices (Bingham, Edmondson, & Stryker, 1983) developed by the Girls Club of Santa Barbara and sold nationally in book form. In her 1987 review of pregnancy prevention programs, Sandra Hofferth considered the approach promising but the evidence on effectiveness as pregnancy prevention inconclusive. Since then, preliminary evidence on the STEP program of Public/Private Ventures (1987) and the Teen Outreach Program of the Association of Junior Leagues (Allen, Hoggson, & Philliber, 1990; and Philliber & Allen, this volume) confirms that the approach has merit.

The original version of Taking Care of Business was called Choices: Career Awareness; it incorporated several activities from the *Choices* book and one or two from *Life Planning Education*. Designed as nine 2-hour sessions for young women aged 15-17, the goal of the program was to motivate participants to avoid pregnancy by abstaining from sexual intercourse or using effective and consistent contraception. The program focused on the individual futures of young women and included goal-setting, sex role stereotyping, assertiveness, abstinence, sexual responsibility, contraception, information about sexually transmitted disease, career planning, and communication skills.

In general the objectives, approach, and even most of the activities in the three curricula for Growing Together, Will Power/Won't Power, and Taking Care of Business remained substantially the same over the course of the study, so that the authors are fairly confident of having performed a reasonable test of the effectiveness of each component. Taking Care of Business probably changed the most of the three, moving more toward pregnancy prevention activities and away from career awareness and household budgeting activities, meanwhile dropping the copyrighted materials from other sources. The young women who participated in Taking Care of Business reported liking it and learning from it, but schedule conflicts with work and school activities made recruitment challenging and attendance more sporadic than was true of Will Power/Won't Power. A few young women participated in a second level of the program, but this was not a popular option.

Health Bridge

As early as 1980 very positive results in pregnancy prevention were being reported from a school-based clinic, the Maternal and Infant Care (MIC) project in St. Paul, Minnesota (Edwards, Steinman, Arnold, & Hackanson, 1980; Hayes, 1987). In the ensuing years many clinics have been established in and near schools. Kirby has evaluated school-based clinics (this volume) and noted that they generally have been effective in meeting their goals of providing primary health care, but that only 15-20% of the activity of school-based clinics was in reproductive and contraceptive services. In most cases, he reported, the availability of clinics did not dramatically increase the use of contraception by teens, partly because the clinic was not the source of birth control for the majority of sexually active teens, and partly because many sexually active teens would have used birth control anyway (Girls Incorporated, 1990, citing personal communication from Kirby).

Zabin reported that, as part of a comprehensive program, a storefront clinic near schools in Baltimore was effective in increasing the contraceptive use of sexually active junior high school students (Zabin, Hirsch, Smith, Streett, & Hardy, 1986; see also Zabin, this volume). The Panel on Adolescent Pregnancy and Childbearing of the National Research Council concluded that "making contraceptive methods available and accessible to those who are sexually active, and encouraging them to diligently use these methods, is the surest strategy for pregnancy prevention" (Hayes, 1987, p. 177).

The Health Bridge component of the Girls Incorporated Preventing Adolescent Pregnancy program is more a delivery system than a program with a curriculum. It was designed to be the youth organization's answer to a school-based clinic, linking educational services in the Girls Incorporated center with comprehensive health services, including reproductive health services, in the community. The goal of the program as it relates to pregnancy prevention is to reduce the incidence of unintended pregnancy among the young women who are having sexual intercourse, by reducing the psychological and logistical barriers to effective contraception.

The key characteristics of Health Bridge are those that professionals in school-based, school-related, and free-standing centers have reported as being important in pregnancy prevention. They include *accessible services* with both health education and medical services provided in a convenient location; *anonymous services* in a context in which both adults and peers can assume that the services being used by the teen are for an earache or a school physical rather than for reproductive health; *comfort with health personnel* by having a clinic staff person, usually a nurse, spend time at the Girls Incorporated center and become a trusted and familiar face, thereby encouraging the young women to use the clinic and to approach her with sensitive health issues; *case management* with informal intake interviews, referral of participants to the clinic, and follow-up to be sure that medical recommendations are being pursued correctly; and *health education conducted by clinic staff* either alone or with Girls Incorporated staff to increase the visibility of the clinic linkage and to promote trusting relationships and positive health habits (Girls Incorporated, 1990).

The Girls Incorporated affiliates worked diligently to establish appropriate relationships with comprehensive clinics, but building the bridge took from 6 months to 2 years. The bridges established in the four sites represented a range of adherence to the model. For example, in one site the health professional who visited most often was the clinic's social worker; in another the nurses who visited were volunteers from the local nurses' association, only some of whom had direct connections with the Health Bridge clinic. Sustained case management was more the exception than the rule. In general more variation occurs among the sites in this component than in the others.

Methods

Data Collection and Measurement

The principal measuring instrument was the annual survey, a questionnaire administered to the participants four times over a 3-year period: at the beginning of each program year (October 1985, 1986, 1987) before programming started, and at the end of the last program year (October 1988). For this report a 2-year time period was used to maximize the sample size. The annual survey included questions about sexual behaviors, attitudes toward pregnancy, educational and career expectations, and social and economic background.

Originally, eight Girls Incorporated affiliates, four acting as experimental sites and four as control sites were included in the research. Initial data analysis revealed, however, a substantial difference existed between the subjects from experimental sites and the subjects from control sites in several background characteristics usually associated with early pregnancy. Despite the project staff's effort to obtain comparable groups in terms of sociodemographic characteristics, the subjects from control sites turned out to be younger, predominantly white, and living in two-parent households. On the other hand, the subjects from experimental sites were older, mostly African-American, and living in households without fathers. Thus the young women from experimental sites were at higher risk of becoming pregnant than were those from control sites. Hence, in this report the program participants and the nonparticipants serving as a comparison group are from the four experimental sites.

The four Girls Incorporated affiliates, then Girls Clubs, that acted as experimental sites were selected from among communities that had an adolescent pregnancy rate higher than the national average. Each site administered all four components of the Preventing Adolescent Pregnancy program and contributed to the further development and refinement of the model. Within each site, as many as possible of all girls and young women aged 12-17 were recruited as project participants and retained as participants for the duration of the study. Project participants were encouraged also to participate in all program components for which their age qualified them during the entire period of the study. Thus girls and young women volunteered to enroll in the program, and those who did not enroll were used as a comparison group.

In both the original eight-site design and in the eventual reliance on volunteers and nonvolunteers from the experimental sites, the design was less than ideal because of the absence of random assignment to the interventions. This factor was taken into account in designing the annual survey as well as the other instruments and procedures. Specifically, the survey included a range of variables that the literature associates with early experience of pregnancy, allowing for careful tests of self-selection bias. Thus though nothing substitutes for random assignment in eliminating self-selection bias, the current study allows for testing and reporting of its likely influence.

Sample

A total of 343 girls and young women, aged 12-15 when the study began, comprised the sample. This group had the opportunity to participate in two or more program components during a 2-year period. The 12-15 age range maximized the sample size while limiting the age range, so that age would not account for most of the variance in the outcome variables. The girls and young women constituting the sample completed at least three consecutive annual surveys—in most cases the last three of the four—and had never been pregnant prior to their initial survey. About 69% (237) of the subjects, designated as program participants, participated in at least one program component at some time during a 2-year period. About 31% (106), designated as nonparticipants and serving as a comparison group, did not participate in any of the four components. Among the program participants, 133 participated in one program component, while 104 participated in two or more program components.

Test for Self-Selection Bias

Common sense would suggest that the young women who volunteered to participate in two or more program components might also be those at lower risk of pregnancy than those who participated in only one program component or did not participate at all. A number of variables often associated with early pregnancy were measured in the annual survey to allow for a test of self-selection bias. The measures of background characteristics (shown in Table 5.1) were compared among nonparticipants, participants in *one* program component, and participants in *two or more* program components. Table 5.1 indicates that the three groups of subjects were alike in all background characteristics. They were similar in age, racial and ethnic background, educational expectation, degree of association with others who experienced teenage pregnancy, and level of sexual activity at the baseline. In addition, the three groups of subjects were similar in family structure—a small proportion live in a household with a father and a much smaller proportion yet live in a household with siblings.

Findings

As noted in the introduction, a major hypothesis of the study was that a comprehensive approach to pregnancy prevention would be more effective than a single approach. The analysis presented here tests that hypothesis by comparing those who participated in two or more program components with nonparticipants and those who participated in one program component on two outcome variables: sexual intercourse without birth control, and pregnancy experience of the participants.

**Sexual Intercourse
Without Birth Control**

Table 5.2 shows the proportion of young women who reported having sexual intercourse without birth control during the last 4 weeks of the 2-year period. The table indicates that those who participated in two or more program components were as likely to engage in sexual intercourse without birth control as nonparticipants. The table also indicates that those who participated in two or more program components were significantly less likely to have sexual intercourse without birth control than those who participated in a single program component. Only 8.9% of those who participated in two or more program components had sexual intercourse without protection, compared with 20.6% of those

Table 5.1 Sociodemographic Characteristics of 12- to 15-Year-Old Women According to Number of Programs Attended

| | Number of Programs Attended | | |
| | 0 | 1 | 2 or more |
Characteristics	(N = 106)	(N = 133)	(N = 104)
Older than 13	48.1 (106)	40.6 (133)	38.5 (104)
Mother's education higher			
than high school	37.2 (102)	40.5 (126)	35.8 (95)
Live in household with a father	32.6 (95)	33.3 (123)	33.3 (90)
Live with siblings	6.9 (87)	14.7 (102)	13.8 (80)
Job as a source of income	92.1 (101)	88.1 (118)	85.6 (90)
Unemployment as a source of income	16.2 (74)	12.9 (85)	14.7 (68)
Welfare as a source of income	19.4 (72)	16.7 (90)	28.0 (75)
Racial and Ethnic Group			
Black	82.1 (106)	84.2 (133)	82.7 (104)
White	12.3 (106)	9.0 (133)	12.5 (104)
Hispanic and others	5.7 (106)	6.8 (133)	4.8 (104)
Religion			
Catholic	12.4 (105)	14.6 (130)	9.7 (103)
Protestant	51.4 (105)	49.2 (130)	56.3 (103)
Other	36.2 (105)	36.2 (130)	34.0 (103)
Academic performance			
(GPA higher than 2)	66.0 (100)	62.6 (123)	62.3 (101)
Educational expectation	68.6 (105)	76.5 (132)	79.4 (102)
Mother pregnant before 18	47.5 (99)	47.5 (125)	37.6 (101)
Sister pregnant before 18	14.6 (96)	16.4 (116)	15.0 (94)
Girlfriend pregnant before 18	56.4 (101)	58.1 (117)	64.0 (100)
Sexually active at baseline	31.1 (106)	32.3 (133)	27.9 (104)

NOTE: Numbers without parentheses are percentages.
Numbers in parentheses are the bases, which are the numbers of young women who answered the question. Based on t-tests there were no significant differences among the groups on any of the background characteristics.

who participated in one program component. The odds ratio of 2.7 means that those who participated in one program component were more than two and a half times as likely as those who participated in two or more program components to engage in this risky sexual behavior. Those who participated in only one program component, however, were also more likely to engage in sexual intercourse without birth control than were nonparticipants. Although the difference was not statistically significant, this finding was contrary to the desired outcome. Overall, participants

Table 5.2 Comparison of 12- to 15-Year-Old Women Who Participated in Various Numbers of Programs According to Having Sexual Intercourse Without Birth Control During the Last 4 Weeks of a 2-Year Period

Number of Programs Attended	Number of Young Women Who Had Sexual Intercourse Without Birth Control	Number of Young Women Who Participated in the Study	Percentage of Young Women Who Had Sexual Intercourse Without Birth Control	Odds Ratio	p-value
0	13	104	12.5	1.5	0.408
1	27	131	20.6	2.7	0.018
2 or more	9	101	8.9	1.0	—

NOTE: The odds ratio for each group was based on the contrast between that group and the participants who attended two or more programs.

and nonparticipants had similar likelihood of engaging in sexual intercourse without birth control.

To determine whether the findings remained when other factors were held constant, multiple logistic regression analysis was applied. Although no background characteristics differentiated the three groups of subjects as indicated by the tests for self-selection bias, age and having a girlfriend who was pregnant before age 18 emerged as important predictors of pregnancy (discussed in the next section). Thus these two variables were included as control variables in the analysis, using whether the subjects engaged in sexual intercourse without birth control during the previous 4 weeks of the 2-year period as the dependent variable.

Results of the analysis are shown in Table 5.3, which indicates the same pattern of relationship as the bivariate analysis between having sexual intercourse without birth control and the number of program components attended. Those who participated in two or more program components were less likely to engage in sexual intercourse without birth control than those who participated in one program component. The difference was nearly significant ($p = .068$) when other variables were controlled. The odds ratio of 2.2 indicates that those who participated in one program component were more than twice as likely as those who participated in two or more program components to engage in unprotected sexual intercourse. But those who participated in two or

Table 5.3 Results of Logistic Regression Analysis on Having Sexual Intercourse Without Birth Control During the Last 4 Weeks of a 2-Year Period Among 12- to 15-Year-Old Women ($N = 311$)

Variable	Logistic Regression Coefficient	p-value	Odds Ratio
Nonparticipant	.450	0.337	1.6
One-program participant	.793	0.068	2.2
Older than 13	.123	0.737	1.1
Girlfriend pregnant	1.044	0.015	2.8

NOTE: The nonparticipants and one-program participants were contrasted with two- or more-program participants, which was the omitted category in the dummy-coded variable.

more program components were not different from the nonparticipants in terms of likelihood of engaging in sexual intercourse without contraception. Also, the difference between those who participated in one program component and the nonparticipants diminished (not shown in the table) so that the likelihood of engaging in this risky behavior of the two groups was at similar levels (odds ratio = 1.4).

In sum, young women who participated in two or more program components were less likely to engage in sexual intercourse without contraception than were those who participated in one program component. This finding was nearly significant. Those who participated in two or more program components were not significantly different from nonparticipants in likelihood of engaging in sexual intercourse without birth control. Also, those who participated in one program component were as likely as nonparticipants to engage in sexual intercourse without protection.

Pregnancy Experience

The bivariate relationship between the number of program components participated in and pregnancy experience is shown in Table 5.4. Pregnancies in this analysis were those that occurred within the last 12 months of the 2-year period, as reported in the last survey taken. This measure allows time for participation in two or more program components prior to assessing the effect of participation on pregnancy, thus testing the hypothesis that a comprehensive approach is more effective.

Table 5.4 Comparison of 12- to 15-Year-Old Women Who Participated in Various Numbers of Programs According to Pregnancy Experience During the Last 12 Months of a 2-Year Period

Number of Programs Attended	Number of Young Women Who Experienced Pregnancy	Number of Young Women Who Participated in the Study	Percentage of Young Women Who Experienced Pregnancy	Odds Ratio	p-value
0	13	106	12.3	2.8	0.062
1	9	133	6.8	1.4	0.527
2 or more	5	104	4.8	1.0	—

NOTE: The odds ratio for each group was based on the contrast between that group and the participants who attended two or more programs.

Table 5.4 shows the percentage distribution of young women who reported in their last survey becoming pregnant within the last 12 months, according to the number of program components they had attended. It indicates that those who participated in two or more program components were less likely to experience pregnancy than nonparticipants. Only 4.8% of those who participated in two or more program components reported becoming pregnant during the last 12 months. In contrast, 12.3% of nonparticipants experienced pregnancy. This finding was nearly significant ($p = .062$). Participants who attended two or more program components and those who participated in a single program component had similar levels of pregnancy experience. Those who participated in one program component (6.8%) were less likely to become pregnant than nonparticipants (12.3%), although the difference was not statistically significant. Overall, those who participated in one or more program components were significantly less likely (5.9%) to experience pregnancy than those who had attended no program components (12.3%; $p = .049$). The odds ratio of 2.2 suggests that nonparticipants were more than twice as likely as the participants to experience pregnancy (not shown in the table).

To determine whether the differences found in the bivariate analysis remained when other variables associated with pregnancy were controlled, multiple logistic regression analysis was conducted on the experience of pregnancy (Table 5.5). As mentioned earlier, although none of the background characteristics differentiated the three groups

Table 5.5 Results of Logistic Regression Analysis on Becoming Pregnant During the Last 12 Months of a 2-Year Period Among 12- to 15-Year-Old Women (*N* = 311)

Variable	Logistic Regression Coefficient	p-value	Odds Ratio
Nonparticipant	.931	0.099	2.5
One-program participant	.354	0.552	1.4
Older than 13	.860	0.082	2.4
Girlfriend pregnant before age 18	1.064	0.075	2.9

NOTE: The nonparticipants and one-program participants were contrasted with two- or more-program participants, which was the omitted category in the dummy-coded variable.

of subjects, age and having a girlfriend who was pregnant before age 18 were found to have a significant association with pregnancy when taken together. Thus both were included in the logistic regression analysis to control for their effects on the outcome variable. The pattern of relationships in the logistic regression was much the same as in the bivariate analysis, with nonparticipants being about two and a half times as likely as those who participated in two or more program components to have become pregnant within the last 12 months prior to the last survey. This finding became marginally significant (*p* = .099). Young women who participated in one program component again had levels of pregnancy experience similar to those who participated in two or more programs. In contrasting participants in one program component with nonparticipants (results not shown in the table), the nonparticipants were almost twice as likely as the participants in one program component to have become pregnant. This finding, however, did not reach statistical significance. Overall, the difference between participants (attended one or more program components) and nonparticipants was substantial and marginally significant when adjusted for age and having a girlfriend who became pregnant at age 18 (results not shown in the table). Nonparticipants were more than twice as likely as participants to have experienced pregnancy (*p* = .092).

In sum, young women who participated in two or more program components were less likely to have experienced pregnancy than nonparticipants. The difference was marginally significant when age and having a girlfriend who became pregnant before age 18 were held constant. No significant difference was found between young women

Table 5.6 Comparison of 12- to 15-Year-Old Women Who Participated in *One* Program According to Pregnancy Experience During the Last 12 Months of a 2-Year Period

Program Attended	Number of Young Women Who Participated in One Program	Number of Young Women Who Experienced Pregnancy	Percentage of Young Women Who Experienced Pregnancy
Will Power/Won't Power	84	3	3.6
Growing Together	15	2	13.3
Taking Care of Business	25	3	12.0
Health Bridge	9	1	11.1
Total	133	9	6.8

who participated in two or more program components and who participated in one program component in likelihood of becoming pregnant. The participants in one program component were less likely to have become pregnant than were nonparticipants, although the difference failed to reach statistical significance. Overall, young women who attended one or more program components were less likely to have become pregnant during the last 12 months of the 2-year period than those who attended no program components. This finding was marginally significant.

**Pregnancy Experience and Patterns
of Program Participation**

Tables 5.6 through 5.8 present the pregnancy experience of the young women according to their patterns of participation in the program components. Table 5.6 shows the percentage distribution of pregnancy experience, according to which component of the program the 133 young women who attended only one program component had participated in. By far the greatest number of these (84) had participated in Will Power/Won't Power, and a relatively low 3.6% of them experienced pregnancy. The remaining percentages are above 10%, suggesting that participation in a single program component other than Will Power/Won't Power may not have been associated with less likelihood of pregnancy for this group of young women, though the sample sizes are small.

Table 5.7 Comparison of 12- to 15-Year-Old Women Who Participated in *Two* Programs According to Pregnancy During the Last 12 Months of a 2-Year Period

Program Attended	Number of Young Women Who Participated in Two Programs	Number of Young Women Who Experienced Pregnancy	Percentage of Young Women Who Experienced Pregnancy
Will Power/Won't Power and Growing Together	32	0	0
Will Power/Won't Power and Taking Care of Business	4	1	25.0
Will Power/Won't Power and Health Bridge	18	0	0
Taking Care of Business and Health Bridge	16	1	6.3
Total	70	2	2.9

Table 5.7 shows that only 2 of the 70 young women who participated in two program components over the 2 years experienced pregnancy during the previous 12 months. Not all the logical combinations of two programs actually had any participants; in particular, 32 young women who attended Growing Together had also participated in Will Power/ Won't Power, but none had participated only in Taking Care of Business or Health Bridge in addition to Growing Together. The largest number attended the two programs for younger girls, Growing Together and Will Power/Won't Power, and none of these participants reported pregnancy experience. None of the 18 participants in Will Power/Won't Power and Health Bridge reported a pregnancy in the last 12 months. The two young women in this group who reported pregnancies had participated in Will Power/Won't Power and Taking Care of Business, and in Taking Care of Business and Health Bridge, the two programs for young women aged 15-17.

Table 5.8 shows that only 1 of the 28 participants who had attended three program components reported experiencing a pregnancy within the last 12 months. This one pregnancy was reported by a young woman who had participated in Will Power/Won't Power, Growing Together, and Taking Care of Business. No pregnancies were reported by young women who had participated in one of the two program components for

Table 5.8 Comparison of 12- to 15-Year-Old Women Who Participated in *Three* Programs According to Pregnancy Experience During the Last 12 Months of a 2-Year Period

Programs Attended	Number of Young Women Who Participated in Three Programs	Number of Young Women Who Experienced Pregnancy	Percentage of Young Women Who Experienced Pregnancy
Will Power/Won't Power, Growing Together and Taking Care of Business	9	1	11.1
Will Power/Won't Power, Taking Care of Business and Health Bridge	8	0	0
Growing Together, Taking Care of Business and Health Bridge	11	0	0
Total	28	1	3.6

girls aged 12-14 and both program components for young women aged 15-17.

Based on the pregnancy experience of young women and their pattern of participation in the program components, Will Power/Won't Power appeared to be the most effective single program component. This finding raised the question of whether participation in Will Power/Won't Power alone was effective in preventing pregnancy. To address this issue, multiple logistic regression was conducted using participation in Will Power/Won't Power as an independent variable. To control for the effect of the other program components, participation in these program components was entered in the logistic regression equation. Also, age and having a girlfriend who experienced teenage pregnancy were held constant.

Results of the analysis (shown in Table 5.9) indicate that the relationship between participation in Will Power/Won't Power and becoming pregnant during the last 12 months of the 2-year period was not significant. Thus Will Power/Won't Power or any of the other program components taken singly did not reduce the likelihood of becoming pregnant among young adolescents aged 12-15 during the last 12 months of the 2-year period.

Table 5.9 Results of a Logistic Regression Analysis on Becoming Pregnant During the Last 12 Months of a 2-Year Period Among 12- to 15-Year-Old Women Who Participated in Any of the Four Programs

Variable	Logistic Regression Coefficient	p-value	Odds Ratio
Will Power/Won't Power nonparticipant	.559	0.296	1.7
Growing Together nonparticipant	−.595	0.317	0.6
Taking Care of Business nonparticipant	.719	0.236	2.1
Health Bridge nonparticipant	.198	0.759	1.2
Older than 13	1.130	0.044	3.1
Girlfriend pregnant before age 18	.998	0.093	2.7

Discussion

This analysis tested the hypothesis that a comprehensive approach to primary prevention of adolescent pregnancy for young women is more effective than a single approach. That is, the Girls Incorporated program Preventing Adolescent Pregnancy consisted of four components, two each for two age groups and each with different objectives related to enabling young women to avoid pregnancy. The question is whether the components work together toward pregnancy prevention. Analyses were conducted on two outcome variables—sexual intercourse without birth control (a measure of behavior putting one at risk of pregnancy), and pregnancy experience.

Participants and nonparticipants were not randomly assigned but instead chose their level of participation. Tests for self-selection bias indicated that the groups were not significantly different on any background variables ordinarily associated with risk of early pregnancy.

Young women who participated in two or more program components were less likely than those who participated in one component to engage in the risky behavior of having sexual intercourse without birth control during the previous 4 weeks of the 2-year period. This finding was nearly significant. Neither the participants in two or more program components nor the participants in one component, however, were significantly different from the nonparticipants in the likelihood of having sexual intercourse without contraception. Thus the findings on this risky behavior are inconsistent and difficult to explain.

On the incidence of pregnancy, young women who participated in two components were less likely to become pregnant than nonparticipants, a marginally significant result. Though no significant difference was found in pregnancy experience between young women who participated in two components and those who participated in one, a 50% (but nonsignificant) reduction occurred in pregnancies when comparing participants in one component with nonparticipants. Thus the difference between participation and nonparticipation is interpreted to be the programmatically important one, even though the difference reached marginal significance at the level of two or more components. A ceiling effect may be operating so that participating in a second, third, or fourth component does not substantially reduce the likelihood of pregnancy beyond participating in the first program component. Overall, participation in one or more components was related to less likelihood of becoming pregnant, a marginally significant result. These findings provide weak support for the hypothesis that more comprehensive program participation is better than no program participation or a single approach in preventing teenage pregnancy.

Still unclear is how the programs might be working to prevent pregnancy. The expectation is that the programs reduce the likelihood of engaging in the risky behavior of having sexual intercourse without birth control. But the findings are inconsistent—overall the young women who participated in programs were less likely to become pregnant but not less likely to have sex without birth control than the nonparticipants. Possibly the program participants who were sexually active were using more effective methods of birth control than the sexually active nonparticipants, though this relationship has not been tested. Another possibility among these young adolescents is that they may be using effective methods ineffectively, resulting in pregnancy in spite of their efforts to prevent it. Nevertheless, the findings fail to support the hypothesis that comprehensive participation leads to reduction in risky sexual behavior.

The bivariate analyses suggested that Will Power/Won't Power, the assertiveness program for girls aged 12-14, was the most effective component, based on experience of pregnancy. Further analysis was thus conducted to test whether the prevention of pregnancies could be attributed to participation in Will Power/Won't Power alone. The results indicated that neither Will Power/Won't Power nor any other single component taken alone was responsible for the reduction in pregnancy.

Programmatic Recommendations

Girls Incorporated conducted a longitudinal study of a comprehensive model of pregnancy prevention attuned to the age and developmental stage of girls and young women ages 12-17. First, one important finding is simply that some of these young women reported having sexual intercourse without birth control and some reported experiencing pregnancy. This finding suggests that young women at risk of pregnancy are not only those who are socially isolated and that the young women who participate in Girls Incorporated (and by inference in other community-based organizations) are not systematically drawn from some segment of society immune to pregnancy risk. This in turn suggests an important role for community organizations, as well as schools, families, and providers of health services, in intervening to help young people avoid pregnancy in their teen years.

Second, the findings presented here are encouraging, though not dramatic, in suggesting that offering programs carefully designed to prevent pregnancy is worth the effort, and a comprehensive approach is worth the additional trouble. It seems that some merit exists in the comprehensive approach and no one program can account for all the pregnancies apparently prevented.

Perhaps even more than the moderately encouraging results of these data, the experience of designing, developing, testing, and refining the program components has yielded insights about the developmental appropriateness of various approaches to pregnancy prevention. By the time the curricula were published and training was offered to Girls Incorporated affiliates across the nation, Will Power/Won't Power had been conducted at least 56 times by the affiliates acting as experimental sites, Growing Together had been conducted more than 30 times, and Taking Care of Business more than 20 times. Refinements in the existing curricula and priorities for the next "level" of each of these components was based largely on the assessments of the trained staff who were conducting the sessions. As noted earlier, the participants were not at all eager to sign up for a second "level" of a program with the same name in the second and third years, so the final curricula incorporate the best topics and activities from all the versions of each program component.

Growing Together Revisited

The staff who delivered Growing Together in the experimental sites immediately reported difficulty in recruiting pairs of parents and daughters to participate. To get any group together, the sites offered light meals and child care for younger children during the sessions, transportation, and parent-to-parent contact to remind participants of each meeting. These special services are still recommended, because it is quite difficult for many low-income and single-parent families to participate in such programs without them. But it soon became clear to the staff that many girls aged 12-14 considered themselves too old for this program, at least in some communities.

Staff reported that girls at ages 9 and 10 had rapport with their mothers and thought of them as trustworthy and knowledgeable, but by the time girls were ages 12 and 13 their mothers had curiously lost much of their intelligence and knowledge—a developmental phenomenon noted by many parents and other experts. Many mothers in turn, they reported, were intimidated by their daughters' apparent knowledge of reproductive anatomy and other issues in sexuality. And staff noted that tension was already present in many parent-daughter pairs over expectations for dating, dress, and unsupervised time. The data later told us that about one fifth of the girls this age in the experimental sites had initiated sexual intercourse. These issues were addressed to some degree by adapting the curriculum during the study, but the major lesson is that this program in family communication about sexuality, now that the study is over and the age range can be changed, is recommended and being implemented for girls aged 9-11 and their parents.

Will Power/Won't Power Revisited

From the beginning Will Power/Won't Power was popular with both girls and staff members at the experimental sites. The exercises identifying social and peer pressure to be sexually active, considering the consequences of sexual involvement and pregnancy at their age, developing and practicing assertiveness skills, and rehearsing resistance to pressure lines and avoidance of risky situations seemed both enjoyable and developmentally appropriate.

Several changes and additions to Will Power/Won't Power are included in the published version. One is the formation of a sorority of the participants, pledging to support one another's decisions to resist pressure in social situations, during the seventh of the eight sessions. The theme that peer pressure is negative but peer support can be positive is emphasized throughout the program and is consolidated in the session on sisterhood. Even more practice in assertiveness is included in the final than in the initial version, along with more discussion of the right to decline sexual involvement. More guidance is given for leaders in including girls who have already initiated sexual intercourse in the decision to abstain until they are older.

In the analysis reported here, Will Power/Won't Power seems to be an effective component of the comprehensive approach. As noted earlier, the development of resistance skills based on social learning theory has positive evaluation results in other programs for early adolescents. In Girls Incorporated this component is the least expensive component to implement. Because staff already have many of the small-group, interactive skills needed to implement the program, it can be offered during regular center hours, and recruitment requires no extraordinary effort. Girls Incorporated will continue to recommend that affiliates implement Will Power/Won't Power as a program girls this age have a right to, and as a possible help in their avoiding pregnancy. Some young women, even if they delay the initiation of sexual intercourse, eventually become sexually active while still in their teens, and they need information and resources for practicing effective contraception.

Taking Care of Business Revisited

Building on the experience of staff who implemented it, the published version of Taking Care of Business includes far fewer pencil-and-paper exercises than the initial version. The final version is a balance of information, resources, and skills for avoiding pregnancy and sexually transmitted disease, including a positive and realistic look at abstinence as an option, with activities and resources for setting goals, and planning for further education, career, and family life.

Middle adolescents aged 15-18 are more difficult than younger girls for Girls Incorporated (and probably other youth organizations) to recruit and retain. The experimental sites were most successful when they already had a contingent of teens involved or made Taking Care of Business part of youth employment or career exploration opportunities. Girls Incorporated suggests conducting a needs assessment before delivering Taking Care of Business, and offering it if a life-planning course of high quality is not already available at school or in other community organizations. Though conducted by adults during the study, the current recommendation is to train and include peer educators, especially college students, in delivering the program. Programs that pursue the life options model seem to provide teens aged 15-18 with information, intellectual and emotional support, and skills in assertiveness and decision making that may help them avoid pregnancy during the teen years.

Health Bridge Revisited

Health Bridge was by far the most expensive and most difficult of the components to establish. The affiliates worked diligently to work through doubts raised by their volunteer boards of directors, to find compatible clinics sympathetic to teens' health needs, to establish mutually satisfactory arrangements and eventually contracts with the clinics, and to raise the funds to put Health Bridge into place on an ongoing basis. They went through false starts and periods of frustration. Among the clearest messages once the bridges were in place is that girls younger than 15 were much more eager to spend time with the nurse at the Girls Incorporated center and more willing to admit they needed information and advice than those aged 15-17 who were eligible to participate. Thus the published guide and training team recommend that Health Bridge be planned for girls and young women aged 12-18. The set of educational resources developed to accompany the Health Bridge delivery system intentionally has not been published, to focus attention away from the educational services and toward the critical connections and individual attention that seem to reduce the barriers to effective contraception among sexually active young women.

Discussions with colleagues suggest that the combination of affordable, accessible, and anonymous medical services; a knowledgeable and nonjudgmental health professional familiar to the teen; and assertive intake and follow-up on health, including reproductive health, is available in relatively few communities. The combination can be and has been accomplished in some school-based and school-related clinics. The Health Bridge experiment suggests that some version of it can be accomplished by a youth organization or other community group. Some communities might need a broader network of services, but evidence from other studies and indications from this one suggest that access and diligence in contraceptive use are key components of a comprehensive approach to adolescent pregnancy prevention.

Recommendations for Evaluation

The study of the Girls Incorporated Preventing Adolescent Pregnancy program is one of the few of this scope and duration undertaken directly by the research staff of a community-based organization. The commitment of the participating experimental (and control) sites led to the collection of a data set of significant size and quality, one of the few longitudinal data sets on the sexual behavior of adolescents, especially those at high risk of pregnancy, and one of very few evaluating interventions designed to prevent pregnancy.

The decision was deliberately made at the design stage to use tests of self-selection, and experimental and control sites, rather than random assignment, to establish comparison groups. In this study the selection and maintenance of control sites in other cities was expensive, very difficult for them as they felt pressure to "do something" about high levels of adolescent pregnancy, and as it turned out, not productive because the background characteristics and pregnancy risk of the control sites were too different from the background characteristics of the experimental sites in spite of careful site selection. By serendipity the comparison groups from the experimental sites turned out to be a preferable substitute for the control sites: the young women function in the same environments and have quite similar backgrounds to those who participated in the program. Though this was anticipated to some degree and diligence was exercised to keep the nonparticipants for the duration of the study, one would hesitate to design a full study in which those who did not volunteer for the program constituted the comparison group. They might be systematically different; and knowing the pool of nonparticipants needed to be a certain size could undermine efforts to recruit every eligible participant into the programs.

A form of random assignment to experimental and control groups that violates as little as possible the principle that beneficial programs in a youth organization should be open to all members who are eligible by age, previous participation, and other normal criteria solves many of the problems of scientific evaluation. The advice is to use random assignment any time a practical and ethical system to do so can be devised, and otherwise to create a comparison group in the same city as the experimental group. Finding comparable individuals or organizations may be a serious challenge, however. One reason the response rates were maintained at a relatively high level in this study is that the national organization has considerable leverage with all the cooperating sites, built on mutual esteem, pass-through funds, reasonable responses to their hardships, and a competitive process to choose them. It would be very difficult to sustain this relationship with organizations that had little to gain from a successful evaluation. The researcher would need substantial resources to be able to track and attract the control subjects.

In the ideal world the program components would be implemented, refined, and established in final form before a quantitative evaluation was undertaken. The decision was made in 1985 that enough was known about these four pregnancy prevention models to begin implementation and testing at the same time, and though not ideal, the same decision would probably be made today. In this study a conflict existed between sustaining the quasi-experiment by adhering to the established age groupings of 12-14 and 15-17, and revising the age groups recommended for Growing Together and Health Bridge. The research design held sway, and the programs were adapted only after the 3-year period of the study.

Practically speaking, it would have been very difficult indeed to stretch the research process out even further by testing the programs extensively (presumably in other affiliates to avoid contaminating the study sites) before collecting baseline data. For example, affiliates that have begun to implement the program and their funders are understandably impatient for news about whether the program is effective in preventing pregnancy. In part as a response to the urgency felt in Girls Incorporated communities to "do something" about this important problem, the programs were made available to affiliates for implementation before the quantitative analyses were being reported. Adding another 2 or 3 years to the process of research and development might well have exceeded the limits of patience in these communities, leading affiliates to adopt other and probably untested interventions.

Despite the large total sample size, the design required grouping of subjects and the control of a number of variables. The resulting sample sizes for a given program year were small. More definitive tests and conclusions thus had to wait until the 3-year sample could be combined. Though the early years were well spent in coding, file construction, discussion with a distinguished panel of advisors, and exploring various strategies for analysis, much of the final work has been done at a rapid pace since the final data were collected in January 1989. The published curricula thus reflect the experience of the practitioners and only the earliest results of the quantitative research. The disadvantage of this is mitigated by the advantage of having a trained implementation team ready to accept adaptations to the curricula as further research results become available.

Summary

Girls Incorporated conducted a longitudinal study of a comprehensive approach to helping young women aged 12-17 avoid pregnancy in the teen years. Participation in one or more components of the program was associated with a 50% (but not statistically significant) reduction in the incidence of pregnancy, and participation in two or more components was marginally significant in reducing pregnancy. No single program component accounted for the reduction, suggesting that it may be important to offer program components for different age groups and with different objectives. The pattern of sexual intercourse without birth control was inconsistent, leaving unexplained the mechanism by which the program worked to reduce pregnancy. Overall, the findings were encouraging, though not dramatic, that the program implemented by this youth organization helped reduce the risk of pregnancy among the young women who participated. Girls Incorporated recommends that its affiliates implement the comprehensive program Preventing Adolescent Pregnancy.

References

Alan Guttmacher Institute. (1981). *Teenage pregnancy: The problem that hasn't gone away*. New York: Author.

Allen, J. P., Hoggson, N., & Philliber, S. (1990). School-based prevention of teenage pregnancy and school dropout: Process evaluation of the national replication of the Teen Outreach Program. *American Journal of Community Psychology, 18*(4), 505-524.

Bingham, M., Edmondson, J., & Stryker, S. (1983). *Choices: A teen woman's journal for self-awareness and personal planning*. Santa Barbara, CA: Advocacy.

Chilman, C. S. (1980). *Adolescent sexuality in a changing American society*. Bethesda, MD: Public Health Service, National Institutes of Health.

Coles, R., & Stokes, G. (1985). *Sex and the American teenager*. New York: Harper & Row.

Dryfoos, J. G. (1983). *Review of interventions in the field of prevention of adolescent pregnancy: Preliminary report to the Rockefeller Foundation*. New York: Rockefeller Foundation.

Edwards, L., Steinman, M., Arnold, K., & Hackanson, E. (1980). Adolescent pregnancy prevention services in high school clinics. *Family Planning Perspectives, 12*, 6-14.

138   A Comprehensive Age-Phased Approach

Ellickson, P. L., & Bell, R. M. (1990). Drug prevention in junior high: A multi-site longitudinal test. *Science, 247,* 1299-1305.

Fox, G. L., & Inazu, J. K. (1980). Mother-daughter communication about sex. *Family Relations, 29,* 347-352.

Furstenberg, F. F., Jr., Herceg-Baron, R., Shea, J., & Webb, D. (1986). Family communication and contraceptive use among sexually active adolescents. In J. B. Lancaster & B. D. Hamburg (Eds.). *School-age pregnancy and parenthood: Biosocial dimension* (pp. 251-261). Hawthorne, NY: Aldine de Gruyter.

Furstenberg, F. F., Jr., Lincoln, R., & Menkin, J. (Eds.). (1981). *Teenage sexuality, pregnancy and childbearing.* Philadelphia: University of Pennsylvania Press.

Girls Incorporated. (1990). *Health bridge: A collaborative model for delivering health services to young women ages 12-18.* New York: Author.

Hayes, C. D. (Ed.). (1987). *Risking the future: Adolescent sexuality, pregnancy and childbearing* (Vol. 1). Washington, DC: National Academy.

Hofferth, S. L. (1987). The effects of programs and policies on adolescent pregnancy and childbearing. In S. L. Hofferth & C. D. Hayes (Eds.). *Risking the future: Adolescent sexuality, pregnancy, and childbearing* (Vol. 2). (pp. 207-263). Washington, DC: National Academy.

Howard, M., & McCabe, J. B. (1990). Helping teenagers postpone sexual involvement. *Family Planning Perspectives, 22,* 21-26.

Hunter-Geboy, C., Peterson, L., Casey, S., Hardy, L., & Renner, S. (1985). *Life planning education: A youth development program.* Washington, DC: Center for Population Options.

Kirby, D. (1984). *Sexuality education: An evaluation of programs and their effects.* Atlanta: U.S. Department of Health and Human Services.

McAnarney, E. R. (1982). *Report on adolescent pregnancy to the William T. Grant Foundation.* New York: William T. Grant Foundation.

Nicholson, H. J. (1988). Teen pregnancy: Prevention is critical. *Youth Policy, 10*(5), 26-29.

Ooms, T. (Ed.). (1981). *Teenage pregnancy in a family context.* Philadelphia: Temple University Press.

Public/Private Ventures. (1987, Spring/Summer). STEP: Cohort II finishes strong. *Public/Private Ventures News,* pp. 1-2.

Treboux, D., & Busch-Rossnagel, N. A. (1990). Social network influences on adolescent sexual behaviors. *Journal of Adolescent Research, 5,* 175-189.

Zabin, L. S., Hirsch, M. B., Smith, E. A., Streett, R., & Hardy, J. B. (1986). Evaluation of a pregnancy prevention program for urban teenagers. *Family Planning Perspectives, 18,* 119-126.

6

Life Options and Community Service

Teen Outreach Program

SUSAN PHILLIBER
JOSEPH P. ALLEN

Introduction

Teen Outreach is a school-based program for adolescents that was designed originally to prevent early pregnancy and to encourage regular progress in school. The program seeks to reach its goal through a combination of small group discussion strategies using its own curriculum and by providing volunteer service experience in the community for its young participants. It is, in other words, a program in the "life options" tradition of teen pregnancy prevention programs (Dryfoos, 1990; Hayes, 1987) and a program that has amassed several years of evaluation data showing positive results.

AUTHORS' NOTE: Teen Outreach and its evaluation are funded by the Charles Stewart Mott Foundation, the Lila Wallace-Reader's Digest Fund, and other foundations. We are grateful for their support. The program is coordinated by the Association of Junior Leagues International, to whom the authors express appreciation for their support and assistance in gathering these data. The authors also wish to thank Kathy Arnold and Merry Oakley of Philliber Research, who have patiently coded, computer-entered, and processed these data. Most important, we wish to thank the Teen Outreach facilitators and their Junior League colleagues from throughout the United States and Canada who have gathered the data and run the programs that made this evaluation possible.

In 1981, the Junior League of St. Louis assumed a major role in promoting and funding the Teen Outreach program, which had begun in 1978 as a collaborative effort between the Danforth Foundation and the St. Louis Public Schools. In 1983, funding was obtained from the Charles Stewart Mott Foundation to begin a 3-year national replication of Teen Outreach. By 1987, a second 3-year national replication effort began under the direction of the Association of Junior Leagues International, in cooperation with the American Association of School Administrators.

Teen Outreach has maintained a nationwide evaluation system to monitor program outcomes since 1984. This chapter reports the data produced by that system, with special emphasis on data from the fifth year of this monitoring, the 1988-1989 school year. This latter year is emphasized because it is the most recent for which analysis is complete and because it was the first year in which the program had any substantial number of teens who were assigned randomly to the program or control groups for evaluation. In addition, however, the chapter compares these last year results with those from the other four years of evaluation in order to make clear the general pattern in program outcomes for Teen Outreach.

Program Components

Teen Outreach is a school-based program that is most often run through the collaborative efforts of a local Junior League, local school personnel, and, when the League is not the funder, a local funder as well. The program has two main components: use of a curriculum in small group discussion sessions led by a facilitator, and involvement of young people in volunteer service in the community.

The curriculum and volunteer service are the core components of Teen Outreach and are shared by all its sites nationwide and in Canada. Beyond these commonalities, however, are variations in program implementation, shown in Table 6.1. Most Teen Outreach programs are offered after school hours, with about one third offered during school; slightly less than half are offered for credit.

The students in Teen Outreach meet at least once per week throughout the school year and engage in discussions on such topics as understanding themselves and their values, communication skills, human growth and development, issues related to parenting, and family relationships and community resources. While the curriculum does contain

Table 6.1 Selected Variations in the Teen Outreach Program Among Sites: 1988-89

Percentage of Programs Offered

During school	31%	For credit	46%
After school	69%	No credit	54%

		Reported Coverage of Unit		
Curriculum Unit	*None*	*A Little*	*A Lot*	*Almost All*
Orientation	6	31	23	40
Volunteer experience	6	31	34	28
Understanding yourself	0	11	51	37
Values	3	31	34	31
Life planning	8	26	43	23
Communication	6	28	37	28
Life pressures	11	23	23	43
Family	6	31	34	28
Relationships	6	20	37	37
Growth/development	23	40	14	23
Parenting	28	31	23	17
Issues in parenting	28	43	11	17
Community resources	20	43	26	11

some traditional sex education information, this is not its primary emphasis. In fact, as the data in Table 6.1 show, the curriculum units on these topics are covered less thoroughly by facilitators than are other topics.

The style of the curriculum is to utilize group discussions and activities that are facilitated rather than taught. The best facilitators in the program become mentors and friends for their Teen Outreach students and create a support-group environment in which students are assured of understanding and confidentiality from both peers and the facilitator. Facilitators for the program often receive training at the annual national Teen Outreach conference, in which a variety of workshops are held to acquaint them with the structure of the program, its curriculum, and the facilitator style that the program seeks. Some facilitators have been trained by those who have been running the program in their local areas or by personnel from the Junior League.

The volunteer activities in the program vary widely in their settings and tasks, reflecting variations in community needs and in the ages and

142   Life Options and Community Service

Table 6.2 The Growth of Teen Outreach, 1984 to 1990

School Year	Students	Cities	Sites
1984-85	148	8	9
1985-86	444	16	24
1986-87	632	15	35
1987-88	782	14	44
1988-89	1028	28	60

circumstances of the Teen Outreach students. These activities are most often coordinated by the local Junior League and have included work in hospitals and nursing homes, participation in walkathons, work at the school itself, tutoring for younger students, and many other types of work.

Teen Outreach sites do not all offer the same number of classroom hours or the same number of volunteer hours for each student. The minimum standards at Teen Outreach sites are that students should meet for 1 hour per week for a year and that each student should perform a minimum of 1 hour per week of volunteer work.

Characteristics of Teen Outreach Students

Table 6.2 shows the growth of Teen Outreach since 1984. The number of Teen Outreach sites increased from 9 in the 1984-85 school year to 60 in 1988-1989. During the same period of time, the number of students enrolled in the program increased by almost seven-fold, to over 1,000 in the 1988-1989 school year. Teen Outreach has always been located in geographically dispersed areas of the United States. The first Canadian site was added in the 1985-1986 school year.

Local Teen Outreach sites range in size from 5 students in Bristol, Rhode Island, to 23 students in Charlotte, North Carolina. Middle schools, junior highs, and senior highs all serve as sites for Teen Outreach. The average Teen Outreach site enrolls 15 students in a single section of the program.

Teen Outreach students enter the program in a variety of ways. At most schools, they volunteer to participate, responding to announcements of the program on posters or in the school media. At other sites, students are sought out by the Teen Outreach facilitators or by school counselors because they are believed to be "high risk" for school leaving or pregnancy. At still other schools, facilitators seek out students who are not yet exhibiting negative behaviors but who could become high risk. Table 6.3 shows the characteristics of the national sample of Teen Outreach students and their comparisons in 1988-1989. Data for each of the 5 years of evaluation show similar characteristics.

Over 75% of those enrolled in Teen Outreach nationwide are females. They range in age from 11 to 21, with an average age of 14.9 years. A similar range occurs in grade level, with students as young as the fifth grade and as old as high school seniors. About 40% of the Teen Outreach students are black, another 40% are white, and 13% are Hispanic. Those in other race/ethnicity groups include mostly Native Americans and Asians.

About 41% of these young people come from nonintact families, and about a fifth have mothers and fathers with less than a high school education. Much variation exists in the socioeconomic level of the families of Teen Outreach students, however, since almost 30% of their mothers have at least some college education. In each year of the evaluation, the Teen Outreach and comparison students have been generally well matched on the characteristics shown in Table 6.3. In 4 out of the 5 years, however, some variables were not matched. For example, in 1988-1989, students in Teen Outreach were significantly more likely than their comparisons to be female. In Years 3 and 4, more Teen Outreach students than comparisons came from nonintact families, and in Year 1, Teen Outreach students came from school grades lower than did the comparison students. In each year's analysis, these differences were controlled in the multivariate analyses, as will be illustrated below.

The Evaluation Design

The evaluation design for Teen Outreach relies on the utilization of common reporting forms at all sites. Each site recruits a local comparison group at the beginning of the school year, preferably using true random assignment procedures. When this is not possible, the comparison students are generally named by the program participants as young people they know who might have filled out the intake form "about like you did." In 1988-1989 five sites were able to use randomization

Table 6.3 Demographic Characteristics of Teen Outreach and Comparison
Students: 1988-89

Characteristics	Teen Outreach Students N = 495	% = 100	Comparison Students N = 490	% = 100
Sex				
Male	116	23.6	159	32.5
Female	375	76.4	330	**67.5
Age				
11-13	52	10.6	61	12.5
14	144	29.5	142	29.0
15	143	29.2	131	26.8
16	80	16.4	82	16.8
17	52	10.6	47	9.6
18-21	18	3.7	26	5.3
Average		14.9		14.9
Grade				
5-7	32	6.5	46	9.4
8	70	14.3	53	10.9
9	169	34.3	182	37.5
10	105	21.4	100	20.5
11	73	14.9	60	12.3
12	42	8.6	46	9.4
Average		9.5		9.4
Sibs				
0-1	163	33.2	145	29.7
2-4	229	46.6	245	50.2
5 or more	99	20.2	98	20.1
Average		2.8		2.9
Race				
Black	197	40.1	191	39.1
White	199	40.6	209	42.7
Hispanic	66	13.4	62	12.7
Asian	3	0.6	6	1.2
Native American	23	4.7	17	3.5
Other	3	0.6	4	0.8
Lived with				
Mother and father	288	58.8	281	57.6
Mother only	171	34.8	161	33.0
Father only	9	1.8	9	1.8
Guardian	10	2.0	13	2.7
Other arrangement	13	2.6	24	4.9
Mother's education				
Less than high school	99	20.3	85	17.5
High school graduate	181	37.0	173	35.6
Some college	89	18.2	89	18.3

Table 6.3 Continued

Characteristics	Teen Outreach Students N = 495	% = 100	Comparison Students N = 490	% = 100
College graduate plus	52	10.6	74	15.2
Don't know	68	13.9	65	13.4
Father's education				
Less than high school	83	16.9	75	15.4
High school graduate	147	30.0	140	28.8
Some college	64	13.1	64	13.1
College graduate plus	63	12.9	93	19.1
Don't know	133	27.1	115	23.6

NOTE: **Difference between the Teen Outreach and comparison students is statistically significant at $p < .01$. The totals vary somewhat from 495 (Teen Outreach students) and 490 (comparison students) due to missing information on some variables.

procedures to assign students to their Teen Outreach or control groups. This chapter presents data separately for these five randomized sites, as well as for the total program samples in each year.

The evaluation of Teen Outreach has always monitored the following outcome variables for both program students and their comparisons: school suspension, failure of courses in school, dropping out of school, and pregnancies.

In 1988-1989, data were also gathered on arrests, skipping school, use of alcohol or marijuana, having sexual intercourse, using contraception when sexually active, joining after-school activities, getting an award, getting on the honor roll, and educational aspirations.

These outcomes were added to produce a fuller picture of other impacts that Teen Outreach might be having on young people and to include some positive outcomes to those already monitored.

The evaluation is thus somewhat demanding for a school-based program of this kind, in that it measures almost exclusively behavioral outcomes, neglecting the traditional emphasis on participant testimonials, knowledge change, or attitude change. The evaluation system for Teen Outreach seeks to report outcome measures on these variables at the end of the school year for all students originally enrolled in the program, regardless of their attendance at the program or their volunteer work patterns. Data are collected, however, on how much exposure to Teen Outreach each student receives.

Table 6.4 Information on the Evaluation Samples

Year	Total Number of Sites	Sites Participating in Evaluation	Prercentage Loss to Follow-up Between Intake and Exit*	# Teen Outreach Students	# Comp Students
1984-85	9	9	10.2	151	151
1985-86	24	22	4.0	444	542
1986-87	35	35	3.8	632	848
1987-88	48	44	5.8	823	912
1988-89	60	35	10.1	495	490
1988-89 Random assignment sample	5	5	0.0	79	89

NOTE: *Among participating sites.

Table 6.4 shows how many of the Teen Outreach sites in each year participated in the evaluation and the rates of loss to follow-up in each of these years. When the number of Teen Outreach sites was small, every effort was made to ensure full participation in the national evaluation. As the number of sites has become larger, participation in the evaluation (which must, of course, be voluntary) has been less, even while the actual number of students on whom data are available continues to grow. Only in the 1988-1989 school year was the participation rate in the evaluation worrisome. This lower participation rate was most probably due to the difficulty of maintaining communication with the rapidly growing number of sites participating in Teen Outreach. Unfortunately, it is not possible to tell how sites that participate in the evaluation may differ from those that do not. A 5-year comparison of the characteristics of students in the program for whom data were reported in the evaluation, however, demonstrates little change. A random sample of about one third of the program sites has been chosen in 1990-1991 to participate in the national evaluation.

For sites that have furnished evaluation information, loss to follow-up between program intake and exit has been acceptably low. This rate has not risen above 10.2% and in most years has been considerably lower. The rate of loss is slightly higher among comparison students than among Teen Outreach students, as might be expected.

Since the sample size in 1988-1989 permitted such an analysis, the demographic characteristics of Teen Outreach students who were lost were compared with those same characteristics among the comparison students who were lost. Age, gender, race, parents' education, or family intactness did not differ, but the two lost samples did differ in two other ways. The lost Teen Outreach students were more likely to have received awards in school in the previous year than were the students from the comparison group who were lost. Also, the lost Teen Outreach students were less likely to report being previously suspended than were the lost comparison students. Since overall loss was so low, these differences are unlikely to affect the conclusions reported here. Also, these variables on prior status of Teen Outreach and comparison students are controlled in relevant analysis.

Risk Factors at Program Entry

Table 6.5 shows the baseline or program entry measures of program outcomes for students in the 1988-1989 sample. Again, these data are similar across all 5 years. It is important to examine these factors as they appeared when the Teen Outreach and comparison students entered the program year in order to (a) describe the kind of population being served by Teen Outreach, and (b) ensure that these are indeed two well-matched groups of students.

In the year before entry into the program, over 4% of the Teen Outreach students had already been pregnant at least once. Over 17% of them had been suspended, and 5% of them reported having been arrested. Almost 40% reported failing courses in the year before the program began, and more than 30% had skipped school. More than a third had used alcohol or marijuana during the past month, and more than a fifth had had intercourse during that month. Only 41% of those having had intercourse had used any form of contraception.

On the positive side, almost 60% said they had received some kind of an award. Slightly more than a fourth were on the honor roll in the previous year. Virtually all the students asserted at the beginning of the school year that they intended to complete both high school and college, an overstatement of likely achievement.

Again in each year of the evaluation, one or another of these factors has not been perfectly matched between Teen Outreach and the comparison groups. For example, in 1988-1989, the Teen Outreach students

Table 6.5 Status of Teen Outreach and Comparison Students at Intake: 1988-89

Characteristics	Teen Outreach Students N = 495	% = 100	Comparison Students N = 490	% = 100
Negative Behaviors				
Ever been pregnant or				
caused a pregnancy	22	4.5	38	*7.8
Last year ever -				
get suspended	85	17.3	86	17.6
get arrested	25	5.1	27	5.5
fail courses	190	38.8	190	39.2
skip school	151	30.9	141	29.1
Last month ever -				
used alcohol/marijuana	129	33.7	121	31.7
had intercourse	81	21.2	84	22.4
used contraception	33	40.7	47	55.9
Positive Behaviors				
Last year ever -				
get awards	283	57.9	251	*51.3
get on the honor roll	126	25.7	149	30.5
Educational Aspirations				
Complete high school				
likely	480	98.0	474	97.7
unlikely	10	2.0	11	2.3
Complete college				
likely	397	81.0	387	79.6
unlikely	93	19.0	99	20.4

NOTE: *Difference between the Teen Outreach and comparison students is statistically significant at $p < .05$.

were significantly less likely than their comparisons to have been pregnant before they began Teen Outreach. Teen Outreach students were also more likely to have gotten awards prior to the start of the program year.

The Outcomes of Teen Outreach

Figures 6.1 through 6.4 show the impact of Teen Outreach on the four major outcome variables of interest: pregnancy, school suspension, course failure, and school dropout. Figure 6.1 shows the percentage of Teen Outreach and comparison students who became pregnant during

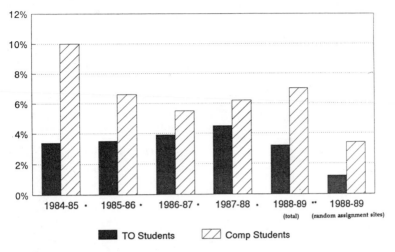

Figure 6.1. Percentage Pregnant or Causing Pregnancy.

each of the 5 program years and in the random assignment sample in 1988-1989. The percentage data shown in this figure and in the three to follow are without any controls for background differences between these two samples of students. The figure also shows, however, the results of multivariate analyses using logistic regression. In each year, grade level of the students and prior suspension history were included in the multivariate equation. In addition, other variables were introduced into these equations if the Teen Outreach and comparison students differed on the variable (e.g., gender in 1988-1989) or if the variable might confound the results (e.g., failing courses was also controlled in the suspension equation). The specific variables in each equation thus varied somewhat from year to year. The asterisks at the bottom of each year's data indicate whether participation in Teen Outreach was still significantly related to the outcome variable of interest, net of these other variables.

Figure 6.1 shows that in all six samples, Teen Outreach students had lower pregnancy rates during the program year than did the comparison students. In all but the random assignment sample (which was too small to permit analysis), participation in Teen Outreach was significantly related to having a lower pregnancy rate.

Figure 6.2 shows the percentage of Teen Outreach and comparison students who were suspended from school in each of the six samples.

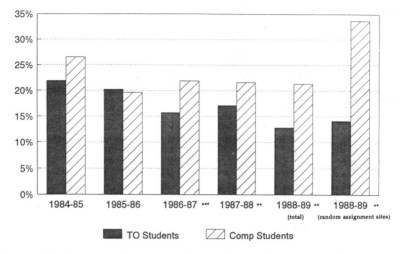

Figure 6.2. Percentage Suspended During Program Year.

In five of the six samples shown, Teen Outreach students had lower rates of school suspension than did comparison students. In four of the samples, including the smaller random assignment sample, participation in Teen Outreach was significantly related to lower rates of suspension, net of grade, prior rates of suspension, failing courses, and selected other variables introduced in a given year to control for sample differences.

In Figure 6.3, comparable data are shown for rates of failing courses during the program year among Teen Outreach and comparison students. Again, in five of the six samples, Teen Outreach students were doing better at the end of the program year. In four samples, participation in Teen Outreach was significantly related to lower rates of course failure, net of grade, prior rates of failure, and other necessary variables introduced in a given equation to control sample differences.

Figure 6.4 offers data on school leaving in the same six samples. In all six samples, Teen Outreach students had lower rates of dropping out. Again, in four samples, participation in Teen Outreach was significantly related to lower rates of dropping out when grade, pregnancy during the program year, and selected other variables were controlled.

As noted above, the 1988-1989 evaluation data set also included some additional outcomes not common to all six samples. An examination of these outcomes showed that participation in Teen Outreach was

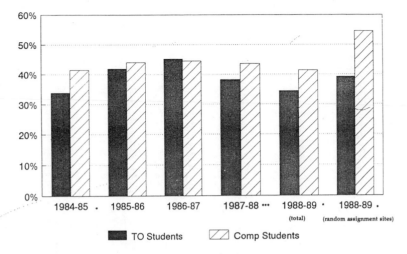

Figure 6.3. Percentage Failing Courses During Year.

significantly related to not getting arrested, skipping school less frequently, more regular use of contraception among sexually active students, getting awards, and getting on the honor roll, again net of the prior history of these behaviors and selected background characteristics. Participation in Teen Outreach was not significantly related to less use of alcohol or marijuana or to raising aspirations to finish high school, although both of these differences favored Teen Outreach students.

Correlates of Teen Outreach Success

In data published elsewhere (Allen, Philliber, & Hoggson, 1990), the correlates of successful change among students in Teen Outreach have been examined. The focus of this analysis was to assess under which conditions and for which kinds of participants this program was most successful. This analysis found that the sites that served primarily older students had lower levels of student problem behaviors at program exit, after controlling for problem behaviors at entry. In addition, programs that most fully implemented the volunteer component had greater success.

Equally important are the findings on which variables did not seem related to program success. Analysis has not found any relationship between gender of students and program success. Minority status of students is likewise not related to success, nor is parent education.

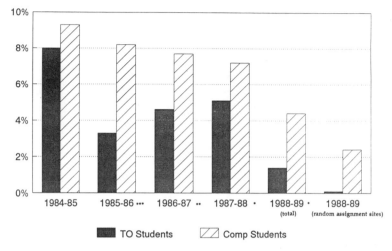

Figure 6.4. Percentage Dropping Out of School.

Several program characteristics or variations are also not related to program success. These include classroom hours, whether credit is offered for participation, whether the program is offered during or after school, and the amount of the curriculum used.

The higher success rate of the program among older students is not surprising in one sense, since Teen Outreach was created originally for high school students. On the other hand, it may be that the evaluation of the program is not currently measuring enough outcome variables appropriate to younger students.

The importance of the volunteer component is to be expected in light of current theories of empowerment and ecological development (Bronfenbrenner, 1979; Rappaport, 1987). The opportunity of young people to become help givers may indeed be an important experience in their development. Still, this research cannot demonstrate a causal link between these experiences and positive outcomes. It may be that some other factor not yet measured completely (such as a caring facilitator who works hard to provide successful volunteer experiences and who cares, in general, about his or her students) produces this finding.

It is gratifying for any program to discover that it is equally successful with both males and females and with those of different racial/ethnic groups. Similarly, for purposes of program replication, it is encouraging to find that when the program is offered and whether or not it is attached to course credit, makes little impact on its success.

The lack of relationships between classroom hours and amount of curriculum use and program success pose interesting questions. Certainly it seems reasonable to posit that number of classroom hours should be less important than the quality of those hours. The curriculum used in the Teen Outreach program does include discussions around topics that should support the development of life options to pregnancy and other negative behaviors. The activities in the curriculum and the style in which they are offered to students, however, are intended to facilitate group bonding and trust among Teen Outreach group members and their facilitator. Thought of in that context, then, it seems likely that the sheer amount of such material used may be less important than the way in which it is delivered. Indeed, case reports from facilitators suggest that they use a variety of supplemental materials to keep their discussions timely and responsive to student needs.

Conclusions

This chapter has presented data on program outcomes in Teen Outreach from six different samples. These data were gathered over 5 different school years. Only one of these samples utilized random assignment to create a control group. Unfortunately, this was the smallest sample of the six. Still, in all of these samples, the results are similar.

Almost all of the differences between the Teen Outreach and comparison students are in the desired direction: Teen Outreach students generally had fewer pregnancies, fewer courses failed, fewer school suspensions, and lower rates of school dropout than comparison students. More important, in each of the samples, the Teen Outreach students had significantly lower rates than did comparison students in half or more of these negative behaviors, even when prior risk and background characteristics were controlled.

These are results that, to our knowledge, are not duplicated by any other program of this kind in the nation. The random assignment results obtained in 1988-1989 add yet additional strength to the conclusion that Teen Outreach is a program that works.

We hasten to add that such a positive conclusion is supported more by the weight of evidence here than by the rigor of the research procedures used in each year. In only one sample were all the Teen

Outreach and comparison students assigned randomly, and this sample is the smallest of the six, leaving too little power to detect statistical significance except in the case of the largest differences, and limiting the capacity for multivariate analysis. At many Teen Outreach sites, participants were self-selected. Also, these data are from self-reports, and future studies will need to validate these with more objective sources of information such as report cards. Still, the weight of evidence here is overwhelmingly positive.

If these effects for Teen Outreach are real (as they appear to be), the evaluation design has not yet revealed for how long they last. While some 1-year follow-up data have been gathered from subsets of the youth enrolled and their comparisons, this question of the length of effects will need further research.

Given these cautions, however, it may still be worth discussing why Teen Outreach appears to be often successful in lessening school problems and postponing pregnancy. Indeed, the program does include elements that are being recommended currently by those who have reviewed what we know about success in these areas (e.g., Dryfoos, 1990; Hayes, 1987; Mueller & Higgins, 1988).

At its heart and when it works best, Teen Outreach includes mentoring from a caring and supportive facilitator, a work experience in the community that offers both the opportunity for skill building and the opportunity to feel needed, and a peer support group atmosphere. In addition, the curriculum concentrates on developing concrete coping skills, as well as the cognitive base necessary to avoid pregnancy. These include skills in assertiveness, in decision making, in use of community resources, and in communication.

The intervention is not a "one-shot" brief program, but rather a year-long effort. In fact, many Teen Outreach students request a second year of participation. While no direct measures of such a dimension have been taken by the current evaluation system, visits to Teen Outreach sites repeatedly confirm the impression that students become proud of their membership in the group and that it comes to function as their "in-crowd" or "clique."

These characteristics of the program, taken together, would seem to account for the general success of the program. Future evaluation of Teen Outreach will focus on increasing the number of sites that can use true random assignment to create a control group, on assembling information on the longer term impacts of the program, and on continuing examination of the conditions under which the program works best.

References

Allen, J. P., Philliber, S., & Hoggson, N. (1990). School-based prevention of teenage pregnancy and school dropout: Process evaluation of the national replication of the Teen Outreach program. *American Journal of Community Psychology, 18,* 505-524.

Bronfenbrenner, U. (1979). *The ecology of human development: Experiments by nature and design.* Cambridge, MA: Harvard University Press.

Dryfoos, J. G. (1990). *Adolescents at risk: Pregnancy and prevention.* New York: Oxford University Press.

Hayes, C. (Ed.). (1987). *Risking the future.* Washington, DC: National Academy.

Mueller, D., & Higgins, P. (1988). *Funders' guide manual: A guide to prevention programs in human services.* St. Paul, MN: Amherst S. Wilder Foundation.

Rappaport, J. (1987). Terms of empowerment/exemplars of prevention: Toward a theory for community psychology. *American Journal of Community Psychology, 15,* 121-148.

7

School-Linked Reproductive Health Services

The Johns Hopkins Program

LAURIE SCHWAB ZABIN

The Johns Hopkins School of Medicine program for the primary prevention of adolescent pregnancy was planned from the outset to serve two major purposes. It sought to design and implement a program that could reduce the rate of unintended conception in an urban junior and senior high school through education, counseling, and medical services; and it sought to document the success or failure of that activity through rigorous process and summative evaluation. The shape of the program that emerged from these twin objectives, and the research model that explored its effects and its costs, will be described in this chapter. It will also address issues that arise when evaluation is undertaken in the school setting, issues relating to access to data, data collection, data management, and analysis. Finally, it will report briefly on program utilization; it will show how the evaluation model permitted an accounting of each program component, the numbers of students who availed themselves of each type of service, and their estimated costs.

The Self Center Program

Rationale

The program, designed and implemented in cooperation with the
Baltimore City Department of Education, had roots in the service and
research histories of its creators. From many years of pediatric experience directing programs for pregnant adolescents and adolescent parents, the principal investigator and the program administrator had
learned many relevant lessons. They had learned that, although adolescents respond well to supportive programs, they frequently do not value
their educational components enough to seek them out if they are not
offered as an integral part of a medical service program. Thus both
education and services in reproductive health should be delivered in one
location. Nonetheless, they are best delivered by a multidisciplinary
staff. To help such a staff function in the best interests of its young
clients, a case-management approach is generally effective; it allows
each discipline to contribute its skills while permitting flexibility in the
roles of the team members as they meet the interrelated problems that
are common among this population. Another aspect of the service
program that derived from prior experience was its emphasis upon small
group work. In an age group in which peers play an important role, more
can often be accomplished in groups of three to five than in the
individual counseling setting in which the counselor may appear to play
a more authoritarian role. Although group work in a classroom setting
and individual guidance were both included in the final model, small
informal groups that coalesced around issues of mutual interest were
frequently the contacts of choice. Because of the developmental status
of the school population, interactive modalities of education were
preferable to didactic teaching; a consistent and caring staff with whom
teenagers could relate over time was an essential component of the
program's effort to build and maintain trust (Hardy & Zabin, 1991).

From the work of the principal investigator for the research portion
of the program came several findings that had implications for the
service model. The risk of pregnancy in the early months of intercourse
was found to be so high that reliance upon traditional reproductive
health services with limited outreach was not likely to succeed; 50% of
all first premarital conceptions in this age group were found to occur in
the 6 months following first intercourse (Zabin, Kantner, & Zelnik,
1979). Compounding these risks, mean intervals of 1 year were observed

between first intercourse and first clinic attendance (Zabin & Clark, 1981). Among young adolescents the proportional risk of pregnancy in the early months of sexual exposure is even higher, suggesting that programs must try to reach 11- and 12-year-old boys and girls if they are to serve those at highest risk before their sexual onset. Other findings suggest that only with early, nonclinic-based intervention could first intercourse be postponed and that only outside the clinic could many of the attitudinal barriers to contraceptive use be addressed. No success has been documented, however, in reducing unintended conception except in the context of accessible family planning services. Furthermore, it was clear that sexually active young women were in need of consistent follow-up if they were to maintain a contraceptive regime and prompt pregnancy testing if they were to make responsible decisions about the outcomes of accidental conceptions.

   Finally, it was apparent from both experience and from the literature that the cognitive and emotional status of young people when they were physically at risk of pregnancy were often such as to limit their ability to respond to episodic intervention, and certainly limited their ability to overcome the multiple barriers to responsible sexual behavior. Developmental age is a critical factor in the design of any intervention; the age range that the program intended to serve required that the needs of young people at very different stages of psychosocial development be appropriately addressed. The importance of developmental issues in adolescent pregnancy prevention is explored in detail elsewhere (Hardy & Zabin, 1991; Zabin, 1990a, 1990b).

The Program Design

   The schools to which the Hopkins team offered the program were the junior and senior high schools within the hospital's geographic community. The model that derived from the service and research experiences described above placed a team consisting of a social worker and often a nurse practitioner or nurse midwife in each school every morning; it utilized the same team in the afternoon in a clinic across the street from one school and a few blocks from the other. These staff, who became acquainted with the students in at least one classroom presentation a semester, were available for individual consultation or small group work in the school health suite. They offered contraceptive services in the clinic, along with continued counseling and education. In the clinic the waiting room became a center for informal education, utilizing audiovisual equipment, games, and small group encounters. Additional educational sessions were guided by a health educator, and clinicians were available at specific times to handle medical problems that required their expertise.

The explicit emphasis of the program was, categorically, upon reproductive health, although referrals were available for other medical problems and counseling often led to broader areas of concern. A multidisciplinary staff was clearly indicated because of the multiple problems so often encountered among the young clients; in fact, the confluence of problem behaviors among those who initiate coitus at young ages was confirmed in data collected in the program and control schools (Zabin, Hardy, Smith, & Hirsch, 1986). At no time, however, did the breadth of the counseling obscure the program's focus upon those reproductive and sexual issues. These were concerns that the students could rarely discuss with other adults; by removing the taboos often placed upon these issues, learning and communication were facilitated. Because the purposes of the endeavor were defined and explicit, the objectives measurable, and the service components directly related to the program goals, a commitment on the part of the research team to an exhaustive and many-faceted evaluation appeared justified. They, in turn, were rewarded with a service staff that appreciated the need for evaluation and were willing not only to invest the necessary time and effort in data collection but also to open their professional activities to rigorous scrutiny. In all the writings devoted to the art and science of evaluation, too little is said of the risks and challenges that it poses to the service providers who are willing to subject themselves to it. Their commitment deserves commendation.

A clear commitment was also made to the program on the part of the principals, the superintendent of schools, the school health committee, and the health department. This commitment included an understanding of the demands of a rigorous evaluation, the inclusion of which was a condition for the private grant that funded the program for 3 years. We attribute the level of support the community and the school authorities gave the program to the investment of approximately a year in the development process. It allowed the team to meet with all the official entities with a legitimate concern for school programs in order to obtain their sanction, as well as those without such authority who nonetheless had an interest in the students and in programs available to them. This effort was crucial to the success of the program.

The Evaluation Model

The evaluation depended upon both a pretest/posttest and an experimental/control model. A junior and a senior high school were chosen by the superintendent of schools as controls; their enthusiasm for the project was especially gratifying because they were not being offered a special program as a bonus for their participation. Measured by the percentage of students eligible for the free lunch program, the control schools had student bodies whose socioeconomic profiles were similar to the experimental schools. Although their populations included white students who were also surveyed, only the black respondents were compared with the all-black student populations of the program schools. On the basis of the data the team subsequently received, the schools appear to have been a good match. Nonetheless, the focus of the evaluation was upon *changes* over time brought about by the program; the control schools were included to determine that the observations were not contaminated by secular change over the program period. Surveys yielded repeated cross-sectional data that, because they were totally anonymous, could not be linked across time periods. Data were collected in the fall of the year the program began, shortly before the school components were inaugurated, and 2 months before the clinic was opened. All four schools participated in the baseline survey and in a similar survey in the spring of the third year. At the close of the first and second year, a survey was given in the program schools so that the effects of brief, as well as longer, term exposure to the program could be assessed.

The evaluation was designed to test the hypotheses that premature conception and childbearing among poor, urban adolescents could be prevented and that the schools were an effective locus in which to reach adolescents for that purpose. One of the principles upon which the proliferation of school-linked programs is predicated is the belief that such programs can reach young people who would not otherwise be served by professional health facilities. If that is the case, such programs ought to be able to demonstrate an impact upon the student body as a whole, not merely upon the self-selected subset who attend its clinic—a subset that might well consist in large measure of those who would have sought similar services wherever they were available. Thus evaluation should not be restricted to those who utilize program services but should include all students who, because they are in a school while a program is in place, have it accessible to them. To expect such effects puts stringent demands upon a program, but if positive changes are demonstrable in the entire student body, that is strong evidence of success. An assessment based upon such effects makes it possible to measure the degree to which the program succeeded, the degree to which its components were utilized overall, and the degree to which they substituted for other services, and thus to measure the true potential of these relatively new designs.

The evaluation of the Self Center, as the students christened the program, was therefore designed from the onset to assess changes in the knowledge, attitudes, and behaviors among entire school populations, based primarily upon data from self-administered questionnaires completed in the program and control schools. The experimental sample consisted of students from the two program schools. In these schools, 667 males and 1,033 females completed the voluntary, anonymous baseline questionnaire referred to as Round I below; they represented 98% of the junior and senior high students present on the day the survey was administered. Because of lower attendance and lower enrollment when subsequent rounds were administered, smaller numbers completed those surveys, although refusal and noncompletion rates remained only about 2-3%. Round II, administered in the program schools at the end of the first year, included 498 males and 793 females; Round III, at the end of year two, included 450 and 764, respectively; and Round IV, the final survey in program and control schools, 506 and 695 students, respectively. In the baseline survey in the control schools, 944 males and 1,002 females are included, and at the end of the project period, 860 males and 889 females. Over 95% of the students in each of the four schools produced records whose completeness and internal consistency qualified them for inclusion in the analysis. Data from these questionnaires, coded and edited twice by different data handlers, were computerized, verified, and cleaned.

In addition to the outcome evaluation built into the project, a process evaluation, a cost study, and a detailed analysis of utilization patterns were provided for in the design of all record systems. Although other sources of evaluation data were less extensive than the survey data, they were invaluable. Cost data were available from the Johns Hopkins University Financial Office, with backup materials provided by the program administrators and staff. All clinic forms, including social work and medical records, registration forms, sign-in sheets, and even a "nonform form" designed to pick up any clinic visit by youngsters whose attendance on a particular day might not otherwise have been recorded, were planned cooperatively by the research and service personnel. All service staff were trained in completing the forms; medical forms were designed with all permissible codes indicated so that even an occasional substitute clinician could follow the correct protocols. The records that contributed most to an understanding of the utilization of staff time were detailed logs maintained by the four key service providers who were in regular contact with the students: the two social workers and two nurse practitioners. The daily logs they maintained were the only forms whose purpose was purely research. They recorded each individual contact with a student in one of many types of service categories. These were then combined by the researchers into the six basic categories of service defined for the study—three types in the schools and three in the clinic. In combination with the financial records, the exhaustive logs made it possible for the research team to estimate the utilization and the costs of each type of service, the proportion of budget required for each location and program component, and the level of cost associated with individual students or cohorts of students who utilized the program in different ways.

Methodological Problems in Evaluation

If more rigorous evaluation is to be undertaken in the future than has been accorded most school-linked initiatives in the past, some of the methodological problems in evaluating programs in the school context may be of considerable interest in their own right. Most of the problems we encountered were not unique to the schools in Baltimore; they can be generalized to other cities, other schools, and other models. Even when cities, school systems, and services differ, generic issues appear to complicate the evaluation process. They make the assessment of change particularly difficult as one seeks to measure program effects in a moving target; classes are changing their membership, and youngsters are growing up. Problems may also be related to the politically charged climate in which these evaluations must be undertaken. Details of the team's methodology and discussions of many of these problems can be found elsewhere (Hardy & Zabin, 1991; Zabin & Hirsch, 1987; Zabin, Hirsch, Smith, Streett, & Hardy, 1986). Outlined here are the issues that are most challenging and that must be understood in order to interpret the results of the present evaluation.

Mobility into and out of individual schools is frequent in most cities, even schools that serve designated communities. This is largely due to normal patterns of graduation and promotion, but it can also be affected by factors relating to individual students, such as transfers or changes in residence, and by institutional factors such as reapportionment and group reassignments. This fluidity is especially common in extensive school systems serving urban populations. Motion into and out of the school makes it difficult to identify a denominator against which behavioral change or the utilization of program services can be measured. This difficulty is especially important when program effects upon the entire student body are used as a key measure of success. Mobility also complicates the definition of exposure groups, as explained below.

Another complication when undertaking a controlled study is the difficulty encountered in most urban school systems in identifying two schools that are clearly comparable. Schools tend to have their own character even when they are following the same guidelines; they often differ in curriculum and administration. They may vary in the economic and racial mix of students because of their geographical settings within the city or because of the ways in which localities allocate pupils and programs within their systems. Sometimes even the proportions of males and females are different. Furthermore, special programs may be offered in some schools but not in others. Even when no confounding programs exist, evaluators in some settings have found that students in one school may have convenient access to services within the community not accessible to those in other schools. Not only does this situation make it difficult to find control schools, it may also limit the ways in which they can be used even after they are chosen. It is safer, therefore, to use controls to establish the presence or absence of secular change, rather than to compare absolute numbers and/or rates at two sites at two points in time. If the possibility of secular change makes it inadvisable to utilize only a pre/post study in a program school without controls, differences between schools make it inadvisable to use comparisons of experimental and control schools at a single point in time as the basis for a program evaluation.

Deriving from these general issues are some of the particular challenges that were addressed in the current study.

1. Even within a single school, attendance can vary between the fall when the baseline data were collected and the spring, when follow-up generally takes place in order to capture those who will graduate and move on. It cannot be assumed that all differences in seasonal attendance are random. For example, although a drop-off in attendance due to transfers or change

of residence may be random, a drop-off due to absenteeism and premature school termination will generally select less motivated students. School systems operating as they do, it is not likely that a new program slated to begin in the fall would be developed long enough in advance of its inauguration to permit the administration of a baseline questionnaire the previous spring; even if that were possible, some students would inevitably be missed. Therefore minor differences in age distribution of school populations will frequently exist between baseline and follow-up data. Unless one controls for exact age by month, these differences can affect results, especially in variables that involve the cumulative initiation of strongly age-related behaviors. Of course, any such differences in the program schools would also appear in the control schools and therefore would not affect comparisons between them. Furthermore, when cumulative measures are used in variables in which exact age is critical, life tables correct for these differences.

2. Because of the students' movement into and out of the schools, and because of the large numbers of students who repeat grades, program exposure cannot be predicted accurately by grade. It is tempting to compare survey rounds in sequential years; that is, no doubt, the simplest way in which to analyze the several waves of cross-sectional data but is not a reliable basis upon which to evaluate program effects. Differentials by individual confound the picture and make it necessary to control for presence in the school while the program is in place in order to get an accurate measure of each individual's actual program exposure.

3. When years of exposure to the program are used to define subgroups for comparison, however, age distributions within subgroups may vary; for example, longer exposure is generally associated with older ages. In the spring, the students who entered a junior or a senior high school in the fall of that school year can only appear in one year exposure groups; students in higher grades may also have been in the school for only one year but are more likely to have been in the school for longer than a year, hence to have had two or three years of program exposure. Again, life table methods correct for age differences; they can also be used to correct for exposure differences and for intervals following first intercourse, as they were in the current study.

In the tables and figures in this evaluation, the basic comparison groups are defined by exposure. Results, however, are reported by grade to minimize age differences, and sometimes even by school or school of origin. Some grades and exposures have cells with small "N"'s and some cells that are inapplicable. (For example, no seventh graders were exposed longer than 1 year, nor eighth graders longer than 2.) When totals are summed across grades, they are controlled for the grade distribution at baseline and/or the grades available at follow-up. Doing the analysis by grade and then summing across grades has an additional advantage: it breaks down the unit of analysis from two—that is, two program schools—to many more. The researchers examine changes over two different time periods—1 year and 2 or more years—in three different groups of the junior high and five for the senior high[1], and then uses a Mantel-Haentzel summed chi-square test to calculate significance across all groups; this gives the researchers greater confidence in the differences they report than if they had used the school as the unit of measurement.

All baseline information is reported as "zero exposure." Round II data, collected in the spring of the first year, represents 1 year of exposure; also exposed for 1 year are a subset of the students interviewed in Round II who entered the program schools in the second year of the program. Two years of exposure were experienced by the remaining students in Round III, and by students who entered a program school in the second year and were interviewed in Round IV. The 3-year exposure group includes Round IV respondents who were in the program school(s) throughout the program's 3 years of operation. Further details relevant to the definition of comparison groups and the methodology used in addressing these problems are described elsewhere (see Zabin & Hirsch, 1987, and the appendix to Zabin, Hirsch, et al., 1986).

Administering the Survey

Before the surveys were administered, parents were informed in parents' meetings of the projected program and the survey. A few days before the survey was to be administered, notices were sent home with all students in the program schools, telling parents that the school was planning to inaugurate the program and explaining its primary objective—the prevention of pregnancy among the students. The use of a very personal, anonymous survey to help plan for that program was detailed. Parents were told that they could call a given number between 8 a.m. and 6 p.m. during the following several days if they wished to ask that their child be excused or if they had further questions. Although the principal and the Johns Hopkins research team were anxious for all students' participation, the parent was assured of the voluntary nature of the survey. Few mothers used the opportunity to call, and those who did call with questions did not ask that their offspring be excused. Often their calls were to express gratitude that something was to be done to help address what they perceived as a serious problem confronting them and their children. (At the control schools, a similar procedure was followed, although the notice to the parents could not promise them a program. Nonetheless, they appeared willing to cooperate.) This means of eliciting parental consent is highly preferable to the demand for positive written permission, a condition that has seriously limited the ability of some evaluations to tap a large enough percentage of the student population. Without a thorough understanding of the procedure on the part of the school administration and without their wholehearted commitment to the process, it is difficult to obtain authorization for the procedures we used—another good reason to invest time and energy in the development of school and community support.

Equally supportive were the students; only an occasional individual declined to take part although the homeroom teachers, briefed in advance, read them a statement that offered them another chance to withdraw. Although homeroom teachers handed out the questionnaires, each member of the research team was assigned four or five classrooms through which to circulate throughout the period. Thus they could respond to questions that the students might not have wished to address to their homeroom teachers. The administration process, originally conceived for research purposes and to aid in the design of appropriate interventions, had another beneficial effect not contemplated in advance: it made the entire student body aware of the forthcoming program and suggested, through the explicit nature of the questions, that discussions of hitherto taboo subjects would be appropriate when the staff became available to them. The researchers suspect that the experience of responding to the questionnaire accelerated utilization of the program in the months ahead.

Evaluation Results

Sexual Activity at Baseline

High levels of sexual activity were reported in the program and the nonprogram schools at baseline (Zabin, Hardy, Streett, & King, 1984). Almost 92% of the boys in the junior high school ninth grade reported having had sexual intercourse, as did boys in the senior high; 54% of the junior high ninth-grade girls, and 79% of the senior high school girls reported coital experience, as well. In the seventh and eighth grades, over 47% of the females had already experienced intercourse. Large proportions reported that they had used a family planning method at some time: approximately 71% of the junior high males and females, and over 89% of the senior high students. Far fewer, however, had used any method at last coitus, a better measure of consistency of use; only 61% of the junior high females and 73% of those in the senior high had used a method of any kind at last coitus. Of the sexually active girls in the seventh and eighth grades, 11% had already experienced a pregnancy, and in the senior high, over 22%. Even these figures were not unusual in similar populations; pregnancy rates in the junior high school at the program and control schools were very similar, and in the control senior high the baseline rates were even higher. On most of the characteristics measured, there was no reason to believe that the students were not broadly representative of young people in an urban school system serving a preponderance of poor black children.

Knowledge and Attitudes

Ten questions were asked of 9th- to 12th-grade students to assess knowledge of the correct use of specific contraceptive methods, and of the risk of pregnancy. Among females, scores on these questions at baseline averaged 6.8, increasing with age from 5.4 among 9th-graders to 7.4 among 12th-graders. A significant increase in knowledge occurred over the program period. Scores increased from 6.8 at baseline to 7.8 after 2 years or more and, for females in the 11th and 12th grades, to 8.2. Significant increase was also observed among males in the program schools at each duration of program exposure. On the other hand, in the control schools, although students started at levels comparable to the program schools at baseline, knowledge scores never exceeded 7.2, and no changes among females or males in the control school achieved significance.

A measure of knowledge frequently assessed in the literature concerns the fertile time of the month. It is generally reported that few young people give correct responses to questions tapping this information, even among young men and women who report that they have had a sex education course. We find that most good sex education courses teach young people that they are at risk at any time; with the often irregular cycles associated with adolescence, that is probably the best protective assumption to make. In view of that lesson, however, the researchers prefer to consider responses correct if students reply that a woman's fertile period is "2 weeks after her period begins" *or* "anytime during the month," rather than coding the latter response incorrect. When coded in this manner, a highly significant increase is found in knowledge among females in the program schools, especially among younger girls. Unfortunately, even with the increases in knowledge brought about by the program, young women rarely exceed a 50% score on this variable. Increases among males in the program schools are small and neither consistent nor significant. A decrease occurs among control school males, however, and among females only an insignificant increase during the same time period. One can begin to see an important pattern of change: younger students come to achieve scores after program exposure that are higher than those achieved by older students prior to the intervention. This is encouraging because an earlier acquisition of knowledge has the potential to reduce the high risks associated with early sexual behavior.

After exposure to the program, fewer male and female students rate withdrawal, rhythm, or douche as "good" or "very good" protection against pregnancy. This trend is already significant among males and females after 1 year's exposure; knowledge continues to improve with longer exposure. The response pattern does not change among nonprogram students. Thus overall, an increase in contraceptive and sexual knowledge appears to occur, a difference that is generally significant in magnitude.

Attitudinal change is small by any of the three attitudinal measures reported here: (a) the proportions of students who hold any positive attitudes toward teenage pregnancy; (b) the percentage who cite a "best" or ideal age for childbearing that is below the age they cite as best for marriage; (c) the percentage who believe that first sex is "okay" when the couple have "just met" or "date occasionally." In a previous study, the researchers had reported a significant relationship between a positive attitude toward adolescent childbearing and the ineffective use of contraception (Zabin, 1985). In the student population, as in the earlier study, few teenagers thought having a child while of school age was a good idea. Although the trend is downward in this measure among females exposed to the program, neither in this nor other attitudinal measures is there marked or consistent change. Large numbers of males and females cite an ideal age for childbearing (or fathering) younger than the ideal age for marriage; in many grades, over 50% share this view. Significantly fewer females hold this view after program exposure than before; among males the downward trend is weaker. In the control schools, however, no such trend was found; in fact, among females an increase is observed. Changes in the third measure, which explores when having sex is "okay," are also inconsistent and insignificant.

The generally insignificant changes in attitudinal variables may reflect the fact that the majority of students held rather positive attitudes toward contraception and rather negative attitudes toward adolescent childbearing even before the program. There was not as much room for significant change as there was in their knowledge and their behavior. Therefore, although the trends appear to be in a direction discouraging to childbearing, improvement in attitude was less consistent and significant than in knowledge scores. The team has since demonstrated that attitudes play a more significant role when they are defined by several variables that tap a single dimension than when defined by a single question (Zabin, Astone, & Emerson, 1990). Using such a construct, consistent attitudes are shown to be associated with behavior, whereas ambivalent attitudes are not. Perhaps with attitudes better defined, change could yet be demonstrated. If students with previously ambivalent attitudes became less ambivalent, that could help explain changes observed in their behavior. That possibility has yet to be explored.

Sexual and Contraceptive Behaviors

The program was designed, and was explicitly committed, to bring about changes in pregnancy rates, including both rates of childbearing and abortion. Clearly, a series of intervening behaviors directly affects those rates, behaviors that a program may or may not be able to alter. These include (a) timing of coital onset, (b) utilization of professional contraceptive facilities, (c) effective use of contraception, and (d) the frequency of coitus among those who are already sexually active. At the outset of the program the team had expected to influence the first three; they had not foreseen the likelihood of change in the fourth parameter, although it was clearly desirable.

The extremely high rates of youthful sexual activity in the study populations made it seem unlikely that a 28- to 30-month program could have much impact upon patterns of sexual initiation. The subset of the population not sexually active when first exposed to the program was relatively small. Figure 7.1 displays the cumulative percentage of ≥15-year-old female students sexually active at each age, comparing the histories of those exposed to the program for 3 years with those of

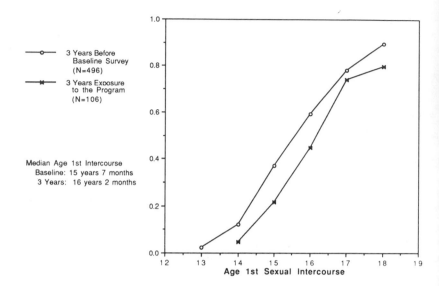

Figure 7.1. Proportion of Senior High School Girls Sexually Active by Age x, in Baseline Data and After 3 Years of Exposure to a Pregnancy Prevention Program.

students responding to the baseline survey in the program senior high school. These life table curves indicate a median postponement of sexual initiation from the age of 15 years and 7 months before the program to 16 years and 2 months after exposure to the entire program, a postponement of approximately 7 months.

Delays were smaller among those exposed for only 1 or 2 years, reflecting the period of time that is required before one can observe the behavioral effects of any intervention. Both the before and after curves in Figure 7.1 show a rapid increase in sexual initiation between the ages of 13 and 16; although the curves are similar, they show a substantial difference in sexual activity at 14 and 15 years of age. Before the program began, approximately two thirds more females were sexually active by age 14 than after 3 years of program exposure. In view of the high risks attendant upon early sexual exposure (Zabin et al., 1979), even a small delay in this age period may have a substantive impact. The relatively small virgin subgroup and the time required to change behavior suggest that, unless intervention occurs early in a population with young ages of sexual initiation, and unless it is in place for a considerable period of time, effects will be limited. Nonetheless, these results suggest that postponement can occur as a result of an explicit program such as this. That is extremely encouraging.

Contraceptive clinic attendance changed dramatically from before to after program exposure, so that by its end, over 70% of the sexually active young women who had been exposed to the program 2 years or more had attended a professional facility for birth control. The proportion of sexually active students who attended clinics (either the program clinic or any other professional individual or facility for contraceptive services) increased significantly at each grade level among both males and females. No consistent pattern of change was evident in the control schools. The junior high school boys attended the clinic in percentages as great or greater than junior high girls, at levels that parallel those reported in the baseline data by *senior* high school females; the program made service to males as important as service to females, and among the junior high school boys that emphasis resulted in their active participation. This evidence suggests that young males can be reached when clinic and outreach staff are willing and able to communicate with them. Positive changes in clinic utilization among the younger girls in the schools were also encouraging.

The timing of first clinic attendance relative to first coitus is shown in Figure 7.2. The curves compare the *timing* of clinic attendance among females exposed to the program for 1 year, to the probability of a similar subset using professional birth control services during a similar interval in the preprogram period. It utilizes only those whose first intercourse occurred within those 12-month periods in order to explore the timing of the clinic visit relative to sexual onset. The percentage of young women who attended such a facility as virgins, in preparation for first coitus, is indicated at the intercept. After program exposure, larger percentages appear to have attended a clinic at every month following first coitus. This is particularly important during the period between first sexual exposure and 3 months thereafter, when the "after" curve shows a steep rise. In view of the high risk of unintended conception during early exposure, that increase should translate into a measurable change in pregnancy rates. Longer exposure to the program had stronger effects: among those exposed for 3 years, 92% of female students age 15 and older had attended some professional services by the end of the observation period. The positive effects of a single year of exposure shown in Figure 7.2 were thus compounded by continued access to the program.

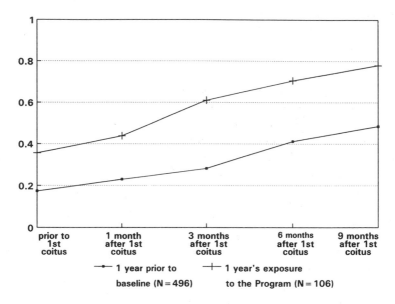

Figure 7.2. Proportion of Seuxually Active Female Students in Grades 9-12*
Who Attended a Birth Control Clinic, by Month Following First Coitus, 1 Year
Before the Survey.

* Excludes students who initiated sexual activity more than 1 year before the survey.

The third behavioral area the program sought to influence was the
use of reliable contraception. That it succeeded is illustrated by the fact
that, at follow-up, in nearly all program school subgroups, fewer than
20% of the sexually active female students exposed to the program for
2 or more years were unprotected by some contraceptive method at their
most recent coitus. At baseline was the expected increase in use of the
contraceptive pill with age from 25% of sexually active 8th-grade girls
to 49% among sexually active 12th-grade girls. After exposure to the
program, all grade levels showed significantly increased usage, but
increases were much greater among the youngest than among the oldest
students. Therefore the large age differentials at baseline (25%-49%)
tended to diminish to 39%-61%. Some of the youngest grades reported
higher levels of effective contraceptive use by the end of the program
than some older grades reported before it began. As mentioned above,
this pattern of change, which disproportionately affected younger girls,
reduced the excess risks of pregnancy typical among this age group.

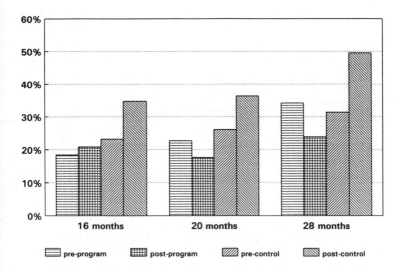

Figure 7.3. Life Table Calculations of Pregnancies Among Sexually Active 9-12th-Grade Females Who Became Pregnant During 16, 20, or 28 Months Prior to Baseline Versus Prior to Follow-Up Surveys.

The improvement is visible even among girls at the 7th and 8th grade levels, at ages at which poor contraceptive usage is generally the rule.

In contrast to the findings among these youthful program school females is the experience of the control schools where younger students continued to demonstrate the limited levels of contraceptive use typical of females who initiate coitus in their early teens. But nonuse was common at older ages, as well. Between 44% and 49% of all the sexually active females in the control schools at follow-up had not used any method of birth control at last coitus; only one grade had attained the levels of protection found in virtually all grades in the program schools.

Pregnancy Rates

The crucial measure of program impact, however, is its effect upon conception. Figure 7.3 illustrates changes in pregnancy rates in the program and nonprogram schools after different intervals of program exposure. It reports the cumulative percentage of sexually active students in grades 9 through 12 who became pregnant during the 16-, 20-, or 28-month periods prior to the applicable survey. Pregnancy rates among girls available for given periods of sexual exposure during the program are compared with pregnancy rates in matched groups of girls available for similar periods of exposure before the baseline interview. (Details of the increment-decrement life table methodology used to obtain these estimates is reported elsewhere [Zabin et al., 1986; Zabin & Hirsch 1987]).

The estimates in Figure 7.3 include young women who transferred to a special school for pregnant girls, if they were in the program or control schools during a relevant interval. They were attributed to their respective cohorts even if they had transferred before the appropriate follow-up survey took place. Including these young women is much more critical to the estimates than including the individuals who leave schools for other reasons; the girls in the special school are not a random selection because they are all pregnant and therefore have a significant impact upon the findings. In this study they represent about 10% to 20% of the pregnant students reported in each school year, and an even higher proportion of those who carry to term; their inclusion in the estimates is vital to the accuracy of the pregnancy rates. Although the researchers did not have the detailed information that a survey would have allowed—information about their knowledge, attitudes, and behaviors—that did not disqualify them from inclusion in the pregnancy estimates.

Figure 7.3 shows a secular increase in pregnancy rates in the control schools, reflecting an increase that was occurring in Baltimore during the program period. A 50% increase during the 16-month exposure period increased by 28 months to an almost 58% increase. (The baseline estimates for the three groups differ because each covers different subsets of the population, a subset with the same exposure prior to baseline as that against which they are compared. This procedure, essential to the comparison, is described in Zabin & Hirsch, 1987, and in the appendix to Zabin et al., 1986.) In contrast to the citywide increase, during the first 16-month exposure period in the program schools, the rate of increase slowed. By 20 months' exposure, a reversal occurs in the trend, a decline of 22.5% in the pregnancy rate; a larger decline, of 30.1%, is experienced among those exposed for the full 28 months the program was in place. Thus the program and control high schools end the program with a very large differential even though they began with pregnancy rates that were similar. Not only in relative but in absolute terms, the program's effects were substantial.

The changes reported here appear robust, as is evidenced by the fact that they emerge when the analyses are performed for different periods of exposure and for different subgroups. Not unexpectedly, abortion rates decreased first. It takes less time to observe changes in abortion rates than in childbearing rates and, because they are all "unwanted" conceptions, they should, theoretically, be even more "preventable." In time, however, the observed reduction in the pregnancy rate reflected the combined effects of reductions in both abortion and childbearing; given time to measure those effects, childbearing rates also declined and contributed to the overall decline in pregnancy.

The data in Figure 7.3 are limited to 9th- through 12th-grade students because information was not collected on the exact timing of pregnancies among the 7th- and 8th-graders. Furthermore, because fewer of these younger girls become pregnant, statistically valid comparisons are difficult to carry out. Can one make any estimate, then, of the impact of the program upon pregnancy rates in the younger group? Increases in pregnancy rates appear to have been even more rapid in the control junior high school during the program period than among senior high school girls. Declines in the pregnancy rates in program schools appear to have been smaller among the younger students than among the older; nonetheless, differentials between program and control schools at follow-up were striking. Thus the program appeared to help the youngest girls largely by helping them avoid the secular increases that were affecting their peers in settings without comparable interventions.

If the data give clear evidence that the program had substantial effects upon pregnancy rates among the sexually active, it remains of interest to explore how the effects were brought about. They can be attributed to demonstrably improved rates of contraception and to improved methods of contraception. In addition to the improvements in contraceptive protection, more recent analysis suggests that the program was associated with reductions in the frequency of coitus, an unexpected but gratifying circumstance. Mathematical models used to decompose changes in the pregnancy rate suggest that the reductions were due as much, if not more, to reductions in coital frequency as they were to improved contraception (Zabin, Becker, & Hirsch, 1989). The use of these models also suggests that the changes in pregnancy rates reported by these young women are credible in terms of their reported behavioral changes. Sensitive and personal areas are being dealt with here. Like other areas that are generally taboo, they are plagued by semantic problems; idioms may differ and, because anonymity is so important to honest response, very little verification is possible. Therefore the correspondence observed between behavioral change and changes in conception is particularly encouraging. It lends considerable strength to the data utilized in this evaluation; indeed, it suggests that evaluations can be based upon retrospective survey data provided by teenage respondents. If asked questions that are appropriate and straightforward, and if granted—and *believe* they are granted—complete anonymity, the students take the process seriously; the vast majority are willing and able to provide credible and useful information.

Program Utilization and the Costs of Intervention

An exhaustive analysis of the components of the program, the time allocated to them, and the students' use of them, was based primarily upon the staff logs but depended upon the availability of complete rolls from the school system. The rolls were used to compute the denominator against which the proportions who availed themselves of each component were measured. Because rolls change constantly, a decision was made to use the November rolls; they are prepared after major changes are made in fall enrollment and before the Christmas holidays, after which most dropouts occur. Thus they are probably maximal. Many students never show up at the schools to which they are assigned; faculty reported that they had never seen many of the students attributed to their homerooms. Therefore estimates of chronic absenteeism per grade for males and females were obtained from the school system so that percentages utilizing each component could be computed not only as proportions of students *theoretically* enrolled but also as proportions of students who could *realistically* be reached.

The six categories of service into which all modalities of student encounters were collapsed for analytic purposes included three in the schools and three in the clinic; they are classroom contacts, small group contacts in the schools, individual contacts in the schools, educational group contacts in the clinic, individual contacts with the social worker in the clinic, and individual contacts with medical staff. On the basis of the rolls, the logs, and other data, it was estimated that 85% of the students were in contact with at least one component of the program, 100% of those who were not chronic absentees (Table 7.1) (Zabin et al., 1988a). This was not unexpected because all classrooms were reached

Table 7.1 Percentage of Students Using Program Services (and Percentage After Adjustment For Chronic Absentees), by Site and Type of Service, According to Gender and School Level

Site and Type of Service	All Students (N = 3,944)	Female Jr. High (N = 1,001)	Female Sr. High (N = 1,163)	Male Jr. High (N = 1,132)	Male Sr. High (N = 581)
Total	84.9 (112.2)	87.1 (119.0)	87.0 (97.8)	82.2 (132.6)	80.7 (90.7)
School					
Class presentation	72.7 (96.1)	81.2 (111.2)	73.0 (83.9)	73.9 (119.1)	61.3 (68.9)
Group discussion	50.6 (66.9)	55.2 (75.6)	55.6 (63.8)	42.0 (67.7)	48.2 (54.2)
Indiv. counseling	15.2 (20.1)	15.3 (20.9)	29.8 (34.3)	4.3 (7.0)	8.8 (9.9)
Clinic					
Group education	26.7 (35.3)	24.2 (33.1)	42.1 (48.4)	21.0 (33.9)	12.4 (13.9)
Indiv. counseling	19.7 (26.0)	14.5 (19.8)	34.3 (39.4)	15.6 (25.2)	9.8 (11.0)
Medical visit	14.5 (19.2)	13.4 (18.3)	34.8 (40.0)	1.8 (2.8)	2.2 (2.5)

NOTE: Chronic absentee rates as reported by the schools were: junior high females, 27%; senior high females, 11%; junior high males, 38%; and senior high males, 11%.
SOURCE: Zabin, L. S., et al. (1988). The Baltimore pregnancy program for urban adolescents: How did it work? *Family Planning Perspectives, 20,* (4), p. 185.

each semester. As Table 7.1 indicates, if the school system's estimates of absenteeism are correct, even some chronic absentees in the junior high were reached by at least one of these sessions.

The importance of the small group work, especially in the schools, is clear in Table 7.1. Although females were more often involved than males, and junior high students more than senior high, these differences are small compared to the differences between the numbers who availed themselves of these services and those who utilized the other elective components of the program. It seems clear that many students who never attended the clinic had multiple contacts through these sessions; this was one of the key objectives of the school components that were designed both to act as a bridge to the clinic *and* to serve the needs of students who either did not need or had access to other clinical services. In reviewing the utilization of clinic services, it should be recalled that Table 7.1 includes young people who are not sexually active. Although many of them attended educational sessions in the clinic, many restricted their contacts to the school setting where they received both the group and the individual guidance they sought. On the other hand, the majority of clinic contacts were made by senior high school females, 46% of whose contacts with the program occurred in the clinic setting.

Overall, 33,388 contacts were recorded between students and staff in the 28-month program, when all six types of encounters are included. The mean exposure per student to the program was about 16 months, but because that included summers and other vacations, that left only an average of 250 school days in which each student had access to the school services; for many, access to the clinic was not as convenient during vacations as it was during the school year. During that period of access, a mean of 10 and a median of 4 contacts took place between all students who used the program and the program staff. The median is considerably lower than the mean because of the repeated involvement of some students with the staff; in addition to members of a Peer Resource team whose contacts were numerous, some particularly needy individuals consumed vast amounts of counseling time. In general, senior high males had the fewest contacts, senior high females the most. The frequency with which junior high males availed themselves of the services was gratifying; they enrolled in the clinic in even greater proportions than junior high females, proving that, with appropriate outreach at the appropriate ages, young men can be served in such a program.

Did the school act as a bridge to the clinic? It would appear so because 86% of the students who came to the afternoon facility had a school contact before they first visited the clinic (Hardy & Zabin, 1991). Of the remainder, about half had a school contact between that first clinic visit and enrollment. Thus the notion that school components could facilitate clinic utilization was apparently correct. But the school base did a great deal more. For almost 70% of the students who had any contact with the program—that is, if the school estimates are at all reliable, 70% of all students who could not be described as chronic absentees—the school components were the only services used. In view of these data, the overall impact of the program upon the student body suggests that nonclinic services rendered in a school setting can have a powerful influence upon knowledge and behavior when those services are delivered in the context of an explicit reproductive health service program.

Programs such as this one, however, are not without financial costs. Costs were computed by dividing the salaries of the four key staff (two social workers and two nurse practitioners) by the time devoted to each of the same six categories of service shown above. Added to their salaries were assigned shares of all other costs, including administrative costs, and other relevant components. For example, all medical staff and materials were included with the nurses' salaries before allocating

Table 7.2 Number of Students Served, Total Expenditures and Costs Per Student, by Gender and School Level

Gender and School Level	N	Total	Costs per Student		
			Average	Maximum†	Minimum
All students	3,349*	$409,140	$122	$3,052	$3
Junior high	1,834	143,106	78	1,680	3
Senior high	1,508	266,001	176	3,052	3
Male	1,400‡	68,438	49	891	3
Junior high	930	47,460	51	815	3
Senior high	469	20,970	45	891	3
Female	1,888‡	340,281	180	3,052	3
Junior high	872	95,397	109	1,680	3
Senior high	1,012	244,868	242	3,052	3

NOTE: *Includes students with gender and/or school level unknown.
†Maximum costs exclude peer resource students.
‡Includes students with school level unknown.
SOURCE: Zabin, L. S., et al., (1988). The Baltimore pregnancy prevention program for urban adolescents: How did it work? *Family Planning Perspectives, 20,* (4), p. 190.

those salaries by time segments, and all educational costs were added to the social work components. Thus the per session costs are inclusive of all program costs and are not merely the costs of the staff time of the provider who rendered the service. (Details of the methodology are described in Zabin et al., 1988b.)

The applicability of the costs computed to other models is complicated by the program's association with a major university medical school, which no doubt had both financial advantages and disadvantages. Personnel costs were probably higher because of this association, and start-up costs lower. The economic use of staff during vacation periods was an advantage, but because the program was heavily staffed, similar services could, theoretically, be offered at lower costs. For example, one could spread the nursing staff between two schools and minimize the large amounts of time devoted to the peer resource group. The figures presented here are maximal, but they permit one to understand the relative costs of various program components and the maximum costs of equivalent services (see Zabin et al., 1988b, for details).

School-based services accounted for 40% of the budget, clinic services for 60%. With a 3-year budget of $409,250 overall, the average cost per student, combining those with all levels of service utilization, was $122 (Table 7.2). Costs per female were almost four times those per male; costs for senior high school students were more than double the costs for students in the junior high. Utilization of the program at many different levels meant that services per individual ranged from a low of $3 for those who experienced only a small group discussion with a social worker in the school setting, to a high of $3,052 for a senior high school female whose needs for individual counseling led to 228 contacts with the program staff.

Because small group sessions in the schools attracted so many students, it is especially encouraging that this activity was extremely cost effective. So many young people utilized the time the social workers made available for this type of consultation that the costs for each student contact were below the per student costs of the classroom presentations even though each of the latter involved many more students. In contrast to the full class period, the spontaneous, small group sessions often lasted only 15 minutes and required no special arrangements or preparation; they were not only an effective educational component but a cost-effective way in which to utilize staff time.

Perhaps the utilization of a wide range of services by those who sought medical consultation in the clinic can be seen as a validation of the original model. Because the majority of enrollees had contact with the staff both in school and clinic and took part in both group and individual counseling, the cost for each student who obtained contraceptive services was approximately $402 when estimated for the entire program period; 1-year costs averaged $188.

The use of high school students as outreach workers and even as counselors for their peers has been promoted not only in the U.S. but in developing countries. The Peer Resource Team in this program was utilized for limited purposes, but especially to give the students a sense of ownership of the program; they publicized it and represented it although their assigned tasks often were limited to management of audiovisual equipment and similar noncounseling activities. The costs attributed to this group, however, were large. The advantages to the team members themselves of their personal involvement with the program staff may have been great, but the costs were high. When their costs are included in the overall estimates, the multiple-year cost per contraceptive patient increases from $402 to $432 because the personal and training contacts of the peer resource students cost over $2,000 each. Thus whatever advantages they may offer, such a team should not be included in an effort to reduce staff costs; the component cost more staff time and attention than it saved.

Individual counseling is expensive. In the clinic, considerable time
was devoted to each session, and some individual counseling was
required for all who sought contraception. The mean cost per clinic
counseling session was approximately $42, school sessions $28. The
lower per visit cost for medical consultation than individual counseling
in the clinic, despite the higher pay received by medical personnel and
the inclusion of medical supplies, physicians, and medical support staff
costs in the estimate, is dramatic evidence of the time these often
extensive sessions required. The high cost of counseling necessarily
raises the question: Is unlimited consultation with a social worker a
necessary component of such a program? All programs may not be able
to invest so much in this component, but because it was seen as one of
the program's most important contributions, there is no guarantee that
without it the same effects could be ensured.

Summary and Conclusion

At the time the evaluation described here was first published, in 1986,
there was an uncomfortable sense that the problem of adolescent unintended conception was intransigent. Although creative programs had
been essayed in many communities, no strong evidence existed that
pregnancy rates could be reduced or that any particular intervention
deserved to be replicated. It was not surprising that the findings reported
here received nationwide attention. It was of special interest that they
demonstrated that abortion and pregnancy rates could be reduced and
sexual onset postponed by one and the same program. Many who
opposed both sex education and contraceptive services for adolescents
believed that the provision of contraceptive services, or even open
discussion of the responsibilities associated with sexual intercourse,
would increase sexual activity. On the basis of the data presented here,
that hypothesis must be rejected. Not only was sexual onset postponed
among those not yet sexually active, but the frequency of coitus was
reduced among those who had initiated intercourse, even while those
who continued their sexual activity were protected by more effective
contraceptive use.

Because program acceptance and utilization was high, it was possible
to affect the intermediate behaviors that can, in turn, account for a reduction in pregnancy rates. Timely clinic attendance was increased dramatically, use of effective contraception was improved, and unprotected coitus

was reduced to extraordinarily low levels. The effects were especially dramatic among the younger girls and boys whose preprogram levels of protection were minimal. They exceeded the magnitude of change that was predicted when it was hypothesized that the program could have a measurable impact upon pregnancy rates. Many more young people learned to make responsible sexual decisions for their futures. Furthermore, the savings that accrued to the community as a result of these reduced pregnancy rates were substantial. Both in human and financial costs averted, the project was a major success. Little doubt exists that such services, or services approximating them, could be delivered at lower cost. The effectiveness of the small group sessions and the low costs related to them suggest their importance in future models. They permit a small staff to reach large numbers of students, and their popularity recommends them in both school and clinic settings. The school components were relatively inexpensive and, with the presence of the staff in the schools, the nearby, free-standing clinic proved highly accessible to students and acceptable to the school community. The clinic could operate without the strictures so often imposed upon an on-campus facility. It combined proximity with the best counseling and medical care a major health and academic institution could provide. In view of the political difficulties in delivering appropriate services within the schools, and the limitations often associated with vacation schedules and early afternoon closings, the location of the clinic just outside the school would appear justified. The way in which the students used the school components, however, often as a bridge into the clinic, suggests that a visible relationship between clinic and school can be crucial; it was represented in this model by the presence of the same staff in both locations.

What can be concluded about the evaluation model? The use of the entire school population as the denominator for assessing utilization, and the designation of all students responding to the questionnaire as the denominator for measuring change, challenged the program in the extreme. It met that challenge. The findings permit the conclusion that the program had an effect even upon those who did not utilize all it offered and that its relationship with the school had a beneficial effect upon many who never entered the clinic. As valuable as self-administered questionnaires are in assessing change, individual data on program utilization has an important role, as well. Without recording each encounter, analyzing each staff members' functions, and tracking each student through the program, the team could have reported only *that* it worked, not *how* it worked. It would not have been possible to measure the importance of the school effort or to establish the relatively low cost at which it operated.

The inclusion of data from the school for pregnant girls was crucial in evaluating the fertility effects of the program. It is a procedure recommended wherever such facilities exist. Having noted their importance in the team's estimates, it would seem wise in future evaluations to attempt to determine who has transferred into such schools and, if they are found in a school setting, to administer the same survey that is conducted in program and control schools. Even in the absence of survey data, however, their incorporation in the enumeration of pregnancies is indicated.

The program proved that young men and women will respond to an appropriately staffed, well-conceived program, one that provides them with supportive services, education, a sense of their self-worth, and the means to act responsibly. Not only did the model give students in two schools that opportunity, but by including a strong evaluation component, it was able to demonstrate that it worked. Both the service and the evaluation models are deserving of replication in other similar urban environments.

Note

1. Five rather than four groups are compared in the senior high because one 10th-grade subgroup consists of students who came from the program junior high, and another subgroup consists of those who did not. They are analyzed separately because their exposures differ (see Zabin & Hirsch, 1987).

References

Hardy, J. B., & Zabin, L. S. (1991). *Adolescent pregnancy in an urban environment.* Baltimore, MD and Washington, DC: Urban and Schwarzenberg and The Urban Institute.

Zabin, L. S. (1985). *Correlates of effective contraception among black inner-city high school students.* (Report No. R01 HD17183-02).

Zabin, L. S. (1990a). Early sexual onset. In B. B. Lahey & A. E. Kazdin (Eds.), *Advances in clinical child psychology* (pp. 247-282). New York: Plenum.

Zabin, L. S. (1990b). The two problems of adolescent pregnancy: The effects of age on unintended conception. In M. Perry, J. Money, & H. Musaph (Eds.). *Handbook of Sexology: Vol. 7. Childhood and adolescent sexology.* New York: Elsevier.

Zabin, L. S., Astone, N. M., & Emerson, M. R. (1990). *Pregnancy, "wantedness," and contraception among urban adolescents.* Paper presented at the annual meeting of the American Public Health Association, New York.

Zabin, L. S., Becker, S., & Hirsch, M. B. (1989). *Decomposing pregnancy rates in a school population into proximate determinants.* Paper presented at the annual meeting of the Population Association of America, Baltimore, MD.

Zabin, L. S., & Clark, S. D., Jr. (1981). Why they delay: A study of teenage family planning clinic patients. *Family Planning Perspectives, 13*(5), 205-217.

Zabin, L. S., Hardy, J. B., Streett, R., & King, T. M. (1984). A school-, hospital- and university-based adolescent pregnancy prevention program: A cooperative design for service and research. *Journal of Reproductive Medicine, 29*(6), 421-426.

Zabin, L. S., Hardy, J. B., Smith, E. A.,& Hirsch, M. B. (1986). Substance use and its relation to sexual activity among inner-city adolescents. *Journal of Adolescent Health Care, 7,* 320-331.

Zabin, L. S., Hirsch, M. B., & Smith, E. A. (1986). Adolescent pregnancy prevention program: A model for research and evaluation. *Journal of Adolescent Health Care, 7,* 77-87.

Zabin, L. S., & Hirsch, M. B. (1987). *Evaluation of pregnancy prevention programs in the school context.* Lexington, MA: Lexington.

Zabin, L. S., Hirsch, M. B., Smith, E. A., Streett, R., & Hardy, J. B. (1986). Evaluation of a pregnancy prevention program for urban teenagers. *Family Planning Perspectives, 18*(3), 119-126.

Zabin, L. S., Hirsch, M. B., Streett, R., Emerson, M. R., Smith, M., Hardy, J. B., & King, T. M. (1988a). The Baltimore pregnancy prevention program for urban adolescents: How did it work? *Family Planning Perspectives, 20*(4),

Zabin, L. S., Hirsch, M. B., Smith, E. A., Smith, M, Emerson, M. R., King, T. M. Streett, R., & Hardy, J. B. (1988b). What did it cost? Expenditures on student services in a successful pregnancy prevention program. *Family Planning Perspectives, 20*(4),.

Zabin, L. S., Kantner, J. F., & Zelnik, M. (1979). The risk of adolescent pregnancy in the first months of intercourse. *Family Planning Perspectives, 11*(4), 215-222.

8

School-Based Clinics

DOUGLAS KIRBY
CINDY WASZAK

Introduction

Since the first school-based health clinic opened in a Dallas high school in 1970, school-based clinics have been seen not only as a means of providing basic health care to medically under-served teenagers, but also as a promising way of addressing some of the intractable and complex health and social problems, particularly unintended pregnancy, that face young people.

Currently over 196 school-based clinics operate in middle, junior, and senior high schools in 33 states (Waszak & Neidell, 1992); they may be found in most major cities and many rural areas. These clinics often serve low-income, predominantly minority youth with limited access to other sources of health care. School-based clinics provide these youths with a wide range of medical and counseling services, including primary health care, physical examinations, laboratory tests, diagnosis and treatment of illness and minor injuries, immunizations, gynecological exams, birth control information and referral, pregnancy

AUTHORS' NOTE: This chapter is based upon an article that appeared in *Family Planning Perspectives* (Kirby, Waszak, & Ziegler, 1991). The research was conducted by the Center for Population Options and was supported by grants from the Ford Foundation, the William T. Grant Foundation, and the Charles Stewart Mott Foundation. The article represents the views of the authors and not necessarily those of the foundations, their trustees, or their officers. We are also indebted to the many clinic administrators and staff who discussed their clinic operations with us; to Dr. Claire Brindis, who collected the survey data in the San Francisco site; and to the thousands of students who completed questionnaires.

testing and counseling, referral for prenatal care, nutrition education, weight reduction programs, and counseling for substance abuse. A few dispense contraceptives, offer prenatal care on site, and provide day care for children of students. School-based clinics are well used by students in the schools they serve. On the average, about half the students in each school enroll in the clinics; that is, they complete a registration form and obtain parental permission. In some schools the proportion is much higher. About 8 in 10 of those enrolled actually use the clinics' services. For almost half of those enrolled, school-based clinics are the sole or primary source of health care (Kirby & Lovick, 1989).

Relatively little research has been done on the clinics' impact upon student sexual behaviors, partly because most of the growth in school-based clinics has occurred in the last few years. A few studies, however, provide some evidence that clinics can have a positive impact in this area.

The most widely quoted findings are those based upon the St. Paul clinics (Edwards, Steinman, Arnold, & Hakanson, 1980). The investigators reported substantial proportions of students using the clinics for reproductive health services, remarkably high contraceptive continuation rates, and large decreases in birth rates. Because of data limitations, however, it is not clear whether a real decline in birth rates occurred; a more recent study of the St. Paul clinics used more valid methods of estimating birth rates and did not reveal a significant impact upon birth rates (Kirby et al., in press).

Additional evidence for the effectiveness of school-linked services was found in a study examining an experimental pregnancy prevention program that combined classroom presentations and counseling in two inner-city Baltimore schools with reproductive health services provided to the students at a nearby clinic (Zabin, Hirsch, Smith, Street, & Hardy, 1986). That study is described more fully in this volume.

As the school-based clinic movement stood on the brink of its third decade, however, it was appropriate to assess more definitively than before the impact of these clinics upon students' use of reproductive health services and sexual risk-taking behaviors. Thus in 1984 the Center for Population Options began an evaluation of a diverse group of clinics located in different parts of the country. The project sought to assess the students' utilization of clinic services and the clinics' impact upon use of medical services generally. It also sought to determine what, if any, effect the clinics had upon students' absenteeism, illegal drug use, alcohol consumption, cigarette smoking, sexual activity, use of birth control methods, and pregnancy. This chapter focuses upon the reproductive health services of school-based clinics and their impact upon sexual and contraceptive behaviors as shown by that study.

The Sample of Clinics

When the clinics were selected in 1984-1985, clinics were operating in only 17 cities or communities. Thus the selected clinics represented about one-third of the sites known at that time. The selected clinics were in high schools in Gary, Indiana; San Francisco, California; Muskegon, Michigan; Jackson, Mississippi; Quincy, Florida; and Dallas, Texas. Thus they were located in different parts of the country, in both rural and urban communities, and in different political and cultural milieus. The remaining sites were excluded because (a) the school clinics did not serve sufficiently large proportions of the student population to have a significant impact upon the student population schoolwide, (b) they were participating in other evaluation projects that might conflict with this one, (c) approval could not be obtained from the school boards, or (d) various logistical arrangements could not be completed in time for participation.

Some of the characteristics of the clinics are summarized in Table 8.1. By definition, all of the clinics were located on school grounds. The only partial exception is the Quincy clinic. After being located on campus for 18 months, the clinic (that was housed in a trailer) was moved about 100 yards across a small dirt road that led to the school parking lot. Thus the clinic became technically off campus, but it remained physically accessible to students who could obtain passes from teachers or others to attend the clinic during the school day. This evaluation covers both the 18 months when it was on campus and the following 6 months when it was adjacent to campus. (Data collected after the clinic was open for 12 months and still on campus were nearly identical to those collected after the clinic was open for 24 months and across the road.)

All six clinics served low-income populations with large percentages of minority students. In five of the six schools the students were predominantly black, but the San Francisco student body also had substantial proportions of Hispanic and Asian students. Four of the clinics had been open for at least 3 years before the study; the Dallas clinic had been open for 14 years. The two remaining clinics, Quincy and San Francisco, opened after the study began and, consequently, the

Table 8.1 Characteristics of Schools and School-Based Clinics, by Site

	Gary	San Francisco	Muske-gon	Jackson	Quincy	Dallas
School						
Enrollment[a]	1700	1800	800	700	800	1100
Racial/ethnic composition (%)[b]						
Black	98	30	94	99	89	76
Hispanic	1	20	1	0	0	21
Filipino	0	37	0	0	0	2
White	0	3	4	0	11	1
Other	1	10	1	1	0	0
Total	100	100	100	100	100	100
Clinic						
Date opened	1981	1985	1981	1979	1986	1970
Staff						
Physician	2[c]	1[c]	1[c]	1[c]	1[c]	2[d]
Nurse practitioner	1	1	2[c]	1[c]	1	2
Nurse	0	0	0	1[c]	0	1
Nurse assistant	0	0	0	0	0	2
Secretary/receptionist	1	1	1[c]	0	1	2
Social worker	1	2[c]	0	0	1[c]	1
Health educator	0	1	1	1[c]	0	0
Family planning services						
Sexuality education in classroom	No	Yes	Yes	No	No	No
Strong AIDS education program in classroom	No	Yes	No	No	No	No
Strong focus on pregnancy prevention	No	No	Yes	Yes	Yes	No
Pregnancy testing/counseling	Yes	Yes	Yes	Yes	Yes	Yes
Contraceptive counseling	Yes	Yes	Yes	Yes	Yes	Yes
Contraceptive prescriptions	No	No	Yes[e]	Yes	Yes	Yes
Contraceptive dispensation	No	No	No	Yes	Yes	Yes
Effective contraception follow-up system	na	na	No	Yes	Yes	No

NOTE: [a]Approximate enrollment at time of study.
[b]Based on Student Health Survey data.
[c]Parttime.
[d]One full-time, one part-time.
[e]Vouchers were issued to obtain contraception at a nearby family planning clinic.
na = not applicable

first 2 years of their operation were assessed. All the clinics were staffed by part-time or full-time physicians and part-time or full-time nurse-

practitioners. The size of the staff, however, varied considerably from
10 full-time staff and 2 part-time staff at the Dallas clinic to 4-6 mostly
part-time staff at the other sites. All the clinics provided primary health
care, and all provided both contraceptive counseling and pregnancy
tests. They differed considerably, however, in their emphasis upon
reproductive health and their provision of sexuality education and
family planning services.

Gary

The Gary clinic placed more emphasis upon providing information
and counseling and less emphasis upon treating medical problems or
writing prescriptions. Increasing the use of birth control methods and
reducing pregnancy were not its major goals. In the past, the clinic did
not raise issues of family planning with the students, but if the students
mentioned the subject or asked questions, the clinic provided students
with information and counseling, conducted pelvic exams if appropriate, and referred students to other family planning providers. Contraceptives were not prescribed or dispensed at the clinic itself.

San Francisco

The San Francisco clinic gave more emphasis to preventing the
spread of AIDS and STDs more generally and to preventing pregnancy.
It developed excellent AIDS education and sexuality education programs; the former included a presentation by a charismatic person with
AIDS who talked to each class for an hour. According to the staff,
students were quite moved by the speaker and voluntarily sent him
letters. The clinic educator gave many presentations in the classrooms
on sexuality education, trained about 20 peer counselors, and counseled
a few students in the clinic each day.

Despite its emphasis upon reducing AIDS and unintended pregnancy,
the clinic did not prescribe or dispense contraceptives. When students
asked for condoms, they were referred to other sources. Condoms were
readily available in the community, both at drugstores and at a community health clinic about 1 1/2 miles away. Even though the clinic staff
did not prescribe contraceptives, they did strongly encourage students
who were having sex to use condoms (and sometimes pills in addition).

All of the clinic and school AIDS activities were greatly reinforced
by the larger San Francisco community. San Francisco, which had one

of the highest rates of AIDS, implemented a variety of media and other public health programs to reduce the transmission of the AIDS virus, and subsequently experienced a major decline in the transmission of the AIDS virus. Thus students were exposed to a wide variety of public health campaigns promoting the use of condoms as a way of preventing the disease, including the presentation of factual information on television and in posters, with fairly graphic demonstrations of proper use of condoms. Other clinics in the community, both public and private, made it a policy to give condoms to anyone requesting them, without having to register or complete any forms.

Muskegon

Because of the high pregnancy rate in the Muskegon high school, both the Muskegon school and clinic devoted considerable attention to pregnancy prevention issues. This was the only school clinic in the country administered by Planned Parenthood. The school health teacher discussed teenage pregnancy and STDs for about 2 to 3 weeks in the classroom. The clinic staff also implemented or coordinated a variety of additional sexuality education programs in the school. In the clinic itself, clinic staff did not prescribe or dispense contraceptives, but they did provide consultation and education, conduct pelvic exams, and issue vouchers for birth control pills that enabled students to obtain pills at the Planned Parenthood clinic about a mile away. The education and counseling were thorough, but obtaining birth control pills often required four visits. Females could go directly to Planned Parenthood for pills, and males could obtain condoms there or purchase them in many neighborhood drugstores or gas station bathrooms, but unless they went through the school clinic, the services and contraceptives were not free of charge. Most of the high school students came from a nearby middle school, which had a clinic that provided education on sexuality and reproductive health.

Jackson

The high school provided little sex education in the school, but the Jackson clinic appeared to focus more upon high-risk students and risk-taking behaviors than did some of the other clinics. Sexually active students were identified during a psychosocial assessment completed during each student's first clinic visit. Appointments were made promptly with the nurse-practitioner for counseling about abstinence and birth control methods and then with the clinic physician who dispensed birth control pills and/or condoms. The clinic had an effective tickler (or reminder) system in place. If females using birth control pills did not return within 2 months for additional cycles of birth control pills, they were asked to come to the clinic.

Quincy

Because of the high pregnancy rates in the Quincy community, family planning was also given considerable emphasis in the Quincy clinic. The clinic staff gave some presentations in health classes and other classes about the clinic, sexuality, and health more generally but did not provide a complete sexuality unit to most students. In the clinic during routine clinic visits, if students gave any indication that they might be having sex, the nurse-practitioner probed to determine whether the student was having unprotected sex. If so, abstinence and family planning methods were discussed as appropriate, and appointments were made for birth control methods that were dispensed in the clinics. After the clinic had been in operation about 6 months, it implemented a tickler system to ensure that students returned for their family planning appointments. In general, these family planning protocols were quite thorough, but staff were insufficient to provide this care to large numbers of students.

Dallas

The oldest school-based clinic in the country, the Dallas clinic was also the largest in terms of both space and staffing. Unlike the other clinics in this study, the Dallas clinic served any adolescent, aged 12-18, regardless of whether that adolescent attended the home high school. All entering students were given appointments for a health maintenance exam, which included visits with the physician or nurse-practitioner, social worker, screening nurse, and dentist. During these visits, staff discussed a wide range of potential medical and psychosocial problems with the students. Issues involving sexuality were discussed at this time and during any other routine visit. Staff counseled students about abstinence and birth control and provided an appropriate method to females who wanted a contraceptive. No follow-up appointments were made, and no follow-up system was in place, but students were encouraged to return when they needed additional cycles.

Although these six clinics differed from one another, as a group they also differed in two important ways from the current population of school-based clinics. First, five of the clinics were located in predominately black schools, but nationally, school-based clinics currently serve larger white populations than those studied here. Second, three of the six clinics dispensed contraceptives, while less than 20% of school-based clinics across the country currently do so (Waszak & Neidall, 1992). These differences are important to consider when generalizing the findings reported here to the larger universe of school-based clinics; the six clinics are not a representative sample of current clinics, but they do constitute a heterogeneous group of clinics reflecting the diversity of clinics nationwide.

Research Methods

To assess the reproductive health services provided by the clinics and to evaluate the impact of those services, data were collected from two primary sources: clinic records and a student health survey. Site visits and interviews with staff provided additional information. Each clinic kept records of the number of clinic users, the number of clinic visits, the number and type of family planning visits, and, depending upon the particular clinic, the number of students given vouchers for contraceptives or the number of students given contraceptives. These data were collected for each academic year. The student health survey, which provided information on all the students in each school (or samples thereof), included questions about use of the clinic that could be compared with the clinic record data, as well as questions about sexual and contraceptive behavior that could be used to measure the impact of the clinic. These data were typically collected at the end of each academic year.

To evaluate the impact of each clinic, it was necessary to provide some means of comparing student populations in schools with clinics to student populations without clinics. Random assignment to treatment and control conditions (clinic and nonclinic schools) was obviously not possible. Therefore quasi-experimental procedures for comparison were implemented. For each of the four schools with clinics operating at the initiation of the project—Gary, Muskegon, Jackson, and Dallas—a treatment group, comparison group posttest only design was employed. Comparison schools were identified that were as similar as possible to

the clinic schools with respect to relevant sociodemographic characteristics and as geographically close as possible. In Dallas, Jackson, and
Gary, schools with reasonably well-matched student populations were
nearby. In Muskegon, the nearest school with a well-matched population was almost 90 miles away. A major limitation of "posttest only"
quasi-experimental designs is that pretest differences may have existed.
Procedures to measure and control for these differences are discussed
further below.

The remaining two schools included in the evaluation—Quincy and
San Francisco—had not yet opened their clinics when the research
study began, and therefore it was possible to use a pretest-posttest
design, though it was not possible to obtain comparison data from
different schools nearby. Preclinic baseline data were collected, as well
as 2-year post data. In these two schools, this was not a longitudinal
study in which the same students were surveyed both times; rather the
survey data provided a cross-sectional "snapshot" of the student population before the clinic opened and a second snapshot 2 years later.

The sampling frame varied from school to school; in most schools it
was the entire student body, but in the Gary and San Francisco schools,
with 1,700 students or more, samples of classes, stratified by grade level
and level of instruction, were selected.

Procedures for obtaining parental consent for survey participation
varied from school to school. At most schools, parents were notified in
writing and given the opportunity to exclude their child's participation
(passive consent). Because fewer than five parents in each of the
schools at these sites did so, this would not have produced any bias. In
San Francisco, consent procedures changed from passive consent for
the baseline survey to active consent for the second survey. Various
problems (including an immediate deadline) prevented substantial numbers of students from obtaining written consent. In Jackson the need to
obtain active parental consent reduced the sample size in both the clinic
and comparison schools, but the comparability of the samples from the
clinic and the comparison schools should not have been compromised,
because both schools required the same procedure.

In Gary, Jackson, and Dallas the survey was administered first in one
school and then immediately in the other. In Muskegon the survey was
administered first in the clinic school and then about 6 months later in
the comparison school. Finally, in both Quincy and San Francisco the
preclinic and postclinic surveys were administered almost exactly 2
years apart.

The survey was a comprehensive health survey designed to measure sociodemographic characteristics, clinic use, utilization of medical services in general, risk-taking behaviors, sexual activity, use of contraception, and pregnancy. Different versions of this questionnaire were used at different sites, but all versions contained a set of common questions on sexual behaviors analyzed in this chapter.

The survey questions on sexuality included questions used in previous studies. They were pretested with three five-member groups of students for comprehension and clarity of items. To measure the test-retest reliability of items, it was administered twice, 2 weeks apart, to one group of 87 students. The test-retest coefficients of agreement and the correlation coefficients indicated that the items had adequate reliability (Kirby, Waszak, & Ziegler, 1989).

It is also believed that the data on sexual activity and use of birth control were valid. First, the survey data on sexual behavior and contraceptive use were consistent with previously published findings (Clark, Zabin, & Hardy, 1984). Second, survey data on use of the clinic for contraceptives were also consistent with clinic record data.

Pregnancy data, however, should be interpreted cautiously. Some students may not wish to report a previous pregnancy (particularly if it ended in abortion), and a few teenagers may define a previous pregnancy as a pregnancy as such only if it resulted in a live birth. In addition, some of the teenagers who conceived while in high school subsequently dropped out and were not present to complete the survey. Nevertheless, it is not expected that reporting biases differentially affect either the clinic-school or nonclinic-school samples, except possibly in Jackson where the day-care program may have increased the percentage of student mothers who remained in school.

Table 8.2 presents the percentages of students completing the questionnaires out of the total enrollment. The response rates were reduced by (a) intentional sampling of students in Gary and San Francisco; (b) the need to obtain active parental consent in Jackson and San Francisco; (c) inflated enrollment figures, which retained names of dropouts at some of the sites; (d) high rates of absenteeism at most of the sites; and (e) the exclusion of educable mentally disabled students who may not have been able to complete the questionnaire reliably.

The response rates, based upon the number of students who actually attended class the day of the survey and who had parental permission to participate, ranged from 90% to 98%. Thus the survey data should be representative of those students who attended class the day of the

Table 8.2 Survey Sample Sizes by Site

	Gary		San Francisco		Muskegon		Jackson		Quincy		Dallas	
	Non-clinic	Clinic	Pre-clinic	Post-clinic	Non-clinic	Clinic	Non-clinic	Clinic	Pre-clinic	Post-clinic	Non-clinic	Clinic
Students enrolled in school	1900	1700	2050	1789	1683	802	1120	708	767	815	1469	1129
Usable questionnaires	667[a]	668[a]	892[a]	433[a]	1177	480	565	317	608[b]	731[b]	918	524
Percentage of total enrollment[c]	35	41	44	24	70	60	50	45	79	90	62	46

NOTE: [a] A representative sample of classes were selected to intentionally reduce the completed sample size.
[b] In Quincy, questionnaires were collected only from grades 10 through 12.
[c] The response rates, based on the number of students who actually attended class the day of the survey and who had parental permission to participate, ranged from 90% to 98%.

195

survey and had parental permission. The survey data may not be representative, however, of students who were absent, especially those who were frequently absent for reasons other than occasional illness. Once again, it is not expected that this bias will affect either clinic or nonclinic schools disproportionately.

Although the comparison schools in Gary, Muskegon, Jackson, and Dallas were selected to resemble the clinic schools as closely as possible, the schools being compared differed in some social and demographic characteristics. Similarly, in San Francisco and Quincy some differences existed between the baseline and 2-year samples. Therefore, in the outcome data in the survey results reported below, the samples were modified to make the clinic and nonclinic samples more similar in terms of background characteristics. First, in the five sites that had very large percentages of black students in the schools (all sites except San Francisco), all nonblack students were removed from the analysis; this made the clinic and nonclinic samples identical with respect to race and also eliminated any possible interaction effects between race and outcome variables. Second, in San Francisco the 2-year posttest data were weighted so that its racial composition was equivalent to that of the baseline sample. After these two modifications were incorporated, the clinic-school and comparison-school samples did not differ significantly on a large majority of the background characteristics. Where difference did exist, they suggested that students in the comparison schools were slightly more advantaged in terms of employment, welfare, and family structure than were students in the clinic schools.

To further control for any possible impact of these remaining differences upon outcome variables, multiple regression was employed. The regression coefficients reported in the tables below measure the relationship between being in a clinic school and various outcome variables, statistically controlling for the following carefully selected background characteristics: age, number of patients, receipt of food stamps, receipt of free lunches, grade point average, and future academic plans.

The communities in which the schools were located might also have varied in ways that would have different effects upon the clinic and comparison schools. In Gary, Jackson, and Dallas the clinic schools and their respective comparison schools were reasonably close to one another and had no known programs that would have had a major impact upon the students.

At three sites, however, the issue of possible confounding factors was more complex. In Quincy, before the school-based clinic opened, students received passes from the school to attend a nearby public health clinic that provided reproductive care. When that clinic moved several miles away, students could no longer attend that clinic, and the public health department opened the school clinic. Thus in that site, this study measured the impact of services provided at the school versus services provided several blocks away.

In San Francisco the community changed quite dramatically during the 2 years covered by this evaluation. AIDS became a far more salient issue, and the community implemented numerous programs to reduce the transmission of the AIDS virus. Moreover, condom use increased substantially among adolescents nationwide during this time (Sonenstein, Peck, & Ku, 1989), and it could be expected that this increase would occur where AIDS was a prominent health issue. In Muskegon the comparison school was 90 miles away, and it is difficult to know in what ways the communities might have differed. Moreover, the Muskegon surveys were administered at the clinic and nonclinic schools at two different times of the year—in the spring and fall, respectively. Therefore in these two communities it is more difficult to attribute clinic school and comparison (or preclinic) school differences to the school clinics.

Results: Services Provided

These school-based clinics were comprehensive clinics designed to provide a variety of needed health services to adolescents. Both clinic records and the survey data confirmed that the clinics did provide a large amount of health care. In five of the sites at least 60% of the students had previously used the clinic, and in Dallas 83% had done so. Only in the San Francisco school had only 48% of the students ever used the clinic (that had been open only 2 years). Furthermore, in four of the sites at least 63% of the students used the clinic during the preceding year. In four of the sites students made about 2,400 to 4,400 visits per year. Muskegon counted only 1,859 visits, while Dallas counted 4,489 student visits plus an additional 6,000 visits by adolescents not attending the Dallas home school. Of those students who used the clinics, about half visited them one or two times per year.

As discussed above, clinics varied in the extent to which they addressed reproductive health. This is demonstrated by the proportion of total visits to the clinic that were for reproductive health and by the

Table 8.3 Total Number of Clinic Visits and Percentage Made for Reproductive Health Care, by Type of Care, According to Site

	Gary	San Francisco	Muske-gon	Jackson	Quincy	Dallas
Total number of visits	2791	2357	1859	3341	4399	4489[a]
Visits for reproductive health care (%)	15	9	27	37	30	38
General gynecology	1	2	na	4	3	12
Contraceptive counseling, prescription, and/or dispensation	8	4	25	28	24	14
Pregnancy test	2	2	2	3	na	8
Prenatal care	na	na	na	2	3	3
STD testing	4	1	na	na	na	1

NOTE: Based on clinic records; na = not applicable.
[a]Visits from students at clinic school; another 6,000 visits were from other adolescents.

proportion of all students in the school who used the clinic for such services. Of all the visits, between 9% and 38% were for reproductive health in general; the proportions of visits specifically for family planning were much smaller and reflected the types of services available (Table 8.3). In the Gary and San Francisco clinics, which did not prescribe or dispense contraceptives, 8% and 4% of the visits respectively were for contraceptive counseling and referral; in Muskegon, which provided vouchers for contraceptives, the proportion of visits for contraception was 25%; and in Jackson, Dallas, and Quincy, which dispensed contraceptives, the proportions ranged from 14% to 28%. These percentages indicate that reproductive health services were an important component of those clinics providing vouchers for or dispensing contraceptives. Yet these data also demonstrate that these clinics were not primarily family planning clinics—between 62% and 91% of the visits were not for reproductive health.

The proportions of students using the clinics for contraceptive services also varied greatly according to the services available. In Gary and San Francisco, which did not dispense contraceptives, only 5% and 3% of the students respectively used the clinic for contraceptive counseling. In contrast, 21% of the Muskegon students used the clinic for contraceptive counseling, and 17% of the students obtained contraceptive vouchers from the clinic; in Jackson, Quincy, and Dallas, between 22% and 26% of the students obtained contraceptives from the clinic.

In the four schools that provided contraceptives (or vouchers) the proportion of sexually experienced female students who obtained contraceptives through the clinic varied from 23% ($N = 67$) in Muskegon to 32% ($N = 154$) in Quincy, 39% ($N = 111$) in Jackson, and 40% ($N = 182$) in Dallas. The proportion of sexually experienced males in those schools who obtained condoms from the clinics ranged from 12% ($N = 41$) in Muskegon to 18% ($N = 93$) in Quincy. The proportions for males are lower than those for females, probably because condoms could be obtained without a doctor's prescription and because efforts to increase use of contraceptives focused upon females.

These percentages should be viewed cautiously. Although the numerator includes all students who ever used the clinic for contraception, some of them may have used the clinic only a small number of times, and probably only a small percentage of these students received continuous contraceptive coverage through the clinic. Thus the numerator may overestimate coverage of the students. On the other hand, the denominator includes all sexually experienced students, even those who had sex only once and did not subsequently need contraception. Consequently it may underestimate the clinics' coverage of those students who continued to have sex.

An analysis of clinic records indicated that a substantial percentage of female students who obtained birth control pills either did not return to the clinic for prescriptions for subsequent cycles of pills or did not return in time to allow continuous contraceptive coverage for 6 months or more. They may have stopped having sex, graduated from school or left school for other reasons, obtained contraceptives elsewhere, or simply had unprotected sex.

Impact upon Sexual Activity

The data from the student health survey were used to assess the impact of the school-based clinics upon sexual activity among students at their respective schools. Three questions concerned sexual activity: "Have you ever had sex?" and if yes, "How old were you when you first had sex?" and "How many times have you had sex within the past 4 weeks?" The resulting data were first analyzed using percentages and either chi-square tests or t tests of significance (Table 8.4); then multiple regression was used to control for respondents' background characteristics (Table 8.5).

Table 8.4 Measures of Sexual Activity Among High School Students, by Gender, According to Site and Presence of Clinic[a]

Measure and Gender	Gary Non-clinic	Gary Clinic	San Francisco Pre-clinic	San Francisco Post-clinic	Muskegon Non-clinic	Muskegon Clinic	Jackson Non-clinic	Jackson Clinic	Quincy Pre-clinic	Quincy Post-clinic	Dallas Non-clinic	Dallas Clinic
Ever had sex												
Males												
%	87	82	63	58	93	91	93	96	92	91	92	87
N	294	274	426	204	432	183	242	119	315	235	432	175
Females												
%	60	63	37	46[c]	72	69	75	82	82	82	76	80
N	341	386	420	226	497	248	273	190	283	352	449	218
Age at first intercourse[b]												
Males												
Mean	12.7	12.5	13.3	13.3	u	u	11.5	12.0	11.7	11.9	11.4	12.4[d]
N	251	220	238	115	u	u	218	110	286	206	379	148
Females												
Mean	14.8	14.4	15.0	14.8	u	u	14.3	14.8[d]	14.3	14.3	14.4	14.4
N	201	238	145	101	u	u	196	153	230	285	334	168
Frequency of sex in last 4 weeks[b]												
Males												
Mean	2.8	2.6	2.9	2.4	4.2	3.7	3.7	3.6	3.3	3.8	3.2	3.2
N	246	222	247	110	382	156	221	109	272	202	375	137
Females												
Mean	1.8	2.1	3.3	2.1	2.6	2.5	2.8	2.2	2.5	2.9	2.2	2.5
N	197	239	151	98	346	166	196	148	223	280	316	164

NOTE: [a]To control for race, the results in Tables 8.4 to 8.9 for all sites except San Francisco are weighted to equal the racial distribution of the preclinic sample. For San Francisco, the postclinic data are based on blacks only.
[b]In this measure and in subsequent tables, analysis restricted to sexually active students.
[c]Difference significant at $p < .05$, as determined by χ^2 test.
[d]Difference significant at $p < .01$, as determined by t test.
u = unavailable.

Table 8.5 Unstandardized Regression Coefficients, by Measure of Sexual Activity and Gender, According to Site

Measure and Gender	Gary	San Francisco	Muske-gon	Jackson	Quincy	Dallas
Ever had sex						
Males						
Coefficient	−.05	−.08	−.02	.01	−.00	−.07[c]
N	558	589	596	353	538	595
Females						
Coefficient	.04	.11[a]	−.08[a]	.04	.01	.03
N	720	615	729	458	624	658
Age at first intercourse						
Males						
Coefficient	−.25	.09	u	.50	.05	.95[c]
N	464	332	u	321	481	521
Females						
Coefficient	.09	−.01	u	.32	.13	.03
N	435	230	u	345	505	498
Frequency of sex in last 4 weeks						
Males						
Coefficient	−.16	−.79	−.42	−.56	.22	.08
N	461	332	521	322	463	507
Females						
Coefficient	.35	−.99	−.32	−.68	.21	.03
N	432	234	500	340	495	476

NOTE: See Note [a] in Table 8.4. The following background variables were statistically controlled in the regression equation: gender, age, grade point average, plans for school future, family receipt of food stamps, receipt of free lunch, and number of parents in the household.
[a]Difference between clinic and nonclinic school significant at $p < .05$, as determined by "change in F" test.
[b]Difference between clinic and nonclinic school significant at $p < .01$, as determined by "change in F" test.
[c]Difference between clinic and nonclinic school significant at $p < .001$, at determined by "change in F" test.
u = unavailable.

Ever Had Sex

When the percentages of students in the clinic schools who had ever had sex were compared with the percentages of students in their non-clinic comparison schools, the data revealed that in four of the sites no differences existed for either males or females that approached statistical significance (Table 8.4). In the San Francisco site, however, female students (but not male students) were more likely to have ever had sex

2 years after the clinic opened than before the clinic opened ($p = .04$). (Notably the San Francisco site neither prescribed nor dispensed contraceptives.) In the Dallas site male students in the clinic school were less likely to have ever had sex than their male counterparts in the comparison school, but the difference fell just short of significance ($p = .06$).

When the background characteristics of the respondents were statistically controlled using regression analysis, again no significant differences were found between the clinic and nonclinic comparison schools in three of the sites. This time, in both the San Francisco and Dallas sites, the differences discussed above were statistically significant. In addition, in Muskegon the regression coefficient revealed that, after controlling for background characteristics, a significantly smaller percentage of female students in the clinic school than in the comparison school had ever had sex.

Results discussed below on the mean age at first intercourse revealed that many of the students surveyed were sexually experienced before entering high school. Because it is unlikely that the school-based clinics affected the sexual activity of the students before they attended the clinic schools, an additional analysis was performed that excluded those students who were sexually experienced before entering high school and that merged the male and female samples (to increase the sample size). Regression analyses (not shown) indicated no differences between the clinic and nonclinic schools in the percentages of students who had become sexually experienced after entering high school.

Age at First Intercourse

The analyses of age at first intercourse and frequency of intercourse were limited to sexually experienced students. In two sites statistically significant differences were found when mean ages of first intercourse were compared using t tests (Table 8.4); using regression analyses (that statistically controlled for background characteristics as previously described), these differences in age remained significant at Dallas but were not quite significant ($p = .06$) at Jackson (Table 8.5). Among the Jackson females the mean age of first intercourse was 14.8 years at the clinic school compared with 14.3 years at the comparison school, while among males in Dallas the mean age was 12.4 years at the clinic school compared with 11.4 years at the comparison school. Similar differences were found among the males at Jackson, but the results were not statistically significant.

Frequency of Intercourse

Neither *t* tests nor multiple regression produced significant differences between the clinic schools and their comparison schools at any site in the frequency of sexual activity during the 4 weeks prior to the survey.

In sum, these data indicate that neither the presence of school-based clinics nor the provision of contraceptive counseling and contraceptives hastened the onset of sexual activity or increased sexual activity. In most cases no statistically significant differences were found; where differences were significant, they were usually in the opposite direction, indicating that the clinics may have delayed sexual activity.

Impact upon Contraceptive Use

The impact of the clinics upon students' use of birth control was measured by asking those students who were sexually experienced whether they or their partner had used any method of birth control at last intercourse (including rhythm or withdrawal), and more specifically whether they had used specific methods of birth control. The results were analyzed first with percentages and either chi-square tests or *t* tests of significance (Table 8.6) and then with multiple regression to control for background characteristics (Table 8.7).

Any Method of Birth Control

Neither analysis found significant differences between the clinic schools and the matched nonclinic schools in Gary, San Francisco, Jackson, and Quincy. In Muskegon, however, both the percentages and the regression coefficients revealed that both the males and the females in the clinic school were significantly more likely to have used some method of birth control the last time they had sex than were the males and females in the comparison school ($p < .001$). In Dallas, females in the clinic school were less likely to have used some method of birth control the last time they had sex than were the females in the comparison school ($p < .05$). This resulted primarily from more use of rhythm and withdrawal by students at the comparison school (data not shown).

Table 8.6 Measures of Contraceptive Use at Last Intercourse Among High School Students, by Gender, According to Site and Presence of Clinic

Measure and Gender	Gary Non-clinic	Gary Clinic	San Francisco Pre-clinic	San Francisco Post-clinic	Muskegon Non-clinic	Muskegon Clinic	Jackson Non-clinic	Jackson Clinic	Quincy Pre-clinic	Quincy Post-clinic	Dallas Non-clinic	Dallas Clinic
Used any method												
Males												
%	69	65	65	74	61	78[c]	58	60	70	73	68	60
N	242	221	256	117	387	165	222	113	210	287	389	144
Females												
%	61	68	67	75	60	75[c]	61	70	74	81	74	63[a]
N	202	239	150	104	358	168	199	153	230	287	333	169
Used condom												
Males												
%	52	48	29	56[c]	41	61[c]	39	40	57	53	33	36
N	242	221	256	117	387	165	222	110	210	287	389	144
Females												
%	27	31	22	38[c]	22	29	25	20	46	48	18	16
N	202	240	150	104	358	168	199	153	230	287	333	169
Used the pill												
Males												
%	10	12	17	24	10	10	18	15	23	28	15	9
N	242	221	257	117	387	165	222	110	210	287	389	144
Females												
%	23	30	18	25	27	36[b]	30	46[a]	29	36	32	30
N	202	240	157	104	358	168	199	153	230	287	333	169

NOTE: See Note [a] in Tables 8.4 and 8.5.

[a] Difference significant at $p < .05$, as determined by χ^2 test.

[b] Difference significant at $p < .01$, as determined by χ^2 test.

[c] Difference significant at $p < .001$, as determined by χ^2 test.

[d] In this table, condom use reported by females and pill use reported by males refers to use by their partners.

Table 8.7 Unstandardized Regression Coefficients, by Contraceptive Use at Last Intercourse and Gender, According to Site

Contraceptive Use and Gender	Gary	San Francisco	Muske-gon	Jackson	Quincy	Dallas
Used any method						
Males						
Coefficient	−.04	.08	.18[c]	.05	.00	−.08
N	456	346	534	327	485	527
Females						
Coefficient	.06	.07	.16[c]	.07	.02	−.10[a]
N	437	237	513	348	505	498
Use of condoms at last intercourse[d]						
Males						
Coefficient	−.04	.27[c]	.20[c]	.06	−.03	.05
N	458	346	534	314	486	527
Females						
Coefficient	.05	.16[b]	.10[a]	−.04	.01	−.00
N	439	237	514	350	505	498
Use of pills at last intercourse[d]						
Males						
Coefficient	.02	.04	.00	−.03	.01	−.07[a]
N	458	346	534	314	486	527
Females						
Coefficient	.04	.07	.08	.13[a]	.03	−.05
N	439	237	513	345	505	498

NOTE: See Note in Table 8.4 and 8.5.
[a]Difference between clinic and nonclinic school significant at $p < .05$, as determined by "change in F" test.
[b]Difference between clinic and nonclinic school significant at $p < .01$, as determined by "change in F" test.
[c]Difference between clinic and nonclinic school significant at $p < .001$, as determined by "change in F" test.
[d]In this table, condom use reported by females and pill use reported by males refers to use by their partners.

Condoms

Neither chi-square analysis nor multiple regression found significant differences at Gary, Jackson, Quincy, or Dallas. Both chi-square analysis and regression analysis, however, revealed significant differences at two sites. In San Francisco, 2 years after the clinic opened, both males and females reported significantly greater use of condoms than they did before the clinic opened. The percentage of males using condoms increased from

29% to 56%, an increase of 27 percentage points ($p < .001$), and the percentage of females reporting their partners used condoms increased from 22% to 38%, an increase of 16 percentage points ($p < .001$). In Muskegon the greater use of any method of birth control in the clinic school was due primarily to a greater use of condoms as reported by males; in the clinic school 61% of the males reported using condoms the last time they had sex, while in the comparison school only 41% of the males reported using condoms, a difference of 20 percentage points ($p < .001$). The multiple regression analysis also indicated that the females in the Muskegon clinic school were more likely to report partner use of condoms than did females at the comparison school.

The Pill

The data from Gary, San Francisco, Quincy, and Dallas revealed no significant differences between the clinic and nonclinic (or preclinic) schools. Moreover, chi-square tests found no significant difference at any site in the proportion of males reporting their partners used the pill. The proportion of females who reported using the pill at last intercourse, however, was higher in the clinic school than in the nonclinic school in Muskegon (36% versus 27%; $p < .05$) and in Jackson (46% versus 30%; $p < .01$).

The regression results were somewhat different. The difference in pill use among females remained significant in Jackson ($p = .02$) but not in Muskegon ($p = .07$). In Dallas the proportion of males who reported that their partner was using the pill at last intercourse was significantly lower in the clinic school than in the comparison school ($p = .03$).

In sum, clinic presence was positively associated with greater use of any method of birth control among both males and females in only one site—Muskegon—and was negatively associated with use of any method of birth control among females in Dallas. When specific methods of birth control were examined, significant differences were found at several sites. In either the percentage results or regression results or both, clinic presence was associated with greater use of condoms as reported by both males and females in San Francisco and Muskegon and with greater pill use as reported by females in Jackson and Muskegon. No significant relationships were found between clinic presence and either condom or pill use in Gary or Quincy, nor were significant relationships found between clinic presence and pill use in San Francisco or condom use in Jackson or Dallas.

These findings are consistent with program efforts in some of these sites: the San Francisco program focused upon AIDS and condom use, the Muskegon program emphasized sexuality education in the classroom and family planning in the clinic, and the Jackson clinic emphasized birth control pills for high-risk sexually experienced females.

Clinic Users and Nonusers

In Jackson, Dallas, and Quincy, comparisons were also made between students in the clinic schools who had used the clinic for contraception and students in the same schools who had not used the clinics for contraception. In all three sites students who used the clinic for contraceptives were significantly more likely to have used an effective method of birth control (condoms or pills) the last time they had sex than were students who did not use the clinic for contraceptives. Nevertheless, in all three sites substantial percentages of students who had not used the clinic for contraceptives used effective methods of birth control.

In Jackson 77% of the students ever using the clinic to obtain contraceptives used an effective method at last intercourse, compared with 48% of the students who had not used the clinic to obtain contraceptives. In Quincy the respective user and nonuser figures were 76% and 61%, while in Dallas they were 67% and 32%. The regression analyses controlling for background characteristics confirmed the significance of these findings (not shown).

These results should be interpreted cautiously, however, because they are undoubtedly strongly affected by a self-selection effect. The students attending the clinic for contraceptives probably were more highly motivated individuals who would have used some type of contraception even if they had to go elsewhere to obtain it. The clinic program simply provided the opportunity for these students to go to the clinic for contraceptives instead of going elsewhere.

Alternative Sources of Contraceptives

The findings thus far have shown that at those sites where contraceptives were prescribed or dispensed, substantial percentages of sexually experienced students used the clinics for contraceptives and that students who used the clinics for contraceptives were significantly more likely to use effective contraceptives the last time they had sex than were students who did not use the clinic for family planning. This difference raises the puzzling question: Why didn't all the clinics prescribing and dispensing contraceptives demonstrate a larger impact upon the contraceptive behavior of sexually experienced students in their respective schools?

The results of another analysis indicate that the primary reason the clinics did not demonstrate a stronger and more consistent impact upon contraceptive use lies in provider substitution (Table 8.8). In Gary and San Francisco, where the clinics did not provide contraceptives, students in the clinic and nonclinic schools found alternative sources of contraception, especially drugstores. In Muskegon, Jackson, and Dallas, students in the clinic schools were less likely than students in the comparison schools to obtain contraceptives from a community family planning clinic or drugstore. In Quincy, after the clinic opened in the school, a dramatic drop (from 35% to 7%) occurred in the percentage of sexually experienced students who obtained contraceptives from the health department.

In order to further investigate this substitution effect, students at the clinic schools in Muskegon, Jackson, and Dallas were asked where they would go to get contraceptives if the school had no clinic. Though their responses were hypothetical, between 78% and 85% of the students at each site claimed they would find another source—another clinic, a doctor, or the drugstore. Between 6% and 13% reported they would have sex without contraception, and 4% to 5% reported they would refrain from sexual intercourse if the school had no clinic. Males in all three sites were more likely to plan to have sex without using contraception than were females.

In Quincy, where the health department was moved from a site near the school to a site farther away from the school grounds when the school clinic opened, an examination of the school clinic records and health department records during the first year after the opening of the school clinic revealed that a nearly even shift of about 100 female clients from the health department to the school clinic occurred. Though undoubtedly these were not the same 100 students, this shift does indicate that the school clinic did absorb those health department clients who were students and is consistent with the survey findings reported above.

Additional information available from the Quincy sample in the postclinic survey demonstrated that sexually experienced students who

Table 8.8 Percentages of Sexually Active Students, by Source of Contraceptives Used at Last Intercourse, According to Site and Presence of Clinic

	Gary		San Francisco		Muskegon		Jackson		Quincy		Dallas	
Source	Non-clinic (432)	Clinic (443)	Pre-clinic (384)	Post-clinic (207)	Non-clinic (663)	Clinic (333)	Non-clinic (422)	Clinic (259)	Pre-clinic (709)	Post-clinic (552)	Non-clinic (709)	Clinic (306)
School clinic	na	na	na	na	na	17[a]	na	30	na	34	na	30
Family planning clinic	14	18	7	7	20	13	15	10	b	b	18	5
Doctor	5	9	b	b	5	10	7	5	b	b	b	b
Health department	b	b	b	b	b	b	b	b	35	7	b	b
Hospital clinic	1	1	4	9	3	3	5	1	b	b	4	1
Drugstore	32	26	18	27	12	9	19	9	15	15	12	5
Friend/relative	6	7	6	10	10	15	9	8	9	6	11	2
Other	1	2	2	1	1	2	1	1	3	2	1	2
Not applicable: used withdrawal or rhythm	5	2	21	10	10	7	3	1	7	10	19	13
Used no method	36	35	36	26	39	24	41	35	28	24	30	39

NOTE: See Note in Table 8.4.

[a]Received vouchers that were redeemed at local family planning clinic.

[b]Information not collected at those locations.

na = not applicable.

typically obtained their contraceptives from the school clinic were not more likely to have used some form of birth control the last time they had sex than were sexually experienced students who typically obtained their contraceptives from the drugstore, doctor, or health department.

Reasons for Not Using Contraceptives

The failure of some clinic sites to increase the use of contraception among students is also partially explained by an analysis of the reasons why students had previously had sex without birth control. Sexually experienced students at four sites—Gary, Jackson, Dallas, and San Francisco—were asked whether they had ever had intercourse without using birth control and, if so, why. They were asked to indicate all the reasons that might apply to their past behavior. Students in the clinic school were not significantly less likely to check any of the potential reasons for failing to use birth control than were students in the comparison school. That is, clinic presence did not appear to reduce the importance of any of the reasons.

The two most common reasons identified were "Didn't expect to have sex" and "Just didn't think pregnancy would occur." In both the clinic and nonclinic schools most of the reasons were not related to access to contraceptives but to the fact that sex was not anticipated or to perceptions of low risk of pregnancy. Some were related to lack of knowledge, some to fear of contraceptives or parents' reactions, and others to a desire not to reduce pleasure. No indication was obvious from these answers that sexually experienced students from the clinic schools were more knowledgeable about pregnancy prevention or more comfortable with contraceptive use than students in the comparison schools.

Impact upon Pregnancy

Students at all six sites were asked whether they had ever been pregnant or gotten someone pregnant and whether they had been pregnant or gotten someone pregnant within the last 12 months. The first question has the advantage that it can measure the impact of the clinic upon all the students' years at the clinic school and can measure pregnancies among those females who gave birth and returned to school, while the question about pregnancy during the last 12 months has the advantage that it is more likely to eliminate the small number of pregnancies that may have occurred prior to the students' coming to the clinic school.

Clinic presence was not associated with lower rates of pregnancy at any of the sites, either at any time or during the previous 12 months (Table 8.9). This was true both for the chi-square results based upon simple percentages and for the regression analyses (not shown). In one site—Dallas—the percentage of females who reported they had ever been pregnant was actually significantly higher in the clinic school than in the comparison school ($p = .02$). This difference was not significant, however, when background variables were controlled through regression analysis.

Timing of Pregnancies
vis-à-vis Clinic Use

In most of the sites, the student health survey asked students who had ever been pregnant (or gotten someone pregnant) whether they had ever used the school clinic, discussed contraception with clinic staff, or received contraceptives from the clinic prior to their pregnancy. The data in Table 8.10 indicate that across the six sites between 44% and 90% of the pregnancies occurred to students who had never attended the clinic. The Dallas clinic had the lowest percentages—44% of the females and 52% of the males—who had conceived prior to using the clinic, possibly because the clinic gave routine maintenance examinations to all incoming students. Even so, almost half of the pregnancies still occurred before any clinic use. Some of those pregnancies may have occurred prior to those students' attending the clinic high school, but this cannot be determined from the data.

Among all the clinics, between 62% and 89% of the reported pregnancies occurred prior to any type of contraceptive counseling with clinic staff, and between 68% and 89% occurred prior to receiving any type of contraceptives from the clinic. These data demonstrate the need for more aggressive outreach to bring students into the clinic before pregnancy occurs. About a fourth of the pregnancies occurred after the students had obtained contraceptives from the clinic—indicating the need for more effective follow-up.

text continued on page 214

Table 8.9 Percentages of High School Students Who Caused a Pregnancy or Experienced One, by Gender, According to Site and Presence of Clinic

Gender and Pregnancy Measure	Gary		San Francisco		Muskegon		Jackson		Quincy		Dallas	
	Non-clinic	Clinic	Pre-clinic	Post-clinic	Non-clinic	Clinic	Non-clinic	Clinic	Pre-clinic	Post-clinic	Non-clinic	Clinic
Males who ever caused a pregnancy												
%	14	17	16	12	13	12	12	18	11	7	11	18
N	238	216	248	110	363	163	221	112	209	271	354	117
Males who caused a pregnancy in last 12 months												
%	7	10	10	8	8	8	6	11	7	6	7	10
N	227	207	232	110	401	167	196	104	209	276	335	116
Females who were ever pregnant												
%	27	21	24	26	20	24	21	25	15	15	18	27
N	201	240	149	102	354	168	204	154	229	285	318	169
Females who were pregnant in the last 12 months												
%	20	11	16	16	14	15	12	14	10	8	10	14
N	196	235	147	101	360	172	196	151	228	280	315	169

NOTE: See Note in Table 8.4.
[a]Significant at $p < .05$, as determined by χ^2 tests.

Table 8.10 Percentages of Students at Clinic Schools Who Were Ever Pregnant (or Caused a Pregnancy) by Timing in Relation to Clinic Use, According to Site and Gender

	Gary		San Francisco		Muskegon		Jackson		Quincy		Dallas	
	Male (32)	Female (53)	Male (10)	Female (20)	Male (21)	Female (40)	Male (19)	Female (39)	Male (19)	Female (45)	Male (21)	Female (48)
Before using clinic for any reason	81	77	80	90	62	70	68	64	u	u	52	44
Before discussing birth control in the clinic	84	89	80	80	81	65	74	77	u	u	67	62
Before receiving prescription/voucher for contraceptives from the clinic	na	na	na	na	90	77	na	79	na	na	na	na
Before obtaining contraceptives from the clinic	na	na	na	na	na	na	68	82	79	76	76	77

NOTE: Data are from student health survey and include all students who were ever pregnant or ever caused a pregnancy regardless of race.
na = not applicable; u = unavailable.

213

Discussion and Conclusions

These school-based clinics were not primarily family planning clinics but were comprehensive health care clinics that provided primary health care and varying degrees of family planning services. Reproductive health services represented a very important component of these clinics but actually constituted only a minority of the visits. Clinics had substantial success in meeting the need for family planning services, even though considerable improvement was still possible. Clinics that prescribed or dispensed contraceptives served far more students than those that provided only counseling, and the three clinics that dispensed contraceptives on-campus served higher proportions of sexually experienced females than the clinic that provided vouchers to obtain contraceptives off-campus. Finally, the clinics provided contraception to much larger percentages of females than males.

Much of the debate over school-based clinics has focused upon whether contraceptive counseling and provision of contraceptives increase sexual activity, either by hastening the onset or increasing the frequency. The results presented here indicate that this was not the case; the preponderance of evidence indicates that the clinics did not increase sexual activity. In most sites no significant differences occurred; when significant differences did occur, most commonly the data showed less sexual activity among students attending the clinic school.

An examination of each clinic's services provides an interesting perspective on the differential impact of the clinics upon use of birth control. Interpretations should be made cautiously, both because of the variety of methodological limitations that vary from site to site and because it is always dangerous to develop ex post facto interpretations.

The Gary clinic, which had no measurable impact upon contraceptive use, did not emphasize pregnancy prevention, did not prescribe or dispense contraceptives, and saw few students for contraceptive counseling and referral.

At the San Francisco school, however, condom use (but not pill use) increased significantly over time. In that school the clinic developed a strong AIDS education program and a peer education program and encouraged condom use. Nevertheless, the clinic could neither prescribe nor dispense contraceptives, and few students used the clinic for counseling or referral. During the 2 years between the pretest and the posttest, AIDS became an especially salient issue in San Francisco, and students were exposed to a wide variety of public health campaigns promoting condom use. During the same period condom use increased substantially among adolescents nationwide, and it might be expected to have increased most in those areas where AIDS became most prevalent and feared. Although it is impossible to determine from the survey data whether school or community interventions had the greater impact upon the students' contraceptive behavior, it seems likely that some combination of clinic, school, and community programs contributed to the increased use of condoms.

Muskegon was the only site at which significant differences occurred between the clinic school and the comparison school on all three measures of contraceptive use. This clinic, the only one administered by Planned Parenthood, gave considerable emphasis to preventing pregnancy. In the classroom the health education teacher and clinic staff gave presentations on human sexuality issues, while in the clinic, staff provided individual consultation on family planning and reproductive health and provided vouchers so that students could obtain birth control pills and condoms free-of-charge at Planned Parenthood.

It is not clear, however, why contraceptive use was higher at the clinic school than at the comparison school. Both schools had strong sex education programs, so the effect of this factor is questionable. Moreover, in the clinic school, during the school year, only an estimated 12% of the sexually experienced males used the clinic to obtain vouchers for condoms at Planned Parenthood, and few females obtained condoms from that clinic. Therefore it is not likely that the vouchers contributed significantly to the large difference in condom use between the two schools. Finally, two methodological limitations existed. First, the Muskegon comparison school was located in a completely different community 90 miles from the clinic school, raising the possibility of other differences in the communities. Second, surveys were administered at the clinic and nonclinic schools at two different times of the year—in the spring and fall, respectively.

Of all the clinic schools, Jackson had the highest proportion (46%) of sexually experienced female students who had used the pill at last intercourse. Notably, it is the only site in which the clinic school, in comparison with the control school, had a much larger percentage of females reporting use of pills at last intercourse. The clinic probably contributed to these differences. The clinic placed little emphasis upon condoms, but it administered risk assessments to students who came to the clinic, carefully followed-up students engaging in unprotected sex, provided birth control pills on site, and followed-up females who received birth control pills. This clinic had the largest percentage of visits for contraception and the second largest percentage of sexually experienced females who received contraceptives from the school clinic.

At Quincy the proportion of females using pills the last time they had sex rose by 7 percentage points in the 2 years after the clinic opened, but that increase was not statistically significant. At first consideration, this finding is disappointing because the Quincy clinic gave considerable emphasis to pregnancy prevention and the school itself provided sexuality education before and after the clinic opened. In the clinic, staff asked students about unprotected sexual activity, dispensed contraceptives, and contacted students who missed family planning appointments.

Two factors partially explain why the clinic did not have a greater impact upon contraceptive use. First, before the clinic opened, students already had access to family planning services through the nearby health department clinic. Second, during its first 2 years the clinic had few staff and considerable turnover, which limited its outreach efforts and the number of students it could serve.

At the Dallas clinic school approximately 40% of the sexually experienced female students received the pill through the clinic; nevertheless, they were not significantly more likely to have used the pill at last intercourse than their counterparts at the comparison school. The reasons for this are not clear. Although the clinic provided health care to many students, it did not focus upon pregnancy prevention, and only 14% of the clinic visits were for family planning. Also, when it dispensed birth control pills to females, it did not set an appointment for the next visit or follow-up patients when their cycles of pills would have run out.

In sum, simply providing contraceptives was not enough to significantly increase their use. School and community programs may have increased condom use in at least one school, and a combination of services including education, counseling, contraceptive provision, and careful follow-up may have increased pill use in at least two schools.

From the data gathered, no indication was given that the presence of any of the school-based clinics reduced the schoolwide pregnancy rates. These findings are consistent with the findings on use of birth control methods in those sites where no significant differences occurred in use of birth control, but they are disappointing in San Francisco, Muskegon, and Jackson, where statistical differences did occur. In San Francisco and Jackson, however, this difference may be partially explained by the fact that significant differences occurred in specific methods of birth control rather than in use of any method. Possible validity problems associated with self-report of pregnancy and the possible dropout problems due to pregnancy may also have obscured some impact upon pregnancy.

Even though many of the students who obtained contraceptives from the clinics may have obtained them from some other source if the clinics had not provided contraceptives, undoubtedly not all of them would have done so. Thus the four clinics that provided contraceptives or vouchers probably prevented small numbers of pregnancies in each school, even though this effect was not large enough to significantly affect the schoolwide pregnancy rates.

Recommendations for Increasing Clinic Effectiveness

School-based clinics for adolescents are still in their own "adolescence." They are new; they are growing rapidly; they are developing and experimenting with a variety of creative and innovative programs to serve youth. In the current highly politicized climate many school-based clinics are prevented from providing potentially effective services to youth. Clinics undoubtedly have the potential to improve the effectiveness of their pregnancy prevention services.

The clinic and survey data discussed above suggest recommendations for improving the effectiveness of clinics. These include:

- *Give a high priority to pregnancy prevention and AIDS prevention.* This may be the most general and most important recommendation. The only clinics that may have affected the use of pills and condoms are those that gave pregnancy prevention or AIDS prevention a very high priority. The other clinics were less effective.
- *Conduct more outreach in the school.* Students' reasons for contraceptive nonuse included lack of knowledge and skills, and many students became pregnant or got someone else pregnant prior to ever visiting the school clinic. Furthermore, two of the apparently effective clinics had developed strong educational and outreach programs in their respective schools.
- *Develop programs to delay and reduce sexual activity.* Large majorities of the students in each school were sexually experienced, and many of these

youth had sex prior to entering high school. Thus programs to delay or reduce sexual activity should begin in elementary and junior high school. Because many students had not yet had sex when they entered high school, however, and because many sexually experienced students had sex only infrequently, such programs in high school may also delay the onset of intercourse or reduce the frequency of intercourse. In two sites some evidence was found that counseling or other school programs might have delayed the onset of intercourse.

- *Identify and target students engaged in sexual activity.* Many sexually experienced students did not use the clinic for contraceptives, and many students became pregnant prior to using the clinic for contraceptives. Although the clinics generally were effective in treating and counseling students who sought specific services, clinics must seek out those at risk who are not already motivated to visit the clinic, if they are to have a significant impact upon sexual risk-taking behaviors. During students' visits the clinic staff should ask students about sexual risk-taking whenever appropriate.

- *Make contraceptives available in the clinics.* The clinics that prescribed or dispensed contraceptives served far more students than those that provided only counseling, and the three clinics that dispensed contraceptives served higher proportions of sexually experienced female students than the one clinic that provided vouchers for students to obtain contraceptives elsewhere.

- *Conduct effective follow-up procedures.* Many females who obtained oral contraceptives from clinics stopped getting them within 6 months. Although some of these females probably stopped having sex or got contraceptives from other sources, some simply engaged in unprotected sex. Effective follow-up procedures may improve contraceptive continuation rates. The Jackson clinic conducted careful follow-up and may have increased use of birth control pills.

- *Emphasize condoms and male responsibility.* The findings in San Francisco and Muskegon suggest that clinics, schools, and communities working together can have an impact upon male use of condoms. At those sites greater differences occurred in condom use than in pill use. In general, males are less likely than females to visit the clinic for family planning, but they can be reached through sports physicals, classroom activities, and other school and community activities. And, of course, females can be taught to exert greater pressure upon males to use condoms.

These recommendations are not necessarily easy to implement. Some of them require additional funding and staffing, and it will still remain difficult to change students' risk-taking behaviors, many of which are deeply rooted in the values and practices of the larger community in which they live. Nevertheless, by adopting some of these recommendations and by giving greater priority to reproductive health, school-based clinics may be able to more effectively reduce sexual risk-taking behavior and reduce adolescent pregnancy.

References

Clark, S. D., Zabin, L. S., & Hardy, J. B. (1984). Sex, contraception, and parenthood experience and attitudes among urban black young men. *Family Planning Perspectives, 16*(2), 77-82.

Edwards, L., Steinman, M., Arnold, K., & Hakanson, E. (1980). Adolescent pregnancy prevention services in high school clinics. *Family Planning Perspectives, 12*(1), 6-14.

Kirby, D., & Lovick, S. (1989). *School-based clinics enter the '90s: Update, evaluation and future challenges.* Washington, DC: Center for Population Options.

Kirby, D., Resnick, M., Downes, B., Kocher, T., Gunderson, P., & Blum, R. (in press). The impact of school-based health clinics in St. Paul. *Family Planning Perspectives.*

Kirby, D., Waszak, C., & Ziegler, J. (1989). *An assessment of six school-based clinics: Services, impact and potential.* Washington, DC: Center for Population Options.

Kirby, D., Waszak, C., & Ziegler, J. (1991). Six school-based clinics: Their reproductive health services and impact on sexual behavior. *Family Planning Perspectives, 23*(1), 6-16.

Sonenstein, F., Peck, J., & Ku, L. (1989). Sexual activity, condom use, and AIDS awareness among adolescent males. *Family Planning Perspectives, 21*(4), 152-158.

Waszak, C. & Neidell, S. (1992). *School-based and school-linked clinics: Update 1991.* Washington, DC: Center for Population Options.

Zabin, L. S., Hirsh, M. B., Smith, E. A., Streett, R., & Hardy, J. B. (1986). Evaluation of a pregnancy prevention program for urban teenagers. *Family Planning Perspectives, 18*(3), 119-126.

9

A Health Beliefs Field Experiment

Teen Talk

MARVIN EISEN
GAIL L. ZELLMAN

Sexuality education has taken on new urgency in recent years. Increasing numbers of births to single teenagers, increasing numbers of coitally active teens, and a decline in the average age at first intercourse have increased the need to encourage more responsible sexual behavior among teenagers (Hayes, 1987). Moreover, the AIDS epidemic has made responsible sexual behavior a life-and-death matter. Prevention of early pregnancy has become a central goal of many sexuality education programs (Hayes, 1987). In many states and localities, publicly funded educational outreach and family planning programs targeted to teenagers are now in place or being developed (Alan Guttmacher

AUTHORS' NOTE: This chapter is based upon a demonstration project that was supported by contracts and grants to the first author from the Texas Department of Human Services; The University of Texas at Austin Research Institute; The Lyndon B. Johnson School of Public Affairs, University of Texas at Austin; The Hogg Foundation for Mental Health; The William and Flora Hewlett Foundation; and NICHD Grant HD-22982. The chapter was written with support provided by The William and Flora Hewlett Foundation, The Kaiser Family Foundation, The C. S. Mott Foundation, and the Northwest Foundation to Social Research Applications. The opinions and conclusions expressed herein are solely those of the authors. They are grateful to Judy Baker for project training, supervision, and administration; and to Robert Timothy Reagan and Max Nelson-Kilger for statistical and conceptual consultation.

Institute, 1989). Most of the educational programs embrace such behavioral objectives as prolonging abstinence, delaying the age of first intercourse, increasing consistent and effective contraceptive use, or now, increasing condom use for both sexes (Alan Guttmacher Institute, 1989; Paikoff & Brooks-Gunn, in press). Even when these programs appear to be carefully constructed and implemented, however, and produce short-term changes in participants' knowledge and attitudes, there is no guarantee that they will impact upon participants' subsequent pregnancy avoidance behaviors (Hofferth & Miller, 1989; Kirby, 1984). Nevertheless, impact remains the key policy concern.

Most of the claims for positive or negative effects of sexuality education upon recipients' sexual and pregnancy avoidance behaviors are not based upon controlled studies of specific sexuality education programs. Rather, they stem from interview data usually gathered retrospectively through survey research (see Eisen & Zellman, 1987; Stout & Rivara, 1989). No consistently positive or negative pattern of findings has emerged from such surveys (Dawson, 1986; Marsiglio & Mott, 1986; Zelnik & Kim, 1982).

Conclusive data from prospective, controlled studies about the effects of sexuality education upon pregnancy avoidance behavior do not exist (see Hofferth & Miller, 1989; Kirby, 1984; Paikoff & Brooks-Gunn, in press). Our own recent review of the primary prevention literature revealed only three published curriculum evaluations with designs rigorous enough to make the link between the intervention and changes in specific individuals' sexual and contraceptive behavior over time. Only one of these evaluations employed random assignment. Schinke, Blythe, and Gilchrist (1981) found that sexuality education, presented to high school volunteers in a classroom small group discussion format, increased consistent contraceptive use 6 months later when compared with no-treatment controls. Kirby (1984) found no consistent effects for seven separate short-term sexuality education programs in delaying first sexual intercourse or in increasing effective postintervention contraceptive use 3 to 9 months later when compared with matched-sample controls. Finally, Howard and McCabe's 1990 effort to postpone sexual intercourse among low-income eighth-graders resulted in significantly more delay through the ninth grade in the experimental group than was found in a no-treatment comparison group from similar area schools. The program appeared to have little effect, however, upon contraceptive usage over the nearly 2-year follow-up period among those who were already coitally active at the time of the posttest.

More outcome evaluation studies of sexuality education are clearly needed. To help fill this need, we conducted a controlled field study of a novel theory-based curriculum. The field experiment implemented and evaluated a public health oriented approach to adolescent fertility control that combined elements of the Health Belief Model (HBM) and Social Learning Theory (SLT). The HBM is a well-known value-expectancy psychological model pertaining to primary prevention (Janz & Becker, 1984; Rosenstock, Strecher, & Becker, 1988). It suggests that, among other factors, the probability that an individual will undertake a particular preventive measure (e.g., contraceptive use) is linked to a number of personal perceptions, including (a) his/her perceived susceptibility to the problem, (b) the perceived seriousness of developing or contracting the problem, and (c) the perceived benefits minus (d) the perceived costs of undertaking the recommended preventive action(s).

The HBM conceptual framework and motivational base seemed especially applicable to teenagers' pregnancy avoidance problems because the four major perceptual components of the HBM—susceptibility, seriousness, benefits, and barriers—suggested salient attack points for strengthening motivation to delay initiation of intercourse and, when having sex, to use contraception. The framework also comfortably accommodated males' perceptions regarding their role in pregnancy avoidance, and an emphasis upon mutual responsibility in sexual and contraceptive decision making.

In the HBM, susceptibility is a cognitive assessment of how likely a person believes it would be for her/him to contract a health-threatening condition if no preventive measures are taken. Teenagers often underestimate their susceptibility to pregnancy or impregnation for many reasons, among them the inability to understand the basic concepts of probability and an unwillingness to accept themselves as sexual beings (e.g., Cvetkovich, Grote, Bjorseth, & Sarkissian, 1975).

Seriousness represents a cognitive assessment of the severity of the consequences a person believes he/she would suffer if he/she were to contract a health-threatening condition. Many teenagers appear to discount the seriousness of early pregnancy, assuming single-parenthood, marriage, or abortion will resolve the problem; or they believe that pregnancy will not interfere with their poorly formed or seemingly nonexistent life goals.

Benefits are often described in the HBM in terms of the perceived efficacy of preventive actions; in the present project, the efficacy concerns how well contraception works. Teenagers generally acknowledge that most methods will work if used correctly; in fact, they sometimes overestimate the effectiveness of such methods as withdrawal and rhythm. We also emphasized the personal responsibility aspect of consistent use; for example, that using contraceptives is an important part of responsible sexual behavior. In addition, we felt that the concept of benefits had to be expanded to include the benefits to be experienced in a protected personal relationship. For instance, contraceptive use by a male can convey to his partner that he respects and cares about her. It may also make sexual intercourse more likely to occur.

Finally, barriers to preventive actions represent a cognitive assessment of the perceived costs of preventive behaviors. For teenagers, these costs are apparent at every point in the sequence of acquiring and using contraceptives. Abstinence too carries its own set of barriers and costs. Maintaining abstinence or insisting upon contraceptive use may be viewed as a sign of lack of love and unwillingness to take a "risk" for love.

The SLT behavior component of the intervention provided participants opportunities to observe both inappropriate and appropriate pregnancy prevention behaviors and to engage in guided practice. Combining the HBM and SLT would successfully counter many teenagers' relatively limited pregnancy avoidance knowledge, improve their interpersonal and communication skills, and increase their contraceptive motivation through active program participation.

Because an HBM-SLT approach to fertility control was untried among teenagers when we began the curriculum development phase (1983), we first fielded and evaluated a relatively small-scale pilot program without a comparison group. The results from the short-term pilot study were encouraging (Eisen & Zellman, 1986, 1987; Eisen, Zellman, & McAlister, 1985) and led to the implementation of the larger demonstration project described here.

In the present field experiment, six community-based family planning agencies and one independent public school district agreed to compare their "usual care" sex and contraception educational outreach curriculum with the HBM-SLT intervention program.

The evaluation component incorporated several design characteristics, such as random assignment of participants to intervention programs, longitudinal data collection, diverse samples, and pregnancy-related behavioral measures, often absent from earlier program evaluations. The objectives of the demonstration were fivefold.

1. To increase unmarried adolescents' knowledge of and motivation for fertility control (i.e., abstinence or consistent use of effective contraception).

2. To determine the relationships among sociodemographic variables, changes in knowledge and motivation for fertility control, and actual changes in coital and contraceptive behavior over a 1-year follow-up period.

3. To compare the impact of the HBM-SLT-based intervention model against a range of community outreach and school-based interventions with respect to participants' subsequent sexual behavior, contraceptive use, and pregnancy status.

4. To compare the impact of the experimental and various comparison programs in a variety of settings that serve populations differing on such characteristics as age, sex, race or ethnicity, previous sexual experience, and rural or urban residence.

5. To determine whether "poor" motivation for fertility control, as measured by HBM-based perceptions and concepts, can be considered a risk factor for adolescent premarital pregnancy, independent of other known factors such as race, ethnicity, and socioeconomic status.

The demonstration project combined diverse agencies, intervention approaches, samples, program settings, and formats into a "forced" comparison with one, generally fixed-format experimental intervention. Nevertheless, it was hypothesized that when data were combined across individual sites, the experimental (HBM-SLT) program, relative to the comparison programs, would lead to (a) lower incidence of transition to coital activity status during the follow-up period, (b) higher incidence of effective contraceptive use at first and last intercourse for those who became coitally active, (c) higher incidence of effective contraceptive use at last intercourse for teenagers who were coitally active prior to he intervention, and (d) more consistent use of effective contraception for all those who were coitally active over the 1-year follow-up. We assumed that the HBM-SLT program model would not be equally effective with all age, gender, racial/ethnic, and sexual status groups or in all study sites. Little empirical basis existed, however, for predicting the direction or the magnitude of potential differences.

Method

Overview of the Study Design

The study design approximated a randomized field trial. Six family planning services agencies and one independent school district (representing a total of eight sex and contraceptive education programs) compared their own "usual care" outreach or regular classroom curriculum with our HBM-SLT-based intervention program. Each agency recruited its study sample by its usual methods; the school district used its eighth- and ninth-grade population. Within an agency's targeted age range (overall range: 13-21), participants were unselected with respect to gender, race or ethnicity, and preintervention coital activity status. In each of the eight study sites or schools, adolescents and young adults were assigned by classroom unit or individually (depending upon agency operating constraints) to the agency's usual program (comparison group) or the HBM-SLT (experimental group). For example, in the agencies that conducted sexuality education as part of summer work-study programs (Sites 1 and 5), ad hoc classroom groups were formed arbitrarily on the basis of students' work schedules, and then classes were assigned randomly to conditions. In the public school classes (Sites 2, 4, and 7), one of the two participating classes in each site was chosen randomly to receive the HBM-SLT intervention (see the Appendix for further information). Data were collected from individual participants at three points during the study period: Before exposure to the intervention (Time 1); immediately following the intervention (Time 2); and 12 months after the scheduled program completion date (Time 3). Individuals were the unit of analysis for all between-group comparisons reported here.

Sample

Educational Outreach Service Providers

Agencies were recruited from a pool of organizations that conducted sexuality education outreach programming with state reimbursement agreements in Texas and with "innovative" information and education (I & E) grants in California. The TDHS Director of Family Planning helped recruit eligible agencies in Texas; the Chief, Office of Family Planning and the Executive Director of the California Family Planning Council referred us to potential program sites there[1] (see Eisen, Zellman, & McAlister, 1990).

A small independent school district in California's San Francisco Bay Area that volunteered to participate in the demonstration as a means of obtaining evaluations of their current ninth-grade Adolescent Family Life curriculum, and of a newly adopted eighth-grade drug education/problem behavior decision-making curriculum was also involved in the project.

The agencies and the school district recruited all teenagers who took part in the study, organized and coordinated the data collection using project forms, and delivered the actual intervention. The agencies were paid up to $5,000, the exact amount based upon the number of teenagers recruited and retained in the sample over the study period. The agency sample represents a relatively broad mix of service provider organizations ranging from an urban Planned Parenthood affiliate to a rural community action program health clinic. Inclusion of the school district permits comparison with school-based curricula. The agencies are not representative of all agencies conducting educational outreach nationally, but they do seem typical of the agencies and community-based outreach programs operating around the country. A summary of study site characteristics is presented in the Appendix.

Adolescent Participants

The study sample was recruited by the agencies from a variety of sources, including public school classes, summer work-study programs run with private sector support, Upward Bound, and a federal Job Corps training program. The agencies recruited from their regular "client" groups and organizations—that is, the same ones they served under reimbursement agreements or grants with state agencies in Texas and California (see Eisen et al., 1990). With the exception of the school system (Sites 2 and 3), all programs had family income ceilings or served low-income, inner-city youth. Information about the population served and specific sample characteristics in each site is also summarized in the Appendix.

Between June 1986 and August 1987, 1,444 adolescents (ages 13-19) from Sites 1-7 completed the baseline (Time 1) interview, and 1,328 (92%) received all or part of the HBM-SLT or the comparison intervention and completed the immediate posttest (Time 2) interview. In keeping with our study design, agencies attempted to reinterview all adolescents who were exposed to any phase of the demonstration 12 months after the scheduled completion date of their particular intervention program even if they did not actually complete it. Between July 1987 and September 1988, some 888 participants (62% of the Time 1 sample and 67% of the Time 2 sample) received the 1-year follow-up (Time 3) interview to assess program impact. Included were 839 participants (58% of the Time 1 sample, and 63% of the Time 2 sample) from the seven sites who completed all three data collection cycles (i.e., baseline, immediate posttest, and 1-year follow-up).[2]

Table 9.1 shows salient sociodemographic, educational, and pre-intervention sexuality status characteristics of the 1,444 adolescents who constituted the present study sample. Of the 1,444 Time 1 interviewees, 52% were females; 15% were white; 24% were black; 53% were Hispanic; 8% were Asians (including recent refugees from Cambodia, Laos, and South Vietnam); 62% reported some previous sexuality education; 37% reported they had had sexual intercourse; 49% said they used contraception at their last intercourse; and of those who used any method, 74% used a condom (see Table 9.1 for other characteristics at baseline of the Time 1, Time 2, and Time 3 samples). The Time 1 sample of adolescents appears to be reasonably reflective of its community populations but certainly is not representative of all teenagers who need or receive sexuality education.

Educational Curricula and Materials

The HBM Educational Curriculum

The experimental intervention was a 12- to 15-hour curriculum intended to increase teenagers' awareness of (a) the probability of personally becoming pregnant or causing a partner to become pregnant; (b) the serious negative personal consequences of teenage maternity and paternity; (c) the personal and interpersonal benefits of delayed sexual activity and consistent, effective contraceptive use; and to decrease their perceptions of (d) the psychological, interpersonal, and logistical barriers to abstinence and consistent contraceptive usage.

The structure of the experimental intervention was designed with the realities of adolescent development in mind (e.g., Cvetkovich et al., 1975). A key feature was the small group discussion format, chosen to accommodate the frequent inconsistencies in teenagers' abstract thinking and to take advantage of their tendency to think in concrete, personalized modes (Schinke, Gilchrist, & Small, 1979). Small groups generally encourage active discussion of information and can be directed to focus upon the personal implications of perceptions and behaviors for each participant. Furthermore, small group discussion appears to help minimize egocentric thinking and increase the likelihood that factual information will be received, understood, and acted upon (Schinke, 1982).

The content of the HBM-based educational intervention program included four broad areas.

Table 9.1 Demographic Characteristics and Intake Sexuality Status of Educational Intervention Participants at Time 1, Time 2, and Time 3 Data Collection

Variable	Time 1 (N= 1444) %	Time 2 (N = 1328) %	Time 3 (N = 888) %
Sex			
Females	52	52	54
Males	48	48	46
Enrollment age			
13-14	29	29	32
15-17	67	67	65
18-19	4	4	3
Race/ethnicity			
White	15	16	17
Black	24	23	22
Hispanic	53	52	51
Asian	8	9	10
Current living arrangement			
With both parent figures	58	58	56
With mother figure only	34	34	37
With father figure only	2	3	3
With neither	5	5	4
Previous sex education course/class(es)			
Yes	62	61	62
No	38	39	38
Educational intervention program (randomly assigned)			
HBM-SLT	50	50	52
Comparisons	50	50	48
Study site			
1	34	36	35
2	7	7	9
3	7	8	9
4	14	11	14
5	17	18	15
6	15	14	14
7	6	6	4
Ever had sexual intercourse			
Yes	37	37	32
No	63	63	68
Missing	<1	<1	<1
Used effective contraception at first sex			
Yes	39[a]	41[b]	43[c]

Table 9.1 Continued

Variable	Time 1 (N= 1444) %	Time 2 (N = 1328) %	Time 3 (N = 888) %
No	59	58	56
Missing	2	1	1
Used condom at first sex			
Yes	78[d]	78[e]	77[f]
No	22	22	23
Used effective contraception at last sex			
Yes	49[a]	50[b]	52[c]
No	50	49	47
Missing	1	1	1
Used condom at last sex			
Yes	74[g]	73[h]	74[i]
No	26	27	26
Contraceptive usage consistency			
Every time	15[a]	15[b]	15[c]
Sometimes[j]	56	55	58
Never	29	29	26
Missing	1	1	1

NOTE: Percentages may not add to 100 due to rounding. [a]$N = 525$. [b]$N = 486$. [c]$N = 280$. [d]$N = 207$. [e]$N = 196$. [f]$N = 121$. [g]$N = 258$. [h]$N = 244$. [i]$N = 147$. [j]Response categories collapsed to include "Most times" + "Sometimes" + "A few times."

1. Presentation of Factual Information. Two project consultants, using materials discussed below, developed a curriculum guide that included coverage of reproductive biology, venereal disease, and contraception. This guide formed the basis for two 2-hour sessions in which the material was presented to experimental subjects in large group lecture format.

2. Group Discussion of Factual Information. These discussions were intended to personalize the factual biological information previously presented. Discussions emphasized basic concepts of probability related to reproductive systems and pregnancy risks; social, educational, and economic consequences of premarital pregnancy and parenthood; and pregnancy resolution options, including adoption and abortion. The goal was for each participant to understand and personalize her/his perception of susceptibility and seriousness and to integrate biological and social factors in calculating his/her own benefits minus barriers score for delaying sexual activity or starting contraceptive usage.

3. Group Discussion of Values, Feelings, and Emotions. These discussions emphasized the personal implications of the curriculum materials for relationships with same-sex peers and opposite-sex boyfriends or girlfriends, as well as for one's own feelings about sexuality. Films, exercises, and role playing specific sexual and contraception-related situations helped stimulate discussion.

4. Making Decisions and Taking Personal Responsibility. These discussions emphasized actual decision making: making personally and sexually responsible decisions and learning new skills to implement those decisions. Skills included learning to say no to boyfriends or girlfriends, to deal effectively with same-sex peers and group pressure, and to communicate more easily and accurately with parents, boyfriends or girlfriends, peers, and important others.

The curriculum was transmitted through a combination of lectures, simulations, leader-guided discussions and practice, and role playing (including gender role reversals). For example, we developed a board game that demonstrated the probabilities of becoming pregnant following unprotected intercourse. Selected "trigger" films that used teenage actors were intended to make participants' perceptions of their personal susceptibility to and serious consequences of pregnancy as concrete and real as possible. Participants generated their own scripts to role-play key sex- and contraception-related situations (e.g., learning to say no to sexual intercourse or unprotected sexual intercourse, and learning to buy over-the-counter birth control materials in a drugstore). All activities were guided and reinforced by group discussion leaders.

Two sorts of materials and curricula were required in the field study: (a) materials to train the study participants in reproductive biology, birth control issues, health belief-related issues, role playing, and communication skills; and (b) materials to train the educational outreach provider staff as lecturers and group discussion leaders.

The reproductive biology materials were drawn from curriculum guides from various family planning agency programs, curriculum guides and instruments from other research studies (e.g., Miller, 1981), and curriculum components that had proved integral to previous sexuality education programs in the national evaluation conducted by Kirby (Kirby, 1984; Kirby, Alter, & Scales, 1980) and summarized in Carrera (1983). In the second year of the controlled field study (1986-1987), the venereal disease portion of the curriculum was augmented with a 15-minute AIDS education component based primarily upon materials provided by the AIDS Foundation of San Francisco. Trigger films, which set up a problematic situation and left the resolution undetermined, were produced by Planned Parenthood affiliates and were available commercially.

After the curriculum materials and delivery approaches targeted to teenagers were selected, developed, and pilot tested, we prepared a training manual for group discussion leaders to use in conducting the experimental intervention. The manual presented an overview of HBM theory, a rationale for extending it to teen pregnancy and STD prevention, tips on running small groups, and commentaries on each of the four (1/2 hour) training tapes created to familiarize the prospective leaders with the program components and specific activities, and to facilitate the presentation of a 12-15 hour program. The tapes used simulations and re-creations of actual program content; they featured adolescents who had "graduated" from the pilot study program and former discussion leaders.

Thus the training manual and tapes, a group discussion curriculum guide, and the reproductive biology curriculum formed the basis for the 2-day training workshops attended by family planning agency educators and school staff who were chosen to deliver the HBM-SLT intervention. During the seminars, the curriculum materials and techniques were discussed at length and the trainees engaged in role playing of the small group curriculum components with study staff. Study staff were also available by telephone for consultation, problem solving, and encouragement throughout the implementation period.

The Comparison Curricula

The Appendix provides brief summaries of the duration, content, and format of comparison programs, which differed one from another. They were similar to the HBM-SLT curriculum and to each other, however, in covering reproductive biology, contraception, STDs, and dating, as well as sexual values, norms, and decision making in both lecture and group discussion formats. No comparison program specifically keyed upon perceived pregnancy susceptibility and seriousness, nor upon perceived fertility control benefits and barriers. Most included course handouts, films, class exercises, and homework assignments. Several programs, including those in the public school district, used commercially available curriculum materials. None indicated more than occasional use of role playing or role reversal techniques. In general, less active student involvement seemed to be written into the comparison curriculum materials than into the HBM-SLT program.

Evaluation Instruments

To assess program impact, various sexuality-related belief, attitude, knowledge, and behavioral measures were developed or, whenever possible, modified from existing measures. Standard sociodemographic and educational items were included at Time 1. In addition, we measured the expectations of Time 1 virgins that they would become sexually active in the next 3 months (using five response categories ranging from "very unlikely" to "very likely," plus "not sure").

Although several previous HBM-based intervention studies have pertained to health promotion (see Janz & Becker, 1984), no studies directly assessed adolescents' fertility control perceptions. Therefore, new items intended to tap the four major perceptual components of the HBM (susceptibility, seriousness, benefits, and barriers) were written. Those items were subjected to extensive scaling and psychometric studies (Eisen, 1985; Eisen et al., 1985), revised, and several additional items included in the present version on the basis of the pilot results.

Table 9.2 presents the final set of items that were developed, grouped by HBM perceptual construct. Adolescents were asked to respond to the items in terms of five-point response categories that ordinarily ranged from "strongly agree" to "strongly disagree," with "not sure" being the fifth category. (Two exceptions to those response categories appear in Items 3, 5, and 6.)

Sexual and contraceptive knowledge was conceptualized to emphasize reproductive physiology knowledge, pregnancy and sexuality myths, and birth control and STD knowledge, as well as birth control method and STD prevention effectiveness. Most items were modified, adapted, or taken verbatim from existent knowledge questionnaires (e.g., Finkel & Finkel, 1975; Reichelt & Werley, 1976). See Table 9.3 for the complete list of items, correct responses, and effectiveness rankings of methods.

Finally, we developed behavioral measures of the major variables necessary to assess program impact upon adolescents' coital status, contraceptive use, and pregnancy avoidance. These measures included whether participants used a contraceptive method or methods at first and most recent sexual intercourse; what specific methods were used, if any; and how consistently contraception was used before and after the intervention. Consistency was measured using a single item with five response options ("never," "a few times," "sometimes," "most

text continued on page 236

Table 9.2 Health Belief Model Items Grouped by Construct Used to Assess Pregnancy and Contraceptive Perceptions (*N* = 35)

Construct	Item No. and Content
Susceptibility to Pregnancy/VD:	(3) If you or your partner used no contraceptives, how likely is it that you/your partner would get pregnant?
	(5) If you had unprotected sex, how worried would you be that you or your partner might get VD?
	(22) Most teenage couples who don't use contraceptives wind up pregnant.
Seriousness of Pregnancy:	(4) A young girl's pregnancy can really hurt her parents.
	(6) If you had unprotected sex, how worried might you be if you or your partner got pregnant?
	(9) If a teenage girl has an unplanned pregnancy, it's not a big problem since she can raise her baby alone.
	(12) An abortion is a pretty simple medical procedure, but it can affect how you feel for a long time.
	(13) With VD getting more common all the time, a teenager who worries about it is being realistic.
	(17) Even though a girl may not think so now, becoming a teenage mother can make it very hard to do all she'd like to later in life.
	(21) Unplanned pregnancy is not worth worrying a lot about because it can be taken care of pretty easily with an abortion.
	(27) Getting married may seem like an easy way to solve an unplanned pregnancy, but a teenage marriage may be more trouble than it's worth.
	(33) If a guy gets a girl pregnant, it's not a big problem since the partners can always get married.
	(35) Even though an abortion may be pretty easy to get, the decision to have one is often difficult and painful.
Benefits of Contraceptive Usage:	(7) If a guy has contraceptives available, a girl is more willing to agree to sex.
	(8) If you use it the right way, contraception makes pregnancy less likely to happen.
	(10) The use of contraception improves a relationship.
	(14) If a girl uses birth control, her partner will know she really cares about herself.

continued

Table 9.2 Continued

Construct	Item No. and Content
	(15) There is not much point in using over-the-counter birth control methods (like condoms, foam)—they really aren't that good at preventing pregnancy.
	(19) It's always a good idea to carry contraceptives because then you can always have protected intercourse.
	(20) I believe contraception is an important part of responsible sexual behavior.
	(23) Using a contraceptive to prevent unplanned pregnancy is a good thing to do.
	(24) You can feel pretty sure that you won't get pregnant if you use contraception every time you have sex.
	(28) If a male uses birth control, his partner knows he really cares about her.
	(31) If a girl uses birth control, her partner will think she's pretty smart.
	(34) If a guy makes sure that one of them is using contraceptives, his partner knows he really cares about her.
Barriers to Contraceptive Usage:	(1) Sometimes it seems that when you try to prevent problems, it is more trouble than it's worth.
	(2) If my girl(boy)friend wanted to have sex but I didn't, I would find it pretty hard to say no.
	(11) The side effects of the good birth control methods are a real problem.
	(16) If I wanted to get a good method of birth control, I know where to get it.
	(18) I would feel pretty comfortable talking to a sexual partner about birth control.
	(25) I have no religious or moral objection to contraception.
	(26) The use of contraceptives makes sexual intercourse seem dirty.
	(29) The whole idea of birth control is embarrassing to me.
	(30) It can sometimes be important to show your love by taking a chance on getting pregnant.
	(32) Having contraceptives with you makes sexual intercourse seem less romantic and exciting.

NOTE: Response categories are five points: (1) strongly agree, to (4) strongly disagree, (8) not sure, except Items 3, 5, and 6. Response categories for item 3 are (1) very likely, to (4) very unlikely, (8) not sure. Response categories for items 5 and 6 are (1) very worried, to (4) not at all worried, (8) not sure.

Table 9.3 Sexual and Contraceptive Knowledge Items Grouped by Index

Construct and Items

Anatomy and Physiology Knowledge (6 items)

Even before a sexually active teenager has her first menstrual period, it is possible for her to become pregnant. (True)

Fertilization is the release of an egg cell from one of a woman's fallopian tubes. (False)

Girls begin to ovulate as much as six months before they begin to menstruate. (False)

Following an egg's release, it is capable of being fertilized for only 24 hours. (False)

Once in the female's reproductive system, a sperm is able to fertilize an egg for 48-72 hours before the sperm dies. (True)

When during her menstrual cycle is a woman most likely to get pregnant if she has unprotected sexual intercourse? (About 14 days before menstruation)

Venereal Disease Knowledge (4 items)

You can catch VD or give it to someone else without knowing it. (True)

VD should be treated because it can cause a person to become sterile. (True)

You are over VD when the symptoms are gone. (False)

Once you have VD, you can't get it again. (False)

Pregnancy and Sexuality Myths (8 items)

A girl cannot get pregnant if:

-she has sexual intercourse for the first time. (False)

-she has sexual intercourse only occasionally. (False)

-she has not had any menstrual periods. (False)

-she does not have an orgasm (doesn't come) during sexual intercourse. (False)

-her partner ejaculates outside her vagina. (False)

-her partner does not ejaculate during sexual intercourse. (False)

If a girl has sex without using birth control over several months and does not get pregnant, she or her partner is probably sterile. (False)

Most teenage boys have such a strong need for sex that they must have it or they can go crazy. (False)

Contraceptive Methods Matching (10 items)

Something that is placed in the vagina that kills sperm. (Foam)

Not having sexual intercourse during the fertile period of the menstrual cycle. (Rhythm)

An object that is placed inside the uterus by a doctor to prevent pregnancy. (Coil, IUD, loop)

Removal of the penis from the vagina before climax (ejaculation) is reached. (Withdrawal)

Washing the vagina after sexual intercourse to remove sperm from it. (Douche)

Something that is taken regularly by mouth to prevent pregnancy. (Birth control pills)

An operation that makes it impossible for a woman to become pregnant. (Tubal ligation)

Not having sexual intercourse. (Abstinence)

continued

Table 9.3 Continued

Construct and Items

    A cup with sperm killer placed in the vagina that covers the opening of the uterus. (Diaphragm and jelly)
    A covering that fits over the penis to prevent pregnancy. (Condom, rubber, safe)
Contraceptive Effectiveness Rankings (11 items)
    Withdrawal (Ninth)
    Condom (Rubber, safe) (Fifth)
    Douche (Tenth)
    Abstinence (First)
    Diaphragm and "contraceptive" jelly (Sixth)
    Birth control pills (Third)
    Foam, "contraceptive" jelly (Seventh)
    Coil (IUD, loop) (Fourth)
    Rhythm (Eighth)
    Tubal ligation (Second)
    Condom and foam (Third [tied])
Venereal Disease Protection (11 items)
    Withdrawal (No)
    Condom (Rubber, safe) (Yes)
    Douche (No)
    Abstinence (Yes)
    Diaphragm and "contraceptive" jelly (Yes)
    Birth control pills (No)
    Foam, "contraceptive" jelly (Yes)
    Coil (IUD, loop) (No)
    Rhythm (No)
    Tubal ligation (No)
    Condom and foam (Yes)

NOTE: Contraceptive Effectiveness Rankings based on Ory, Forrest, & Lincoln (1983).

times," and "every time.") We also asked whether they or their partner(s) had become pregnant since the intervention program.

Because of restrictions imposed by the Institutional Review Boards in Texas on the study design, we were not able to determine participants' age at first sexual intercourse or the number of sexual partners they had had before and after the intervention program. For participants who became coitally active during the 12-month follow-up period, however, we estimated age at first intercourse by adding 6 months (i.e., the midpoint of the follow-up interval) to their ages at Time 1.

Procedure

In general, the experimental and comparison intervention programs were conducted in the context of the client organizations' regular, ongoing training, educational activities, and requirements. For example, the Private Industry Council (PIC) summer work-study programs mandated several hours of sexuality education as part of the basic education component that trainees received and for which they were paid through PIC. Because the demonstration was a controlled field experiment with a longitudinal evaluation component, several modifications were made to usual program delivery procedures. These were related to obtaining parental permission to participate, interviewing teenagers prior to the interventions, randomly assigning them to intervention programs, and extending the length and scope of their usual curricula.

Time 1 Interview

Study participants were interviewed individually before the intervention in each site where time and resources allowed (Sites 1, 2, 4, 5, and 6). Interviews generally took 60-75 minutes to complete. Every effort was made to match participants and interviewers on gender and race/ethnicity. Interviews were conducted by trained agency staff members who were not involved in the program delivery, or by agency and school district student interns as part of their assigned duties. Participants were read the demographic, background, and HBM perceptions sections of the instrument. They were able to choose whether to read the sexual and contraceptive knowledge sections themselves or have the interviewer read them. All participants read and answered the personal sexual behavior section by themselves and then deposited the sections in precoded envelopes that were collated with the other sections of the interview later. The interviewer was available to answer questions or to clarify instructions as needed. In Sites 3, 7, and 8, group interviews were conducted within classroom units with both teachers and agency staff monitoring the group administration and collating the sexuality-related material after the interviews.

Program Implementation

The HBM-SLT curriculum was designed to involve about 4 hours of lectures on reproductive biology and 8-10 hours of small group discussions, usually in 2- to 2 1/2-hour sessions. In the controlled field study, however, the HBM-based programs was shortened in every site, with a maximum of 12 hours allocated to the program. With few exceptions, HBM-SLT and comparison programs were similar in terms of number and length of sessions. This parity was achieved when some agencies stretched or adjusted their regular programs to match the time required for the experimental program.

Time 2 Interview and Time 3 Interview

After the teenagers in each site completed their intervention, they were immediately retested in a group setting on their sexual and contraceptive knowledge and HBM-related attitudes and perceptions. Twelve months after the scheduled date of intervention program completion, participants were reinterviewed individually to collect program impact data. Educational outreach agencies were paid from project grant funds for each completed Time 3 interview. Each agency determined whether or not to pay teen participants for the Time 3 interviews and, if so, what the payment would be. The school district was not paid per completed Time 3 interview because it considered the follow-up to be part of its own program evaluation plan.

Plan of Analysis

To assess the outcomes of the demonstration, we attempted to answer the following questions.

1. Were teens who were not yet coitally active more likely to remain so if they had received the HBM-SLT intervention? Did significant sex or race/ethnicity differences exist in treatment effects between the HBM-SLT and comparison programs?

2. Were experimental program teens who became sexually active following the intervention more likely to report initial and then consistent contraceptive use than comparison program recipients? Did sex or racial/ethnic differences in program effectiveness occur?

3. Did significant increases occur in contraceptive efficiency from Time 1 to Time 3 among coitally active teenagers? If so, was the HBM-SLT program more effective than the comparison programs in producing these improvements? Were there sex or race/ethnicity differences in program effectiveness?

4. Were Time 2 health beliefs and sexual knowledge significant predictors of adolescents' fertility control behaviors (i.e., continued abstinence or

contraceptive usage) at Time 3? Did the perceptual and knowledge changes (if any) mediate or augment relationships between treatment conditions and fertility control behaviors?

Our overall analysis plan involved a four-group approach: we examined Time 1 virgins' abstinence, transition to coital activity, and initiation of contraceptive use separately for each sex; and we examined Time 1 nonvirgins' contraceptive behavior separately for each sex. This analytic approach was adopted on theoretical as well as empirical grounds.

From a general theoretical perspective, the underlying mechanisms and explanations of behavior initiation are likely to differ from those that govern maintenance or strengthening of behaviors (Bandura, 1986). Adolescent fertility control behaviors are probably no exception. Howard and McCabe's (1990) sexual postponement intervention suggest that different issues are likely to surround the initiation of sexual intercourse and of contraceptive use, and the maintenance of contraceptive use. Moreover, the determinants and dynamics of coital activity and contraceptive use generally differ for females and males (Chilman, 1983).

From an empirical standpoint, psychological research has clearly documented that past behavior is the best predictor of subsequent behavior under similar circumstances (Bandura, 1977). Realistically, teenagers who were already coitally active carried their contraceptive histories with them to the intervention and through the follow-up year, so we needed to take these histories into account. For teens who were not coitally active at Time 1 and who became active during Time 2, no comparable contraceptive histories could be brought to bear.

Thus for those who were not yet sexually active, the analytic focus was upon detecting potential treatment group differences in abstinence maintenance; for those who became coitally active, we focused upon contraceptive use, as well as the role of Time 2 HBM scales and sexual knowledge in predicting adoption and continuation of pregnancy avoidance behaviors. When statistically significant changes occurred, further analyses would determine whether they were attributable to treatment group effects and changes in HBM variables from Time 1 to Time 2.

For the coitally experienced at Time 1, we wanted to determine whether exposure to either program significantly increased contraceptive use from Time 1 to Time 3. If it did, then we would test whether the experimental program was significantly more effective than the (combined sites) comparison programs, with Time 1 contraceptive use controlled. Once again we would determine whether the Time 2 HBM scales mediated or augmented the treatment effects for each sex.

Outcome Variables

Abstinence continuation, transition from virginity to coital activity, and use of and changes in use of effective birth control methods at first and most recent postintervention intercourse were measured. Following the delineations in the National Survey of Adolescent Males (NSAM), effective contraceptive methods included pill, condom, diaphragm, foam/jelly, and sponge; ineffective methods were withdrawal, rhythm, and douche (Sonenstein, Pleck, & Ku, 1989b). To assess teenagers' consistent use of effective methods, we computed a weighted composite contraception index.[3]

Data Analysis

Before assessing the immediate and 1-year impact of the educational intervention programs across study sites, several preliminary analyses were conducted. First, we assessed the general representativeness of our baseline sample of adolescents (ages 15-18) by comparing data pertaining to their sexual behavior (collected in 1986-1987) with a nationally representative sample of same-aged females from the 1988 National Survey of Family Growth (NSFG) (National Center for Health Statistics, 1988), and of males from the 1988 NSAM (Sonenstein, Pleck, & Ku, 1989a, 1989b) using methods outlined by Card and Reagan (1989). Second, we determined whether random assignment of participants to HBM-SLT and comparison programs resulted in generally equivalent treatment groups with respect to demographic, background, beliefs, and knowledge variables, as well as pregnancy avoidance behaviors. Next, we examined whether differential participant attrition from the study sample at Time 3 occurred, using discriminant function analysis. Finally, we tested for between-site differences in Time 3 Contraceptive Efficiency among the seven comparison programs by one-way analysis of variance or covariance and post hoc comparisons before deciding whether to combine data across sites.

The main analyses tested for treatment group differences on the three major outcome measures: abstinence maintenance; initiation and consistent use of effective contraception for those who became coitally active; and changes in contraceptive efficiency among those who were sexually active at Time 1. This was accomplished first through bivariate analyses conducted separately for each sex. Then, we examined the relative contribution of age, race/ethnicity, family composition, religiosity, grade-level-for-age, educational aspirations, previous sexuality education, Time 1 and Time 2 sexual and contraceptive knowledge and perceptions, and Time 1 contraceptive use (when appropriate), using a stepwise multiple regression approach (see Eisen et al., 1990 for details).

Results

Preliminary Analyses

Baseline Sample Representativeness

We compared our participants at Time 1 with national samples on two salient variables: "Ever had sexual intercourse" and self-reported use of an effective contraceptive method at most recent sexual intercourse. For males, our Time 1 sample included the same proportion of coitally experienced teenagers (55%) as was contained in the recent NSAM sample (55%) (Eisen et al., 1990; Sonenstein et al., 1989a, Table 1; 1989b, Table 1), but our sample reported significantly fewer individuals using an effective contraceptive method at last intercourse (35% vs. 62%, $p < .001$) (Eisen et al., 1990; Sonenstein et al., 1989b, Table 3). For females, our Time 1 sample contained a somewhat smaller proportion of coitally active teens (34%) than did the adjusted 1988 NSFG sample (40%, $p < .10$) (Eisen et al., 1990; London, Mosher, Pratt, & Williams, 1989, Table 4). Our Time 1 female sample was significantly less likely than the 1988 NFSG sample to have used an effective contraceptive method at last sex (46% vs. 68%, $p < .001$) (Eisen et al., 1990). Thus at baseline our sexually active males and females appeared to be at somewhat greater risk for pregnancy exposure than similar teenagers in recent national surveys (Eisen et al., 1990).

HBM Scales Construction: Factor Analysis of the HBM Items

The 35 items listed were first grouped by the four HBM constructs, as shown in Table 9.2. Seriousness and Benefits were then each divided into two parts. We hypothesized six oblique item groupings, including Perceived Serious Affective Consequences of Pregnancy (Items 4, 6, 12, 13, 17, 27, and 35); Perceived Serious Resolution Consequences (Items 9, 21, and 33); Perceived Interpersonal Benefits (Items 10, 14, 28, 31, and 34), and Perceived Benefits of Effective Birth Control Use (Items 7, 8, 15, 19, 20, 23, and 24). Confirmatory factor analysis revealed that the six hypothesized factors all had eigenvalues >1 and accounted for about 43% of the variance extracted from the correlation matrix containing the 35 items, which was a larger percentage of variance than any of the alternative six factor models tested. On this basis and other standard criteria, we concluded that six hypothesized item groupings constituted HBM-based scales.

HBM Scale Construction: Reliability of the Scales

Internal-consistency reliability estimates were computed for each of the six scales. Five of the six were sufficiently reliable (Cronbach's Alphas >.50) for making group comparisons (Helmstadter, 1964), but the Susceptibility to Pregnancy and STDs measure did not meet minimum standards and was dropped from the outcome analyses.

Time 1 Treatment Group Equivalence

No significant differences were found in reported sexual behavior or contraceptive use variables between participants randomly assigned to the HBM-SLT and comparison conditions. Moreover, only three differences occurred at all across the range of variables examined: Comparison participants had slightly higher educational aspirations, they attended approximately one more sexuality education class meeting on average, and they scored about one point higher on the Sexual Knowledge measure than participants in the HBM-SLT program.

Time 1 to Time 2 Changes in Health Beliefs and Sexual Knowledge

Bivariate Analyses

In order to determine whether teenagers who completed either the experimental intervention or one of the comparison programs increased their perceptions of pregnancy susceptibility, seriousness of pregnancy, benefits of contraception, became more knowledgeable, and decreased their perception of barriers to contraceptive usage from Time 1 to Time 2, seven repeated measures analyses (paired t tests) were performed (not shown). For the HBM scales, all changes were in the hypothesized (i.e., favorable) direction, all were statistically significant for both the experimental and comparison intervention groups ($ps < .01$ to $.001$), but none was very large.

A substantial increase occurred, however, in sexual and contraceptive knowledge immediately following both intervention programs. Each participant's sexual and contraceptive knowledge score was the sum of the number of knowledge items answered correctly, with 50 points possible. The Time 1 mean (M) was 25.12, with a standard deviation (SD) of 7.02. Therefore the average adolescent in this age range answered about half of the items correctly at Time 1. For HBM-SLT participants at Time 2, the average increase was more than 8 points (from 24.68 to 32.85, $p < .001$), while the comparison group increase was very similar (from 25.55 to 32.36, $p < .001$). These increases were greater than one SD and represented an improvement of almost 20% in scale scores. Thus consistent with the results of other intervention studies (Kirby, 1984), a substantial increase occurred in knowledge over the 2- to 3-week program of lectures and small group discussions in both conditions.

Multivariate Analyses

To understand what influenced changes in perceptions and knowledge from Time 1 to Time 2, stepwise regression analyses were performed. For these analyses, treatment group and participants' demographic characteristics were used as predictors of each Time 2 score while controlling that specific scale's Time 1 score. All regression equations were statistically significant ($ps < .001$).

Four consistent patterns of findings emerged (see Table 9.4). First, the experimental and comparison program participants did not differ on any Time 2 health beliefs, net of demographic variables. Second, females' health perceptions were significantly more favorable than males' perceptions on four of the six HBM scales. As common sense might suggest, females saw themselves as more susceptible to pregnancy and perceived both the affective and pregnancy resolution consequences to be more serious for themselves. One significant treatment group by gender interaction effect did occur (not shown): Females in the comparison programs saw themselves as more susceptible to pregnancy than females in the experimental program, while males in the experimental program saw themselves as more susceptible to causing a pregnancy than did their comparison group peers (p <.05). Interestingly, females continued to perceive fewer barriers to birth control use than males after the interventions, despite widespread assumptions that females face more barriers than males in obtaining and using birth control (Nathanson & Becker, 1983). Third, on four of six HBM scales, older adolescents reported significantly more favorable postintervention perceptions than younger ones. Only on the two Perceived Seriousness scales were no age differences detected. Finally, ethnicity was not consistently related to health beliefs, although Hispanic teenagers did perceive fewer Benefits of Birth Control Use on either scale than other groups, and blacks perceived less personal Susceptibility to Pregnancy and STDs, as well as fewer Serious Pregnancy Resolution Consequences than other groups.

A similar analysis revealed, as hypothesized, a significant treatment group effect upon the sexual and contraception knowledge measure when Time 1 Sexual Knowledge scores were controlled. Participants in the experimental intervention had significantly greater knowledge than those in the comparison groups, independent of demographic characteristics (p <.05). Participants' treatment group assignment, however, increased the amount of variance explained in the final step of the equation by less than 1%.

To summarize Time 1 to Time 2 changes, participants in both programs made significant increases in the favorable direction on all six health belief scales and on the comprehensive sexual knowledge measure. However, no significant differences were found in Time 2 HBM perceptions between the experimental and comparison programs. In general, females and older adolescents held significantly more favorable attitudes than males and younger teens, respectively. Finally, the experimental group achieved significantly higher Time 2 sexual and contraceptive knowledge scores than the comparison group, but the effect was small.

Time 3 Attrition Analysis

We determined which variables distinguished Time 3 interview completers ($N = 888$) from noncompleters ($N = 556$) (not shown). For males, age, Time 1 coital activity status, Time 2 Sexual Knowledge, and

Table 9.4 Final Step in Regressions of Health Belief Scale Scores (Time 2) on Selected Demographic Variables and Time 1 Health Belief Scores: Gain Analyses (N = 1325)

Variable/Scale	SUS Beta	SUS T-Value	SERAFF Beta	SERAFF T-Value	SERRES Beta	SERRES T-Value	BENEFF Beta	BENEFF T-Value	BENIP Beta	BENIP T-Value	BARS Beta	BARS T-Value
Pretest scale	.405	16.27***	.494	20.77***	.497	21.02***	.442	17.63***	.550	23.94***	.577	26.16***
Age	.079	3.18**	—		—		.094	3.90***	.064	2.79**	-.056	-2.59**
Sex[a]	.102	4.10***	.102	4.28***	.124	5.27***	—		—		-.125	-5.69***
Hispanic[b]	—		—		—		—		—		—	
Black[b]	-.061	-2.46*	—		-.054	-2.31*	-.077	-3.06**	-.060	-2.63**	—	
Treatment[c]	—		—		—		—		—		—	
Adjusted R^2	= .185		= .268		= .287		= .227		= .315		= .336	

NOTE: SUS = Susceptibility to Pregnancy/VD; SERAFF = Serious Affective Consequences of Pregnancy; SERRES = Serious Pregnancy Resolution Consequences; BENEFF = Benefits of Effective Contraceptive Use; BENIP = Interpersonal Benefits of Contraceptive Use; BARS = Barriers to Contraceptive Use.
a. Females = 1; Males = 0. b. Dummy variable: Yes = 1; No = 0 (relative to all others, i.e., comparison group). c. HBM-SLT = 1; Comparisons = -1. $*p < .10$ $**p < .05$
$***p < .001$

245

treatment group were significant discriminators. Younger males, those without previous coital experience, those who were more knowledge-able following the intervention, and those who attended the HBM-SLT intervention were more likely to complete the Time 3 interview. Among nonvirgins, Time 1 contraceptive usage did *not* differentiate between the completers and noncompleters. Thus more of the coitally experi-enced males left the study sample at Time 3, but they were not poorer contraceptors than those experienced males who remained.

For females, only two variables separated the completers from the noncompleters. Younger participants and those who at Time 1 cited more negative effects of a (near future) pregnancy were more likely to complete the follow-up. No variables significantly differentiated the Time 1 nonvirgins who completed the follow-up interview from those who did not complete it at the $p = .05$ level.

Outcome Analyses: Stability and Change
in Coital Activity Status at Time 3
for Time 1 Virgins

Among the 596 participants who had not had sexual intercourse at Time 1 and who provided coital status data at Time 3, 177 (30%) reported that they had first experienced intercourse since Time 1. Thus 419 (70%) of the sexually inexperienced teens maintained abstinence. In addition, 41 (15%) of 270 participants with coital experience at Time 1 reported at Time 3 that they had had no sexual intercourse since Time 1.

Bivariate Analyses

No significant difference was found between the HBM-SLT and com-parison programs in maintaining participants' abstinence (71% vs. 70%). Females were more likely to remain abstinent than males (77% vs. 61%, p < .001) when data were combined across treatments, age, and race/ethnic-ity. Age at Time 3 was not significantly associated with virginity loss in this combined sample of treatment, gender, and race/ethnicity groupings, although a trend was apparent (< 15 years old = 27%, 15-17 = 30%, and > 17 = 33%). Race or ethnicity was not significantly associated with contin-ued abstinence at Time 3 for the combined sample either (whites = 65%, blacks = 62%, Hispanics = 72%, Asians = 76%, p > .10). Finally, no difference was found between teenagers who reported attending at least one sexuality education class meeting prior to the study and those who

Table 9.5 Final Step in Regressions of Time 3 First Intercourse[a] for Time 1 Virgins on Selected Demographic, Cognitive, Health Belief and Treatment Variables (Females and Males)

Predictor	Females (N = 290)		Males (N = 197)	
	Coefficient	T-Value	Coefficient	T-Value
Expectancy of becoming coitally active, next 3 months	.140	2.35*	.176	2.66**
Black[b]	—		.278	4.18***
Frequency attend church	—		−.174	−2.62**
Educational aspirations	−.131	−2.15*	—	
At grade level for age[a]	.120	2.04*	−.158	−2.41*
Time 1 Serious Pregnancy Resolution Consequences	−.160	−2.38*	—	
Time 1 Barriers to Birth Control Use	−.138	−2.01*	—	
Time 1 Benefits of Effective Birth Control Use	.150	2.41*	—	
Treatment[c]	—		−.430	−2.28*
Age X treatment	—		.389	2.06*
Adjusted R^2	= .089		= .172	

NOTE: [a]Yes = 1; No = 0.
[b]Dummy variable: Yes = 1; No = 0 (relative to all others, i.e., comparison group)
[c]HBM-SLT = 1; Comparisons = −1
*$p < 0.05$
**$p < 0.01$
***$p < .001$

attended none (70% vs 71%). Thus our data indicate that the receipt of previous formal instruction neither prompted nor retarded the initiation of sexual intercourse in the follow-up year.

Multivariate Analysis: Males

As hypothesized, receipt of the HBM-SLT intervention program led to significantly greater continued abstinence (64%) than the comparison programs (56%) among males with demographic, background, and Time 1 and Time 2 knowledge and health belief variables controlled (see Table 9.5, right half).[4,5] A regression model with six variables—HBM-SLT group membership, being nonblack, having lower expectancy of becoming coitally active in the next 3 months, attending church services more frequently, being at or above grade level for one's age, and the treatment program by (estimated) age at first intercourse inter-action—best predicted continued abstinence at Time 3. Inspection of the adjusted group means (not shown) indicated that the HBM-SLT males who became coitally active by Time 3 were significantly older than the comparison males. About 17% of the variance in abstinence stability was accounted for by this six-variable model.

Multivariate Analysis: Females

A six-variable model also emerged as the best fit to the data for females (see Table 9.5, left half). Lower expectancy of becoming coitally active in the next 3 months, higher perceived Barriers to Birth Control Use, greater perceived Serious Negative Consequences of Re-solving a Teen Pregnancy, and fewer perceived Benefits of Effective Birth Control Use (all at Time 1), higher educational aspirations, and being *below* grade level for one's age were significant predictors of continued abstinence for females, but treatment program was not (HBM = 73% vs. comparison = 78%). This six-variable model accounted for almost 9% of the variance in Time 3 virginity status.

To summarize, HBM-SLT program males were significantly less likely to become coitally active than comparison males. HBM-SLT and compar-ison females showed equal likelihood of becoming sexually active during the follow-up year. The one common predictor of the transition to coital activity for both genders was their personal expectation at Time 1 of becoming sexually active in the near future. No Time 2 Health Belief scales were significant predictors; Time 1 Health Beliefs were significant predic-tors for females only. Neither previous sexuality education nor follow-up age were significant predictors of the transition to nonvirginity for either gender. Males who were exposed to the HBM-SLT intervention and who reported becoming coitally active, however, were estimated to be older at first intercourse than those who attended comparison programs and subse-quently became sexually active.

**Outcome Analyses: Initiation of Contraceptive
Use at Time 3 for Time 1 Virgins**

Bivariate Analyses: Males

No significant differences were found between HBM-SLT and com-parison program participants on use of an effective method at first

Table 9.6 Time 3 Contraceptive Usage for Time 1 Virgins (*N* = 153)

Variable	Contraceptive Usage Effective Method First Sex %	Effective Method Last Sex %	Efficiency Mean
HBM-SLT	57	45	8.54
Females			
Total	49	35	6.95
White	44	33	6.33
Black	50	38	9.13
Hispanic	50	35	6.41
Males			
Total	64	55	9.98
White	63	75	12.25
Black	63	63	12.25
Hispanic	64	46	8.63
COMPARISONS	67	65	12.04
Females			
Total	61	65	12.00
White	100	100	17.14
Black	50	83	13.67
Hispanic	50	44	9.29
Males			
Total	71	65	12.08
White	82	70	13.60
Black	83	67	14.50
Hispanic	53	60	9.13

NOTE: Effective methods included pill, condom, diaphragm, foam, and sponge. Contraceptive efficiency is a weighted composition of Consistency X Effective Method (First + Last Sex).

intercourse, use of an effective method at most recent intercourse, or on Contraceptive Efficiency in the follow-up year (see Table 9.6). About 55% of those in the HBM-SLT program and 65% of those in the comparison programs reported using an effective method at their last coitus. Some 64% of HBM-SLT and 71% of comparison males used an effective method at first sex. Thus about 67% of the males who completed either intervention program reported using an effective birth control method at first intercourse. This latter incidence rate is somewhat higher than the rate of effective method use at first sex that was

Table 9.7 Final Step in Regression of Time 3 Contraceptive Efficiency for Time 1 Virgins on Selected Demographic, Health Belief, Knowledge, and Treatment Variables (Females and Males)

Predictor	Females (N = 67)		Males (N = 79)	
	Beta	T-Value	Beta	T-Value
Age	.211	2.00**	—	
Hispanic[a]	—		−.221	−2.11**
Time 1 Interpersonal Benefits of Birth Control	—		−.315	−3.06***
Previous Sex Education[b]	—		.283	2.80***
Time 2 Sexual Knowledge	.306	2.99***	—	
Time 2 Benefits of Effective Birth Control	.260	2.35**	.201	1.90*
Treatment[c]	−.350	−3.39****	—	
Adjusted R^2	= .307		= .231	

NOTE: Contraceptive Efficiency is a weighted composite of Consistency X Effective Method (First + Last Sex). [a]Dummy variable: Yes = 1; No = 0, (Relative to all others, i.e., comparison group). [b]Yes = 1; No = 0. [c]HBM-SLT = 1; Comparisons = −1; $*p < 0.10$; $**p < 0.05$; $***p < 0.01$; $****p < 0.001$

reported by a comparable sample in the 1988 NSAM (67% vs. 57%, z = 1.80, $p < .10$) (Eisen et al., 1990; Sonenstein et al., 1989b, Table 5).

Multivariate Analysis: Males

We continued to find no significant HBM-SLT program effect upon Contraceptive Efficiency when other relevant variables were brought into the analysis, as shown in Table 9.7 (right half). Four variables—previous exposure to sexuality education, perception of the Interpersonal Benefits of Birth Control Use at Time 1, perception of the Benefits of Effective Birth Control Use at Time 2, and not being Hispanic—were significant predictors of Contraceptive Efficiency at Time 3. Males who had prior sexuality education classes, who saw *fewer* interpersonal benefits of using birth control but greater benefits of using effective birth control, were better contraceptors than the others; Hispanics who became sexually active during the follow-up year were significantly less efficient contraceptors than their black and white peers (who did not differ from each other). These four variables accounted for about 23% of the variance in males' Contraceptive Efficiency scores.

Bivariate Analyses: Females

Comparison program participants reported significantly greater contraceptive use on two of the three contraceptive use measures after making their sexual debuts (see Table 9.6). In the HBM-SLT group, 35% reported using an effective contraceptive method at their last sex, while 65% said they did so in the comparison groups ($p < .05$). The groups also differed with respect to Contraceptive Efficiency scores over the follow-up period (HBM-SLT M = 6.95; comparison M = 12.00, $p < .01$). No significant group difference was seen in rates of use of an effective contraceptive method at first intercourse (49% vs. 61%). Comparison of the combined HBM-SLT and comparison group rate (54.6%) with the rate reported in the 1988 NSFG revealed no significant difference between our combined groups and national sample estimates (54% vs. 57%) (Eisen et al., 1990).

Multivariate Analysis: Females

Further analyses revealed that the bivariate treatment differences for Contraceptive Efficiency described above remained when other salient variables were included, as shown on the left side of Table 9.7. Significant positive effects also were found for being older at first sex, having more favorable Time 2 perceptions of the Benefits of Using Effective Birth Control, and greater Time 2 Sexual Knowledge (with Time 1 Knowledge and Benefits controlled). Together, these four variables accounted for about 34% of the variance in females' Contraceptive Efficiency Scores.

To summarize, the patterns of intervention program effects upon contraceptive initiation and maintenance differed substantially for males and females. For males, no significant difference was found between intervention groups. For females, the comparison programs were more effective than the HBM-SLT program. Time 2 Benefits of Effective Birth Control Use scale was an important contributor to Contraceptive Efficiency for both sexes. Time 2 Sexual Knowledge was a significant predictor of follow-up Contraceptive Efficiency for females, independent of the intervention program they attended. The latter finding is especially important because it represents the first time that a direct link between postintervention sexual knowledge and subsequent contraceptive behavior has been reported in a prospective study (Hayes, 1987; Kirby, 1984).

Table 9.8 Time 3 Contraceptive Efficiency Means (M) for Time 1 Non-virgins (N = 220)

Variable	Time 1 M	Time 3 M
HBM-SLT	8.51	11.06
Females		
Total	8.51	9.94
White	9.55	13.09
Black	10.33	10.40
Hispanic	6.83	8.13
Males		
Total	8.51	11.91
White	14.67	18.00
Black	9.25	13.18
Hispanic	6.65	9.58
COMPARISONS	8.03	10.40
Females		
Total	8.63	11.22
White	10.22	12.11
Black	10.68	13.79
Hispanic	5.67	8.56
Males		
Total	7.48	9.46
White	7.44	8.89
Black	7.45	11.50
Hispanic	7.52	7.76

NOTE: Contraceptive efficiency is a weighted composite of Consistency X Effective Method (First + Last Sex).

Outcome Analyses: Changes in Contraceptive Use at Time 3 for Time 1 Nonvirgins

Bivariate Analyses: Males

Contraceptive Efficiency improved about 3 scale points (from M = 8.51 to M = 11.91, $p < .005$) for subjects in the HBM-SLT group, as shown in Table 9.8. Comparison subjects showed some improvement in Contraceptive Efficiency, but it was not as large as for the HBM-SLT group (Time 1 M = 7.48; Time 3 M = 9.46, $p < .10$). Neither group showed significant improvement in effective contraceptive use at last intercourse, although a trend was apparent in the experimental group.

Multivariate Analysis: Males

The statistically significant increases in Contraceptive Efficiency for males in each program allowed us to test one of our major study hypotheses: That HBM-SLT program participation would lead to greater 1-year follow-up Contraceptive Efficiency than comparison program participation, net of other relevant variables. Table 9.9 presents the final stepwise regression model.

A five-variable equation that included Time 1 Contraceptive Efficiency, Time 1 Sexual and Contraceptive Knowledge, being non-Hispanic, Time 1 living arrangement, and treatment program appeared to provide the best fit to the data. Participants who were more efficient contraceptors at Time 1, who had greater sexual and contraceptive knowledge prior to the program, who were non-Hispanics, who lived with both parents (at Time 1), and who participated in the HBM-SLT intervention were more efficient Time 3 contraceptors. Approximately 8% of the variance in Time 3 Contraceptive Efficiency was accounted for by Time 1 Efficiency. Adding ethnicity, living arrangement, and Time 1 Sexual Knowledge almost doubled the initial R^2 (Step 2, $p < .01$), and exposure to the HBM-SLT program contributed an additional 3% to the total variance explained (Step 3, $p < .05$). Thus demographic factors, prior sex knowledge, and intervention group more than doubled the influence of Time 1 contraceptive behavior alone. Together the five variables accounted for about 18% of the variance in contraceptive use at Time 3.

Bivariate Analyses: Females

For HBM-SLT program participants, no significant improvement was seen in Contraceptive Efficiency (Time 1 M = 8.51; Time 3 M = 9.94) or in use of an effective method at last sex from Time 1 to Time 3 (see Table 9.8). For teenagers in the comparison program, average Contraceptive Efficiency increased from 8.63 to 11.41 ($p < .05$). Like the teenagers in the HBM-SLT program, effective contraceptive use at most recent sex did not improve significantly for those in the comparison program.

Multivariate Analysis: Females

We assessed treatment program differences in Time 3 Contraceptive Efficiency scores with Time 1 Contraceptive Efficiency and other

Table 9.9 Stepwise Regression of Time 1 Nonvirgins' Time 3 Contraceptive Efficiency on Selected Demographic, Knowledge, Time 1 Contraceptive Usage, and Treatment Variables: (Males, $N = 115$)

Predictor	Step 1 Beta	Step 1 T-Value	R^2	Step 2 Beta	Step 2 T-Value	R^2 Chg	Step 3 Beta	Step 3 T-Value	R^2 Chg
Time 1 Contraceptive Efficiency	.302	3.37	.083***	.251	2.90**		.234	2.71**	
Sexual Knowledge Time 1	—			.165	1.92}		.183	2.15*	
Hispanic[a]	—			−.263	−2.89}	.095***	−.276	−3.07***	
Family[b]	—			.162	1.80}		.161	1.81*	
Treatment[c]	—			—			.177	2.06	.031**
Adjusted R^2								= .181	

NOTE: Contraceptive Efficiency is a weighted composite of Consistency X Effective Method (First + Last Sex). [a]Dummy variable: Yes = 1; No = 0, (Relative to all others, i.e., comparison group). [b]Composition: 0 = Lives with neither parent; 1 = Lives with one parent; 2 = Lives with both parents. [c]HBM-SLT = 1; Comparisons = −1; *$p < 0.10$; **$p < 0.05$; ***$p < 0.01$

254

Table 9.10 Stepwise Regression of Time 1 Nonvirgins' Time 3 Contraceptive Efficiency on Selected Personal History, Time 1 Contraceptive Usage, Health Belief and Treatment Variables (Females, $N = 92$)

Predictor	Beta	Step 1 T-Value	R^2	Beta	Step 2 T-Value	R^2 Chg
Time 1 Contraceptive Efficiency	.384	3.95	.138***	.265	2.66**	
Previous Sex Education[a]	—			.198	2.07*	
Time 1 Barriers to Birth Control Use				−.228	−2.27*	.098**
Treatment[b]	—			—		
Adjusted R^2					= .220	

NOTE: Contraceptive Efficiency is a weighted composite of Consistency X Effective Method (First + Last Sex). [a]Yes = 1; No = 0. [b]HBM-SLT = 1; Comparisons = −1; *$p < 0.05$; **$p < 0.01$; ***$p < 0.001$

salient variables included. The final stepwise regression results are indicated in Table 9.10. Contrary to our study hypothesis, the HBM-SLT program was no more effective than the comparison programs in improving Time 3 Contraceptive Efficiency.

A three-variable model that included Time 1 Contraceptive Efficiency (Step 1 R^2 = .15) was combined with previous sexuality education and perception of Barriers to Birth Control Use at Time 1 (Step 2, $p < .01$; total adjusted R^2 = .22). Those females who were more efficient contraceptors at Time 1, who had been exposed to sexuality education before our demonstration project, and who saw fewer barriers to birth control use at Time 1 were more efficient contraceptors 1 year after the program.

In sum, the HBM-SLT intervention appeared to be more effective than the comparison program in promoting Contraceptive Efficiency for males. Participation in the HBM-SLT treatment program added significantly to a model that predicted males' contraceptive use at Time 3. For females, the HBM-SLT program exposure did not contribute significantly to the prediction of Time 3 Contraceptive Efficiency. Previous sexuality education, independent of the current intervention program, increased Time 3 Contraceptive Efficiency for females. Finally, Hispanic ethnicity was an important negative predictor of Time 3 contraceptive use for males.

**Outcome Analyses: Incidence of Pregnancy
or Pregnancy Responsibility at Time 3**

Claiming some personal involvement in a pregnancy were 5% of males (11/202) and 11% of females (18/169). The small number of conceptions precluded extensive analysis; however, it was clear that no differences existed between treatment programs in pregnancy responsibility for males (HBM-SLT = 7%; comparison = 3%) or pregnancy for females (HBM-SLT = 9%; comparison = 13%). Conceptions were more numerous among teenagers who had been coitally active at Time 1 than among those who became sexually active during the follow-up year, but we did not test for statistical significance because any difference would almost certainly be attributable to transitioning teenagers' shorter coital history and reporting period (i.e., right censoring). Finally, we examined the relationship between reported contraceptive use at the most recent postintervention intercourse and the incidence of pregnancy or pregnancy responsibility. Again, bearing in mind the small number of pregnancies reported overall, 14% of teenagers who used ineffective or no methods but only 3% percent of those who used effective methods reported involvement in a pregnancy.

Discussion

Summary of Program Outcomes

Sexual experience (Time 1 virginity/nonvirginity) and gender were important mediators of the effects of the HBM-SLT and comparison programs on the key pregnancy avoidance measures. For those who had not had intercourse prior to the intervention, more males in the HBM-SLT than the comparison program maintained their abstinence over the follow-up year ($p < .05$); for females, no difference was found between intervention programs. Female Time 1 virgins who attended the comparison programs were more likely to use an effective contraceptive method at their most recent intercourse and to be more efficient contraceptors than those who attended the HBM-SLT program ($p < .01$); the intervention programs were equally effective for coitally inexperienced males. Both interventions significantly increased contraceptive efficiency. Coitally active teens exposed to either intervention became more efficient contraceptors. For males, the HBM-SLT program led to significantly greater follow-up contraceptive efficiency than the comparison programs ($p < .05$); for females, the interventions produced equivalent improvement. Positive Time 2 perceptions of the Benefits of Effective Birth Control Use predicted contraceptive efficiency for two of the four analytic groupings, as well as predicting transition to coital activity in the follow-up year for males. Finally, exposure to sexuality education prior to the study was associated with greater Time 3 contraceptive efficiency, irrespective of the present intervention program attended, for two of the four groups.

Answers to Basic Evaluation Questions

Our data allow us to address whether short-term educational outreach programs can be effective in strengthening teenagers' fertility control behaviors over a 1-year period. We do so by answering four questions about the HBM-SLT and comparison programs.

First, did a greater proportion of sexually inexperienced teens remain abstinent after exposure to the HBM-SLT than the comparison programs? YES, among males; NO, for females. Only one common predictor of the transition to sexual intercourse existed for males and females: their personal expectation of becoming coitally active in the near future.

Second, among teenagers who become sexually active following the intervention programs, was the adoption of effective contraception greater in the HBM-SLT than the comparison groups? NO. For males, the HBM-SLT and comparison programs brought about equal levels of contraceptive initiation and efficiency. For females, the comparison programs actually appeared to be significantly more effective. However, an examination of the contraceptive methods reported by comparison program females at their most recent sex shows that they relied heavily upon condoms—primarily a male method (condom only = 60%; pill + condom = 10%; pill only = 30%). Thus it is not clear to what extent females' contraceptive decision making and choices were determined or affected by exposure to the comparison programs and to what extent by their partners' influence and choices. Did program effectiveness vary for teens of different racial and ethnic groups? YES. Most notably, Hispanic males reported significantly less contraceptive usage than their black and white peers. Did intervention participants who became sexually active report higher initial contraceptive use than teenagers nationally? YES, males did. When both of our intervention groups were combined, a somewhat greater proportion of males reported using an effective contraceptive method at their first intercourse than did a comparable group of males in a recent national survey ($p <$ .10). No such differences emerged when study females were compared with females from another current national survey.

Third, were significant increases evident in Contraceptive Efficiency from Time 1 to Time 3 among teenagers who had been coitally active at baseline? YES. Was the HBM-SLT program more effective than the comparison programs in producing these improvements? YES, for males.

Fourth, were Time 2 health beliefs and sexual knowledge significant predictors of adolescents' fertility behaviors at Time 3? YES, but not consistently. The Time 1 HBM scales used to assess motivational aspects of pregnancy avoidance often correlated with behavior changes assessed at Time 3; in a few instances, Time 2 scales appeared to mediate these changes. For example, Time 2 measures of perceived Benefits of Effective Birth Control Use and sexual knowledge significantly improve predictions of males' and females' Contraceptive Efficiency in the year of their sexual debuts. These mediational effects did not emerge for teenagers who were already coitally active when the demonstration project began.

Other Noteworthy Findings

The significant association of prior sexuality education experience with Time 3 Contraceptive Efficiency in two of four analysis groups is intriguing. This finding suggests that one major benefit of the current demonstration project, independent of specific treatment program, may have been to provide many participants an opportunity to overlearn sexuality material. Formal sexuality education may be a more incremental learning process than we realized; programs that appear inconclusive or ineffective upon completion or at short-term follow-up may exert a substantial effect later on, perhaps in combination with other interventions.

Implications

Viewed as a whole, what has been learned from the implementation and findings of this theory-driven demonstration project? First, it is possible to carry out a fairly rigorous impact evaluation of community- and school-based intervention programs with adequate funding and an appropriate level of agency/school district cooperation. Second, publicly funded sex and contraceptive education programs as short as 8-12 hours appear to increase many participants' knowledge from Time 1 levels and facilitate some pregnancy avoidance behaviors. Third, differences in programs impact as a function of previous sexual experience, gender, race and ethnicity, and prior sexuality education confirm that intervention programs need to be client-group specific: "One size does not fit all." As health and sexuality researchers and educators have always known intuitively, few if any main effects exist in real world social interventions.

In the present demonstration, the HBM-SLT intervention appeared to work best with males who were coitally experienced at Time 1, and better with black and white males than with Hispanic males. For some educational outreach programs, this sort of client-specific findings may be a starting point for program development or implementation. For example, program developers and administrators may want to target specific client groups and at-risk behaviors. The fact that the HBM-SLT intervention seemed especially helpful to Time 1 nonvirgin males in increasing consistent use of effective methods (including condoms) has important implications for framing and developing more effective AIDS education efforts.

One hypothesis for the relatively greater success with males in the HBM-SLT curriculum is that active involvement and the role playing/interpersonal interaction format forced males to examine and think about their dating and sexual interactions with females in new and unsettling ways. When they did so, they gained new awareness of the pregnancy risks they and their partners face (experimental males scored higher on the Time 2 Susceptibility to Pregnancy and STDs scale than comparison males), as well as some means with which to maintain or improve their pregnancy avoidance behaviors.

The comparison programs seemed to be most effective with females who were not yet coitally active at Time 1, irrespective of race or ethnicity. In contrast with males, females—even the youngest ones in our sample—may be saturated with the threat of pregnancy—the perceived susceptibility and seriousness elements in the HBM—from early on in their socialization. The HBM-SLT approach may have focused too intensively upon topics that females have overlearned. Consequently they may have perceived that they had less to "learn" from the HBM-SLT intervention. Significantly higher scores on the Time 2 Susceptibility to Pregnancy and STDs scale for comparison group females than experimental group females would seem to support this notion. Future research and evaluation demonstrations that apply an HBM-SLT approach may well be able to strengthen the empirical relationships by refining the curriculum components, increasing the duration and salience of the interventions to the targeted groups, adopting standard impact evaluation measures (see Eisen & Brindis, 1989), and improving the measurement of health beliefs.

Finally, despite the limited impact of the HBM perceptual measures in mediating pregnancy avoidance behaviors at follow-up, we believe that an HBM-SLT measurement and intervention approach may still prove worthwhile as a guide to designing and targeting interventions or intervention components. In this context, the HBM measures may hold promise as a screening device to assign participants to program components that directly address their needs (Eisen, 1989). For instance, teenagers who score low on perceived benefits of effective birth control use or high on expectancy to become coitally active in the near future could be directed to programs or program components that are specifically designed to strengthen their perceptions of the benefits of using effective birth control methods or their susceptibility to pregnancy and STDs. In light of Howard and McCabe's (1990) and our findings, we believe that this sort of participant by treatment interaction approach is the next logical step in developing effective sexuality education outreach programs for teenagers.

References

Alan Guttmacher Institute. (1989). *Risk and responsibility: Teaching sex education in American schools today.* New York: Author.

Bandura, A. (1977). *Social learning theory.* Englewood Cliffs, NJ: Prentice-Hall.

Bandura, A. (1986). *The social foundations of thought and action.* Englewood Cliffs, NJ: Prentice-Hall.

Card, J., & Reagan, R. (1989). Strategies for evaluating adolescent pregnancy programs. *Family Planning Perspectives, 21,* 27-32.

Carrera, M. (1983). Sex education: Curriculum issues. *Journal of Research and Development in Education, 16,* 193-206.

Chilman, C. (1983). *Adolescent sexuality in a changing American society.* (2nd ed.). New York: John Wiley.

Cvetkovich, G., Grote, B., Bjorseth, A., & Sarkissian, J. (1975). On the psychology of adolescents' use of contraceptives. *Journal of Sex Research, 11,* 265-270.

Dawson, D. (1986). The effects of sex education on adolescent behavior. *Family Planning Perspectives, 18,* 162-170.

Eisen, M. (1985). *Developing a health-based educational intervention to increase adolescent fertility control.* (Paper No. 7-002). Austin: University of Texas, Texas Population Research Center.

Eisen, M. (1989). *Testing an intervention model for teen fertility control.* (Final Grant Report to NICHD.). Los Altos, CA: Sociometrics Corp.

Eisen, M., & Brindis, C. (1989). Compilation of a prevention minimum evaluation data set (PMEDS). In J. J. Card (Ed.), *Evaluating programs aimed at preventing teenage pregnancies* (pp. 69-75). Palo Alto, CA: Sociometrics Corp.

Eisen, M., & Zellman, G. (1986). The role of health belief attitudes, sex education, and demographics in predicting adolescents' sexuality knowledge. *Health Education Quarterly, 13,* 9-22.

Eisen, M., & Zellman, G. (1987). Changes in the incidence of sexual intercourse of unmarried teenagers following a community-based sex education program. *Journal of Sex Research, 23,* 527-533.

Eisen, M., Zellman, G., & McAlister, A. (1985). A health belief model approach to adolescents' fertility control: Some pilot program findings. *Health Education Quarterly, 12,* 185-210.

Eisen, M., Zellman, G., & McAlister, A. (1990). Evaluating the impact of a theory-based sexuality and contraceptive education program. *Family Planning Perspectives, 22,* 261-271.

Finkel, M., & Finkel, D. (1975). Sexual and contraceptive knowledge, attitudes and behavior of male adolescents. *Family Planning Perspectives, 7,* 256-260.

Hayes, C. (Ed.). (1987). *Risking the future: Adolescent sexuality, pregnancy, and childbearing* (Vol. 1). Washington, DC: National Academy.

Helmstadter, G. (1964). *Principles of psychological measurement.* New York: Appleton-Century-Crofts.

Hofferth, S., & Miller, B. (1989). An overview of adolescent pregnancy prevention programs and their evaluations. In J. J. Card (Ed.), *Evaluating programs aimed at preventing teenage pregnancies* (pp. 25-40). Palo Alto, CA: Sociometrics Corp.

Howard, M., & McCabe, J. (1990). Helping teenagers postpone sexual involvement. *Family Planning Perspectives, 22,* 22-26.

Janz, N., & Baker, M. (1984). The health belief model: A decade later. *Health Education Quarterly, 11,* 1-47.

Kirby, D. (1984). *Sexuality education: An evaluation of programs and their effects.* Santa Cruz, CA: Network Publications.

Kirby, D., Alter, J., & Scales, P. (1980). *An analysis of U.S. sex education programs* (Vol. 1). Springfield, VA: National Technical Information Service.

London, K., Mosher, W., Pratt, W., & Williams, L. (1989). *Preliminary findings from the national survey of family growth, cycle 4.* Paper presented at the Annual Meetings of the Population Association of America, Baltimore, MD.

Marsiglio, W., & Mott, F. (1986). The impact of sex education on sexual activity, contraceptive use and premarital pregnancy among American teenagers. *Family Planning Perspectives, 18,* 151-162.

Miller, W. (1981). *The psychology of reproduction.* Springfield, VA: National Technical Information Service.

Nathanson, C., & Becker, M. (1983). Contraceptive behavior among unmarried young women: A theoretical framework for research. *Population and Environment, 6,* 39-59.

National Center for Health Statistics. (1988). *National survey of family growth, cycle 4.* Washington, DC: Author.

Paikoff, R., & Brooks-Gunn, J. (in press). Taking fewer chances: Teenage pregnancy prevention programs. *American Psychologist.*

Ory, H., Forrest, J., & Lincoln, R. (1983). *Making choices: Evaluating the health risks and benefits of birth control methods.* New York: Alan Guttmacher Institute.

Reichelt, P., & Werley, H. H. (1976). Contraception, abortion, and venereal disease: Teenagers' knowledge and effect of education. *Family Planning Perspectives, 7,* 83-88.

Rosenstock, I., Strecher, V., & Becker, M. (1988). Social learning theory and the health belief model. *Health Education Quarterly, 15,* 175-183.

Schinke, S. (1982). School-based model for preventing teenage pregnancy. *Social Work in Education, 6,* 34-42.

Schinke, S., Blythe, B., & Gilchrist, L. (1981). Cognitive behavioral prevention of adolescent pregnancy. *Journal of Counseling Psychology, 28,* 451-454.

Schinke, S., Gilchrist, L., & Small, R. (1979). Preventing unwanted adolescent pregnancy: A cognitive-behavioral approach. *American Journal of Orthopsychiatry, 49,* 81-88.

Sonenstein, F., Pleck, J., & Ku, L. (1989a). *At risk of AIDS: Behaviors, knowledge and attitudes among a national sample of adolescent males.* Paper presented at the Annual Meetings of the Population Association of America, Baltimore, MD.

Sonenstein, F., Pleck, J., & Ku, L. (1989b). Sexual activity, condom use and AIDS awareness among adolescent males. *Family Planning Perspectives, 21,* 152-158.

Stout, J., & Rivara, F. (1989). Schools and sex education: Does it work? *Pediatrics, 83,* 375-379.

Zelnik, M., & Kim, J. (1982). Sex education and its association with teenage sexual activity, pregnancy, and contraceptive use. *Family Planning Perspectives, 14,* 117-126.

Notes

1. The state of California had no funding relationship with the demonstration project.

2. Data from Site 8 were not included in this report because participants' age range, marital status, and previous parenthood status were substantially different. In addition, data quality was compromised in this site (Eisen, 1989).

3. The Contraceptive Efficiency index for participants with coital experience at Time 1 was computed by the formula: (Effective Method at First Preintervention Sex [No = 0; Yes = 1] + Effective Method at Last Preintervention Sex [No = 1; Yes = 3]) X Time 1 Consistency (range: 1 to 5). The index for all Time 3 nonvirgins was: (Effective Method at First Postintervention Sex [No = 0; Yes = 1] + Effective Method at Last Postintervention Sex [No = 1; Yes = 3]) X Time 3 Consistency (range: 1 to 5).

4. The sample for the remaining multivariate analyses is limited to black, white, and Hispanic teenagers who were exposed to all or part of the intervention in the seven sites ($N = 501$). For these analyses, which rely on responses to complex cognitive variables, the limited English language skills represented in the Asian race/ethnicity category led to unacceptably high levels of "don't know" responses. Consequently, this group was eliminated from further analyses.

5. Follow-up data pertaining to fertility control behaviors (Abstinence and Contraceptive Efficiency) were combined across sites in the following analyses because no significant differences were found between any two sites for either gender (Eisen et al., 1990).

APPENDIX

Site 1—family planning clinic of community action program in rural south central Texas. *Population served:* low-socioeconomic-status 13-19-year-olds in a summer work-study program sponsored by private industry. *Samples:* Sample 1 (July 1986-July 1987) consisted of 288 participants (79% Hispanic, 12% black, 9% white): retention rate was 60%. Sample 2 (July 1987-July 1988) consisted of 200 participants (84% Hispanic, 10% black, 6% white); retention rate was 68%. *Experimental program:* five 2-hour sessions over a 2-week period—4 hours on sex, biology, STDs, and comparative methods; and 6 hours of small group discussion. *Comparison program:* four 2-hour sessions over a 2-week period—2 hours on sex, biology, STDs, and contraceptive methods; and 6 hours of small group discussion on sexual decision making. *Other:* program assignment random, by classroom: program taught by clinic nursing and health education staff.

Site 2—single high school of small, independent urban school district in San Francisco Bay Area. *Sample:* all 100 ninth graders in school, mostly low- to middle-socioeconomic-status 13-18-year-olds (49% white, 14% Hispanic, 12% black, and 25% of other race or ethnicity); retention rate of 76%. *Experimental program:* fifteen 50-minute sessions during 3-week period—4 hours on sex, biology, STDs, and contraceptive methods; and 8 hours of small-group discussion. *Comparison program:* fifteen 50-minute sessions during 3-week period implementing district's usual ninth-grade adolescent family life unit—covering sex, biology, STDs, and contraceptive methods; and including group discussion and class projects. *Other:* assignment random, by classroom: program taught by school social studies teacher and counselors.

Site 3—single middle school of same district as Site 2. *Sample:* all 101 eighth graders in school, mostly low- to middle-socioeconomic-status 13-15-year-olds (57% white, 14% Hispanic, 7% black, and 22% of other race or ethnicity); retention rate of 77%. *Experimental program:* same as Site 2. *Comparison program:* fifteen 50-minute sessions during 3-week period implementing district's newly instituted eighth-grade unit on drug education and responsible decision making—including 4 hours on sex, biology, STDs, and contraceptive methods (with curriculum methods utilizing the health belief model); and group discussion and class projects. *Other:* random assignment by classroom; program taught by school biology teacher and by counselor from district-funded private counseling center.

Site 4—family planning clinic of community action program in rural south-western Texas. *Population served:* low-socioeconomic-status 13-18-year-old students who participated in Upward Bound and summer work-study programs. *Sample:* 199 participants studied April 1987-August 1988 (88% Hispanic, 12% white); retention rate of 62%. *Experimental program:* six 2-hour sessions over 3-week period—4 hours on sex, biology, STDs, and contraceptive methods; and

8 hours of small group discussion. *Comparison program:* two 2-hour sessions over 3-week period—1 hour on sex, biology, STDs, and contraceptive methods; and 3 hours of discussion on responsible sexual decision making. *Other:* assigned randomly, to groups as these were formed in each program cycle: program taught by clinic health education staff.

Site 5—Planned Parenthood affiliate in north-central California. *Population served:* low-socioeconomic-status 14-19-year-old students in a summer work-study program sponsored by private industry. *Sample:* 242 participants studied July 1987-August 1988 (31% black, 27% Hispanic, 14% white, and 28% of other race or ethnicity): retention rate of 57%. *Experimental program:* four 2-hour sessions over 1-week period—2 hours on sex, biology, STDs, and contraceptive methods; and 6 hours of small group discussion. *Comparison program:* three 2-hour sessions over 1-week period—1-2 hours on sex, biology, STDs, and contraceptive methods; and 5-6 hours of discussion on sexual responsibility and decision making with a "peer educator." *Other:* assigned randomly, by classroom: program taught by staff from community education department.

Site 6—community health education unit of county health department in urban central Texas. *Population served:* low-socioeconomic-status 13-18-year-olds in a private summer work-study program. *Sample:* 222 participants studied July 1987-August 1988 (55% black, 37% Hispanic, 7% white, and 1% of other race or ethnicity); retention rate of 57%. *Experimental program:* five 2-hour sessions over 2-week period—4 hours on sex, biology, STDs, and contraceptive methods; and 6 hours of small group discussion. *Comparison program:* five 2-hour sessions over 2-week period—2-3 hours on sex, biology, STDs, and contraceptive methods; and 7-8 hours of group discussion and exercises on responsible sexual decision making, using components from a national family life education curriculum. *Other:* assigned randomly, to groups as these were formed in each program cycle: program taught by unit health education staff.

Site 7—free-standing community health center in San Francisco's East Bay area. *Population served:* low-socioeconomic-status 14-18-year-old students from magnet high school who were taking summer remedial biology classes. *Sample:* 92 participant students July 1987-August 1988 (77% black, 17% Hispanic, 2% white, and 3% of other race or ethnicity): retention rate of 42%. *Experimental program:* five 2-hour sessions during 2-week period of classes—4 hours on sex, biology, STDs, and contraceptive methods; and 6 hours of small group discussion. *Comparison program:* five 2-hour sessions during 2-week period of classes—2 hours on sex, biology, STDs, and contraceptive methods; and 8 hours of group discussion and exercises on responsible sexuality and decision making. *Other:* assigned randomly, by classroom: program taught by staff of community health education department, under agreement with school district.

10

Comparing Adolescent Pregnancy Prevention Programs

Methods and Results

BRENT C. MILLER
ROBERTA L. PAIKOFF

As noted in the preface of this book, the main goal of any prevention effort is to reduce the incidence of a problem behavior or event. Adolescent pregnancy, which is usually unintended and nonmarital, is a problematic event about which there is widespread agreement—such pregnancies would be better avoided or postponed. More consensus occurs around the goal of preventing adolescent pregnancy than about how to achieve this goal.

On Program Models

An early (and apparently naive) belief was that providing more adequate sex education would result in adolescents being less likely to become pregnant. An apt cliché might be, JUST SAY KNOW. In general, though, studies have found sex education to have little or no relationship to adolescent sexual behavior, contraceptive use, or pregnancy (Stout & Rivara, 1989). Knowledge can be viewed as being helpful or even necessary to prevent pregnancy, but knowledge surely is not *sufficient* to avoid pregnancy. Thus as evident in the preceding chapters and other program summaries (Hayes, 1987), pregnancy prevention programs are usually more broadly conceptualized as including values reinforcement, decision making, skill building, contraceptive services, and motivation to avoid pregnancy through life options.

Following the JUST SAY NO antidrug campaign in the late 1980s, it was suggested that adolescents should also JUST SAY NO to sex. An important distinction exists, however, between using drugs and having sexual intercourse. It would be best never to use drugs, and it can be said that doing drugs is always wrong, but that is not the message that most adults would want to be conveyed about having sexual intercourse.

Instead of JUST SAY NO, perhaps a more appropriate phrase would be JUST SAY NOT YET. This phrase communicates that it is the *timing* of sexual intercourse that is at issue, not that it is always wrong. If not now, then when? The Adolescent Family Life Act of 1981 and the Office of Adolescent Pregnancy Programs in the Department of Health and Human Services that has administered the legislation have taken the stand that the emphasis should be on sexual abstinence until marriage. Some program models featured in this book (Howard & McCabe, Chapter 4; Thomas et al., Chapter 2) are based on the less restrictive premise that any delay in sexual initiation could be beneficial, and such programs seek to postpone sexual involvement without specifying for how long.

Instead of, or in addition to, a sexual postponement message, other program models (Barth et al., Chapter 3; Eisen & Zellman, Chapter 9; Kirby & Waszak, Chapter 8; Zabin, Chapter 7) emphasize that whenever sexual intercourse occurs, effective contraception must be used to prevent unwanted pregnancy. This model might be captured by the phrase NOT WITHOUT USING SOMETHING. If contraception is viewed as a central program element, several related issues come into play. Because so many teen pregnancies occur soon after the initial sexual experience (Zabin, Kantner, & Zelnik, 1979), it is important to use contraception from the beginning and then to use it consistently thereafter. It is also important for adolescents to avoid or abandon less effective methods, such as withdrawal, in favor of more effective methods. Further, for contraceptive programs to succeed with adolescents from diverse backgrounds, it is important that contraceptive services be readily accessible to teens at low or no cost.

A final program model might be characterized by the phrase I HAVE OTHER THINGS TO DO. Some programs emphasize giving young people alternative life options, whether or not they address sexual behavior and contraception specifically. Programs like Teen Outreach (Philliber & Allen, Chapter 6) include opportunities for involvement and service in the present, as well as a clearer sense of possibilities for the future. Life Options program models give teens "other things to do," building on the premise that adolescents need motivation and opportunities perhaps as much as they need abstinent values or contraceptive knowledge in order to avoid adolescent pregnancy.

Other more specific ways exist of characterizing the prevention models or approaches presented in this book. Table 10.1 summarizes the main features of these programs. It is worth noting that these programs involved teens of all ages, but especially preteens and young teens, as would be expected of primary prevention efforts. The amount of program contact varied from as few as five sessions in about 2 months (Nicholson & Postrado, Chapter 5) to about once per week for an entire school year (Philliber & Allen, Chapter 6). Some programs (Kirby & Waszak, Chapter 8; Zabin, Chapter 7) were available on an open, walk-in basis throughout the junior or senior high school year. Some programs had later "booster" program follow-ups or linked program components that continued after the first year (Nicholson & Postrado, Chapter 5).

Another program dimension that stands out in Table 10.1 has to do with the site of program delivery; most programs are school-based or school-linked, others are agency- or clinic-based. As also summarized in Table 10.1, some program models (Thomas et al., Chapter 2) emphasized education and instilling knowledge, while other programs (Barth et al., Chapter 3; Eisen & Zellman, Chapter 9; Howard & McCabe, Chapter 4) emphasized learning and rehearsing the skills needed to negotiate sexual and contraceptive decisions successfully. Still other programs referred to or directly offered contraceptive services through which young people can translate their decisions into action. Finally, some of these programs attempted to influence basic values about the appropriateness and timing of adolescent sexual activity.

Program Lessons

Several lessons can be learned from the program models presented in this volume, as well as from other recent sources (Hardy & Zabin, in press; Hayes, 1987, Chapter 6; Ooms & Herendeen, 1990; Paikoff & Brooks-Gunn, in press). These basic principles of adolescent pregnancy prevention programs can be summarized as follows.

text continues on page 270

Table 10.1 Selected Features of Programs Designed to Prevent Adolescent Pregnancy

Chapter/ 1st Author	Target Ages	Number of Contacts	Exposure Time	Delivery Site	Targeted Behavior	Competency Focus	Unusual Features
2 Thomas	11-16	10(1 hr)	6-8 wks	schools	sexual intercourse	knowledge, skills	small group tutors
3 Barth	15.4 (mean)	15 classes	3 wks	schools	sexual intercourse, contraceptive use	knowledge, skills, motivation	teacher training and delivery
4 Howard	8th-graders	10 classes	3 months	schools	sexual intercourse, contraceptive use	knowledge, skills	teen leaders
5 Nicholson	12-14	5 (2 hr) to 9 (2 hr) sessions	1-3 yrs	Girls Incorporated centers	sexual intercourse	knowledge, skills, motivation	age-phased program
6 Philliber	teens	1 hour/week minimum	1 school yr	schools	avoid pregnancy, (no deliberate target behavior)	values, skills, motivation	community service involvement

#	Author	Population	Hours	Duration	Setting	Target behaviors	Outcomes	Description
7	Zabin	Jr & Sr high school students	varied, open access	varied 1-3 yrs	schools and clinics near schools	sexual intercourse, contraceptive use	knowledge, skills	combined education; counseling, & medical services
8	Kirby	12-18	varied, open access	varied	health clinic in schools	contraceptive use, other health behaviors	health promotion	provided health care services
9	Eisen	13-19	12-15 hrs in 8 programs	2-3 weeks	work study programs & schools	sexual intercourse, contraceptive use	knowledge, skills, attitudes, motivation	theory-based; small group discussions

1. *The program goals and objectives must be clear and specific.*
Program goals and objectives cannot be achieved unless they are clearly understood. The overall goal might be to prevent or reduce adolescent pregnancies, but more specific objectives need to be clearly stated, understood, and supported by project staff. Consistent with the goal of preventing adolescent pregnancy are the following more specific objectives: help adolescents acquire the social skills to resist sexual pressures, help adolescents personalize the risks of early sexual involvement, and increase adolescents' use of an effective contraceptive at first sexual intercourse. The programs described in this volume had clearly targeted objectives linked to the goal of preventing adolescent pregnancy. Such concrete objectives as these help focus program efforts toward attaining broader goals.

2. *The target population must be relatively young.* Because adolescents begin having sex in their mid teens, on average, and intercourse occurs in the early or even preteens in some populations (Hofferth, Kahn, & Baldwin, 1987; Zabin, Smith, Hirsch, & Hardy, 1986), adolescent pregnancy prevention efforts must start at young ages. This is especially important when the program objectives are to delay the onset of sexual intercourse and/or increase contraceptive use at first intercourse. Some programs in this book (Barth et al., Chapter 3; Howard & McCabe, Chapter 4) were clearly most effective with those who were young and sexually inexperienced. The Girls Incorporated (Chapter 5) evaluators found that pubertal changes in 12-13-year-old girls increased tensions and made communication more difficult, perhaps suggesting that beginning even sooner (maybe ages 9-11) would be better. Similarly, Postponing Sexual Involvement (Chapter 4) has been revised to include a version for fifth-graders. We think that some parallel exists with the fact that drug and smoking prevention programs have found greater success with preteens and with younger than older adolescents (Ellickson & Bell, 1990).

3. *The program should be intensive.* Simply put, the program must be substantial to have a substantial effect. The program must have a level of intensity commensurate with the expectation that it will change adolescent behavior. Both the number of contacts (classes, sessions, or visits) and their duration over time are important in this respect. Some of the programs described in this volume involved participants at least once a week over an entire school year (Philliber & Allen, Chapter 6). It is usually unrealistic to expect a few sessions delivered over several weeks to have any powerful effect months or years later as adolescents

face the sexual and contraceptive decisions that could place them at risk of pregnancy. Exposure to prevention programs generally need to be more frequent and longer lasting in order to bring about substantial and lasting behavior change.

4. *The program should be comprehensive.* Many programs show increases in knowledge, but often without showing behavior change. It is increasingly clear that several components in concert have the greatest promise of producing behavior change. Comprehensive programs usually include some combination of values and of knowledge-based education, decision making and social skills training, reproductive health services, and alternatives or options that enhance motivation to avoid adolescent pregnancy. Most of the programs featured in this book were built on two or more of these components.

5. *The program should consider leveraging parent and peer support.* The fact that the prevention programs described in this book are school- or clinic-based reflects the advantage that programs gain from being based where the target population is concentrated in large numbers and where (as in schools) they are a semicaptive audience. Such programs can attempt to change and take advantage of peer group norms in classrooms (Barth et al., Chapter 3) or in the entire school, especially when using respected teen leaders as role models (Howard & McCabe, Chapter 4). It might be a disadvantage, however, that school- and clinic-based programs only superficially involve, or leave out entirely, the families of adolescents being served. Programs that more strongly encourage or depend on parental involvement are probably more difficult to implement, especially if they are home-based, and they are impossible to implement independent of self-selection factors, as chapter authors have noted. Although the prevention effects of parent involvement are not yet clear, it would seem that leveraging parental involvement, at least in some families, could bring an additional and important source of influence to bear on preventing adolescent pregnancy.

On Evaluation Designs

A variety of program design, monitoring, and evaluation issues were presented in the introductory chapter, and many of these issues have reappeared in individual chapters. The focal point of the evaluations featured in this book, however, has been impact evaluation—drawing conclusions about program effects. Program developers, evaluators, agency professionals, and policymakers all want to know, Did the program work? or For whom did the program work? While other aspects of program evaluation are important, assessing the program's effects— its impact—is fundamentally important. Below we revisit selected impact evaluation issues in light of the preceding chapters. More advanced treatments of impact evaluation issues are widely available in a variety of methodological literatures. (For broader treatments of these issues specifically focused on adolescent pregnancy prevention, see Card, 1989; Philliber, 1989; Zabin & Hirsch, 1988.)

Comparison Groups

To assess the effect of any program, the fundamental question is, Compared to what? A prepost single group comparison (the one-shot case study) simply compares what a group was like after the program (e.g., the level of sexual behavior, contraceptive use, or pregnancy) with what it was like before. Because so many other things, besides the program, could have affected the group during the interim, such a comparison has little or no scientific validity. So a variety of other comparison groups has been devised.

The ideal comparison group is like the treatment group in every way. Because it is difficult, if not impossible, to find such groups naturally occurring, the ideal scientific procedure is to compose comparison groups by randomly assigning who will receive the treatment and who will not. Evaluation designs that use random assignment are sometimes called *true experiments* (Campbell & Stanley, 1963). As shown in Table 10.2, several of the projects in this book created control groups by randomly assigning individuals (Eisen & Zellman, Chapter 9), classes (Barth et al., Chapter 3), or schools (Thomas et al., Chapter 2) to treatment and control groups. A subset of the Teen Outreach evaluation (Philliber & Allen, Chapter 6) also was based on random assignment of individuals.

The other evaluations featured in this book were based on *quasi-experimental* designs, so named because the comparison groups employed were not created by random assignment (see Table 10.2). Using quasi-experimental designs with nonequivalent control groups is a more serious problem in some evaluations than others. The Teen Outreach comparison group was remarkably similar to the treatment group based mostly on the selection strategy of having participants simply choose a peer who would fill out the survey "about like you did." On the other

Table 10.2 Selected Features of Impact Evaluation Research Designs Used to Study Pregnancy Prevention Programs

Chapter/ 1st Author	Number of Cases	Design	Comparison Group	Outcome Measures
2 Thomas	3,290	true experiment	randomly assigned schools	sexual intercourse, contraceptive use, pregnancy
3 Barth	1,033	true experiment	randomly assigned classes	sexual intercourse, contraceptive use
4 Howard	1,005	quasi-experiment	nonparticipants from records of same hospital	sexual intercourse, contraceptive use, pregnancy
5 Nicholson	343	quasi-experiment	nonparticipants self selected	pregnancy, contraceptive use
6 Philliber	1,028	both true and quasi-experiments	comp. students nominated by participants, some random	school suspension, failing, dropout, pregnancy
7 Zabin	3,944	quasi-experiment	students in other, nontreated schools, and in same schools prior to treatment	sexual intercourse, contraceptive use pregnancy
8 Kirby	12 schools; 6 treatment, 6 control	quasi-experiment	students in other, nontreated schools, and in same school prior to treatment	sexual intercourse, contraceptive use
9 Eisen	1,444	true experiment	randomly assigned individuals or classes	sexual intercourse, contraceptive use, pregnancy avoidance

hand, the original Girls Incorporated comparison group was found to be quite different from participants (Nicholson & Postrado, Chapter 5). Consequently, the strategy was followed of ignoring the original comparison group, and instead, subdividing those who were supposed to participate into those who actually did (participants) and those who were eligible to participate but did not (nonparticipants). This strategy produced relatively equivalent groups. Still, selection bias caused by unmeasured variables (e.g., motivation, ability) remains a major threat to inferences about program effects when the groups being compared in any study have come about by a selective process.

Overall, the evaluation designs of the projects featured in this book show an intriguing diversity of comparison groups. These comparison groups reflect the diverse programs being evaluated, the practical problems of research design, and the ingenuity of the evaluators. The group that received the program has been compared to a group that remained unserved by that program (Philliber & Allen, Chapter 6), to those who received the standard curriculum (Barth et al., Chapter 3; Eisen & Zellman, Chapter 9; Thomas et al., Chapter 2), to those who received alternative programs, to those who were eligible to be served but were not (Nicholson & Postrado, Chapter 5), or to those in demographically similar schools nearby (Kirby & Waszak, Chapter 8; Zabin, Chapter 7).

Dosage

Dosage is the amount of each program component the individual participant actually received. Differences in individual dosage or exposure to an effective program will explain variation in participant outcomes. Dosage can also be thought of in terms of program delivery. The difference between the program as planned and as it is delivered is often substantial. Both program directors/managers and evaluators need to know the extent of this discrepancy. Sometimes the argument is made that monitoring dosage levels is unimportant because actual program implementation will always leave some participants less served, either by their own choice or because of problems in program delivery. Dosage variations will be true of program delivery in the real world, but that is not the issue here. The point is that program effects cannot be assessed without knowing how much of the program was actually delivered to and received by individual participants.

It is our view that not enough attention is paid to the extent of exposure to the program. Teen Outreach is a rare exception in which more subtle findings have been revealed by examining dosage of the intervention (Allen, Hoggson, & Philliber, 1990). In designing a prevention program, we encourage evaluators to collect relevant dosage information in the form of class attendance, clinic visits kept, and so on, that could be *individually linked* to the sexual, contraceptive, and pregnancy outcomes of interest. Program effects can be most precisely determined when it is possible to link individual program dosage and outcome measures.

Measurement

Major difficulties can arise in measuring adolescent sexual and contraceptive behavior and pregnancy experience. It is a credit to the programs featured in this book that they all obtained measures of behavior (see Table 10.2), in addition to the more usual measures of knowledge and attitudes. Even more significant is the range of key variables that were measured, including sexual behavior, contraceptive use, pregnancy, and births. These data are sensitive and oftentimes difficult to collect. The McMaster (Thomas et al., Chapter 2) project "private ballot" is a unique technique devised to address parental concerns about asking their children sensitive personal questions, and at the same time not compromising the scientific need to obtain data about adolescent sexual behavior (Mitchell et al., 1991).

Most of the data used to evaluate pregnancy prevention programs rely on adolescents' own reports of their sexual and contraceptive behavior, and it is obvious why this is the case. Like all self-reports of behavior, however, there are several threats to the reliability and validity of these measures. It has been suggested (Rodgers, Billy, & Udry, 1982) that Murphy's laws could be rewritten to include the following axioms of survey research.

1. No matter how well stated the question, someone will be confused by it.
2. No matter how nonsensitive the question, someone will lie to it.
3. No matter what the question, someone will answer without reading it.
4. No matter how interesting a question is or where it is placed, someone will skip it.

In short, some responses to survey questions inevitably will contain confusion, lies, random responses, and missing data. Even more than adults, adolescents might not answer questions correctly because they do not understand them or because they do not know the answers. These problems are endemic in descriptive self-reports about sex, contraception, and pregnancy, and inconsistencies become more evident when multiple responses are obtained over time (see Howard & McCabe, Chapter 4, Appendix).

A common adolescent sexual behavior question is often phrased something like the following: "Have you ever had sex?" or "Have you ever had sexual intercourse?" One threat to obtaining valid answers to this question is confusion—some respondents do not understand what this question means. Some preadolescent and younger adolescent respondents do not understand what sexual intercourse is. This could be called the "cognitive" source of confusion in adolescent self-report data about sexual intercourse. For example, in the second round of a longitudinal survey, one young teen wrote, "In the first questionnaire I said I'd had intercourse, because I thought I had, but now I really have and I know I hadn't before" (Newcomer & Udry, 1988).

A second, and probably more common, source of confusion arises because adolescents who cognitively understand the concept, perhaps even those who have had coitus, are not necessarily familiar with the term "sexual intercourse." This could be called the "semantic" source of confusion and error in adolescent self-reports of sexual experience. Adolescents are more likely to have heard and used four-letter slang terms or phrases like "getting laid" or "going all the way." Carefully constructed surveys, as in most of the projects described in this book, now contain phrases and synonyms for sexual intercourse to reduce the chance for semantic confusion. The following examples are from the 1981 National Survey of Children (NSC), the 1988 National Survey of Family Growth (NSFG), and the 1988 National Survey of Adolescent males (NSAM).

NSC: Q126: "People refer to sexual intercourse in many ways— 'making love,' 'having sex,' or 'going all the way' . . . Have you done this?"

NSFG: C5: "At any time in your life, have you ever had sexual intercourse (that is, made love, had sex, or gone all the way)?"

NSAM: F6: "Have you ever had sexual intercourse with a girl (sometimes this is called 'making love,' 'having sex,' or 'going all the way')?"

In each of the above examples there seems to be little chance that the questions would be misunderstood by those who understand what the concept of sexual intercourse means. A more detailed measurement strategy, developed by Udry and colleagues at North Carolina and also used in the NSAM, is a list of gradually more intimate sexual behaviors culminating in coitus. It is so specific and incremental that few respondents would be confused about the question of whether or not they have ever had sexual intercourse. Sometimes sexual intercourse is defined as "penis in vagina," perhaps further reducing the chance for misunderstandings.

A third potential source of confusion in adolescent self-reports of sexual intercourse arises because no distinction is made between coercion and consent. This could be called the "consent" source of confusion. Among teenagers who have had sexual intercourse are those who have done so willingly and those who have been involved in incest or who have been otherwise pressured, coerced, or raped. A respondent might report having had sexual intercourse when her only experience was involuntary. Or, conversely, a young woman who had been sexually victimized by incest or rape might answer that she had never had sexual intercourse (willingly). Hence the confusion and potential error in measurement.

One attempt to disentangle this source of confusion is the 1987 National Survey of Children (NSC), which contained the following questions.

M33: "Was there ever a time when you were forced to have sex against your will, or were raped?"

M34: "How old were you the first time this happened?"

M35: "Have you ever (voluntarily) had sexual intercourse with someone of the opposite sex?"

In these 1987 NSC data, about 5% of the respondents answered yes to question M33—that they were forced to have sex against their will (Moore, Nord, & Peterson, 1989). Some confusion probably exists among respondents who have been forced to have sex about whether they should answer yes or no to a general question about whether they have ever had sexual intercourse.

In summary, valid and reliable measures of sexual behavior, contraceptive use, and pregnancy are oftentimes difficult to obtain, but these data are essential to evaluate adolescent pregnancy programs. Parental consent, question wording, and nonvoluntary sexual experiences should all be considered in conducting program evaluation.

Records

Some program evaluations (Kirby & Waszak, Chapter 8; Thomas et al., Chapter 2; Zabin, Chapter 7) are based on records, in addition to self-reports of behavior. A strength of the McMaster program (Thomas et al., Chapter 2) is the potential to use the Ontario health records of fertility-related medical events to validate teen self-reports of pregnancy in the control and treatment groups. This is unusual because the provincial health records are complete for virtually all female participants. These record data might also be useful to find out missing information about cases lost to follow-up, in addition to corroborating self-reports, as was done in the Grady Hospital study (Howard & McCabe, Chapter 4).

In self reports of sexual behavior the more sensitive or threatening the question, the greater the probability that respondents will lie, leave the question unanswered, or give inconsistent responses when asked the same question more than once (Rodgers et al., 1982). External records, however, often are lacking or are not adequate to the task of checking for congruence with the self-report of sexual intercourse. STDs and pregnancy are events for which records are kept, and they imply the occurrence of sexual intercourse, but intercourse does not necessarily result in these events. Intercourse is necessary but not sufficient to produce these recorded events, so the records alone will underestimate the incidence of sexual intercourse.

In the Hopkins study (Zabin, Chapter 7) records and logs meticulously kept by staff improved the ability of the evaluators to measure program utilization. Clinic forms, especially designed to augment the research component, were more reliable sources of information than standard program forms would have been.

Statistical Controls

Groups not composed by random assignment usually differ in some systematic way that is related to how they came to be, (a "selection" effect), and the way(s) that groups differ can easily be mistaken for program effects. Because quasi-experiments rely on the comparison of preexisting groups, it is very important to try to rule out selection bias as a threat to the integrity of the comparisons. In the evaluations featured in this book, it is noteworthy that the researchers attempted to make treatment and comparison groups equivalent (except for their exposure to the program) in several ingenious ways. This is usually done by testing for group differences on a variety of non-outcome variables, and then statistically adjusting the outcome data to compensate for the effects of those variables by which the groups have been found to differ. Another way of saying this is that the evaluator should search for and identify variables on which the groups differ and then make statistical adjustments to examine *net* treatment effects on the outcomes after the effects of these other variables have been removed. The examination of day versus after-school treatments in Teen Outreach (Philliber & Allen, Chapter 6) as a proxy for student motivation is conceptually interesting in this regard.

Another important way of assuring equivalent group comparisons is to obtain baseline measures of the outcomes so that compensation for initial group differences can be made. This can be done statistically by adjusting for preexisting baseline differences between groups in the outcomes being studied. Sometimes, even with random assignment, groups will differ initially on an outcome variable of central interest to the evaluators. This was true, for example, of the McMaster study (Thomas et al., Chapter 2), in which more of the treatment group males began the study having had sexual intercourse than their counterparts in control schools. An alternative way of analyzing these kinds of data, in which the experimental and comparison groups are both measured at two points in time, is to focus on comparing the amount of change (e.g., Zabin, Chapter 7), instead of pretest and posttest absolute values.

On Adolescent Development

The integration of basic developmental knowledge into the delivery of prevention programs and services for adolescents is a recent phenomenon (Paikoff & Brooks-Gunn, in press). Much information exists regarding basic processes of adolescent development that can inform pregnancy prevention programs; likewise, the findings of program evaluation can often provide insights about basic developmental processes. For example, age-linked findings on the Teen Outreach program published elsewhere (Allen, Hoggson, & Philliber, 1990) suggest that classroom components of the program are more effective for young adolescents than for older adolescents. In contrast, the volunteer work component was more effective for older adolescents than for younger adolescents. These findings provide avenues for basic researchers to explore different contextual effects across the adolescent years.

In addition to the Teen Outreach findings with developmental implications, the Girls Incorporated program devised a series of prevention strategies for different-aged adolescents. This program provides an elegant explication of the progression of adolescent needs with regard to pregnancy, from initial programs emphasizing parent-adolescent communication and assertiveness skills to later needs regarding future plans and provision of health and contraceptive services.

Other programs address issues of variation across the adolescent participants on dimensions other than age. For example, both the Eisen and Zellman and the Howard and McCabe chapters discuss variation as a function of sexual experience. In addition, these authors (and Thomas et al., Chapter 2) discuss variation in program effectiveness by gender. While initial programs were conducted and evaluated for all adolescents, these results suggest the importance of focusing programs on particular groups of adolescents. In particular, it seems important to address the unique needs of sexually active adolescents relative to youth who have not yet become sexually active (Chase-Lansdale, Brooks-Gunn, & Paikoff, 1991). Postponing sexual involvement is a more appropriate message for adolescents who have not yet had sexual intercourse. Conversely, sexually experienced adolescents might be less likely to respond to programs that emphasize JUST SAY NO, or JUST SAY NOT YET; for these teens, programs emphasizing effective contraceptive use (NOT WITHOUT USING SOMETHING) and/or life options (I HAVE OTHER THINGS TO DO) might be more effective approaches.

In addition to the issues raised by the chapters in this volume, a number of developmental issues must be considered in future basic and evaluation research on pregnancy prevention, and on healthy teenage sexual development more generally (Brooks-Gunn & Paikoff, in press; Hardy & Zabin, in press; Paikoff & Brooks-Gunn, in press; Zabin, 1990). We also believe research on sociocultural factors, including the media, and on the basic social and cognitive processes (e.g., peer and parent networks, decision-making strategies) are important but neglected concerns. Research is needed to document basic processes of adolescent social and cognitive growth and to link these processes over time to adolescents' social and sexual development. Knowledge about the microlevel processes that facilitate or inhibit early sexual activity and contraceptive non-use could add to our understanding of adolescent development, as well as point out important dimensions that should be taken into account in developing prevention programs.

In short, the interface between basic developmental and program evaluation research represents an exciting new arena for investigators from a variety of disciplines. Researchers studying these issues have the potential of increasing our knowledge regarding adolescent development, as well as enhancing programs and policies that may facilitate more optimal developmental processes for a wider range of adolescents.

Conclusions

It is difficult to design and implement programs that change human behavior. It is no less difficult to evaluate such programs so that clear conclusions can be drawn about their effects. Partly because of the nature of sexual and contraceptive behaviors, and partly because of the age group involved, adolescent pregnancy prevention programs face especially difficult challenges.

For example, some of the programs presented in this book seek to postpone adolescent sexual involvement in a culture that glamorizes sexual behavior. Adolescents on their way toward gaining adult privileges are not easily convinced that they should wait for anything (least of all the physical pleasures of sex), especially when its positive benefits are so alluringly portrayed. The pleasurable aspects of sexual activity for the individual and the couple, pressures and status in their peer group, and social expectations portrayed in the larger culture, are in constant tension with the prevention messages that it would be best for teenagers to postpone having sexual intercourse.

Different obstacles hinder the effectiveness of pregnancy prevention programs that emphasize the use of contraception. The young adolescent has to understand that sexual intercourse leads to pregnancy and that contraceptives can prevent conception. If knowledge and the requisite motivation to avoid becoming pregnant exist, the risk of pregnancy must be personalized to the extent that specific contraceptive plans are made. To contracept effectively, the adolescent must recognize and accept his/her sexuality, anticipate future sexual activity, and plan ahead. Then the social, economic, and psychic costs of obtaining and using contraception must be outweighed by the perceived risks and costs of pregnancy. The use of contraceptives might need to be negotiated with the partner. Further, this kind of complex decision-making process must be repeated regularly because most methods of contraception require action on a daily basis or with every act of sex. Pregnancy avoidance is sometimes difficult for adults, and it should not be surprising that many teens find themselves faced with unintended pregnancies.

Another difficulty for adolescent pregnancy prevention programs is that the negative consequences of early sexual behavior, pregnancy, and parenthood do not seem real to some adolescents, though female adolescent clients of family planning clinics in one study did evaluate adolescent pregnancy and childbirth as negative events, relative to later pregnancy and childbirth (Paikoff, 1990). But for those who are young and healthy, threats to health and future well-being might seem too remote to be easily personalized (Weinstein, 1980). Scare tactics about negative consequences appear to have little effect. To some extent this problem is inherent in human nature, exacerbated perhaps by the adolescent perception of personal invulnerability, the personal fable that "it won't happen to me." (See Furby & Beyth-Marom, in press, for a discussion of how adolescents' risk perceptions might differ from adults' perceptions, given their different developmental concerns.)

In the face of such obstacles, adolescent pregnancy prevention programs must be ingeniously planned, intensively implemented, and carefully evaluated. The programs reviewed in this book have made it clear that no simple solution to preventing adolescent pregnancy exists. Providing knowledge (JUST SAY KNOW) and encouragement for teenagers to wait (JUST SAY NO or NOT YET), and encouraging or dispensing contraceptives (JUST SAY NOT WITHOUT USING SOMETHING) are fundamental approaches. Postponing sexual intercourse and contraceptive approaches are not mutually exclusive: A program that provides contraceptives can also postpone the onset of sexual intercourse as has been demonstrated here (Zabin, Chapter 7). Furthermore, these strategies can be made more effective by increasing motivation and skills to avoid pregnancy and by helping teens understand that they could have much to gain by avoiding pregnancy until they are older (I HAVE OTHER THINGS TO DO). The projects reviewed here provide evidence that programs that are intensive and comprehensive can bring about modest reductions in adolescent pregnancy and parenthood.

References

Allen, J., Hoggson, N., & Philliber, S. (1990). School-based prevention of teenage pregnancy and school dropout: Process evaluation of the national replication of the Teen Outreach Program. *American Journal of Community Psychology, 18,* 505-524.

Brooks-Gunn, J., & Paikoff, R. L. (in press). Sex is a gamble, kissing is a game: Adolescent sexuality and health promotion. In S. P. Millstein, A. Petersen, & E. Nightingale (Eds.), *Promotion of health behavior in adolescence.* New York: Carnegie Corp.

Campbell, D. T., & Stanley, J. C. (1963). *Experimental and quasi-experimental designs for research.* Chicago: Rand McNally.

Card, J. J. (1989). *Evaluating programs aimed at preventing teenage pregnancies.* Palo Alto, CA: Sociometrics Corp.

Chase-Lansdale, P. L., Brooks-Gunn, J., & Paikoff, R. L. (1991). *Research and programs for adolescent mothers: Missing links and future promises.*

Ellickson, P. L., & Bell, R. M. (1990). Drug prevention in junior high: A multi-site longitudinal test. *Science, 247,* 1299-1305.

Furby, L., & Beyth-Marom, R. (in press). Risk-taking in adolescence: A decision-making perspective. *Developmental Review.*

Hardy, J., & Zabin, L. S. (in press). *Adolescent pregnancy in an urban environment.* Baltimore and Washington, DC: Williams and Wilkens and the Urban Institute.

Hayes, C. D. (1987). *Risking the future: Adolescent sexuality, pregnancy, and childbearing* (Vol. I). Washington, DC: National Academy of Sciences Press.

Hofferth, S. L., Kahn, J. R., & Baldwin, W. (1987). Premarital sexual activity among U.S. teenage women over the past three decades. *Family Planning Perspectives, 19,* 46-53.

Mitchell, A., Thomas, H., Devlin, C., Goldsmith, C., Singer, J., Watters, D., & Marlow (1991). *A controlled trial of an educational program to prevent adolescent pregnancy.* Manuscript submitted for publication.

Moore, K. A., Nord, C. W., & Peterson, J. L. (1989). Nonvoluntary sexual activity among adolescents. *Family Planning Perspectives, 21,* 110-114.

Newcomer, S., & Udry, J. R. (1988). Adolescents' honesty in a survey of sexual behavior. *Journal of Adolescent Research, 3,* 419-423.

Ooms, T., & Herendeen, L. (1990). *Teenage pregnancy prevention programs: What have we learned?* Washington, DC: The Family Impact Seminar.

Paikoff, R. L. (1990). Attitudes toward consequences of pregnancy in young women attending a family planning clinic. *Journal of Adolescent Research, 5*(4), 467-484.

Paikoff, R. L., & Brooks-Gunn, J. (in press). Do parent-child relationships change during puberty? *Psychological Bulletin.*

Philliber, S. (1989). Designing and conducting impact evaluations of adolescent pregnancy prevention programs. In J. J. Card (Ed.), *Evaluating programs aimed at preventing teenage pregnancies* (pp. 41-68). Palo Alto, CA: Sociometrics Corp.

Rodgers, J. L., Billy, J. O. G., & Udry, J. R. (1982). The rescission of behaviors: Inconsistent responses in adolescent sexuality data. *Social Science Research, 11,* 280-296.

Stout, J. W., & Rivara, F. P. (1989). Schools and sex education: Does it work? *Pediatrics, 83*(3), 375-379.

Weinstein, N. D. (1980). Unrealistic optimism about future life events. *Journal of Personality and Social Psychology, 39,* 800-820.

Zabin, L. S. (1990). Adolescent pregnancy and early sexual onset. In B. B. Lahey & A. E. Kazdin (Eds.), *Advances in clinical child psychology* (Vol. 13) (pp. 247-282). New York: Plenum.

Zabin, L. S., & Hirsch, M. B. (1988). *Evaluation of pregnancy prevention programs in the school context.* Lexington, MA: Lexington.

Zabin, L. S., Kantner, J. F., & Zelnik, M. (1979). The risk of adolescent pregnancy in the first months of intercourse. *Family Planning Perspectives, 11*(4), 215-222.

Zabin, L. S., Smith, E. A., Hirsch, M. B., & Hardy, J. B. (1986). Ages of physical maturation and first intercourse in black teenage males and females. *Demography, 23,* 595-605.

Index

Abstinence. *See* Sexual abstinence
Adolescent childbearing, 3
Adolescent development:
  basic research needs, 280
  decision making, 85, 114
  implications for prevention program design 10, 158, 227, 279-280
Adolescent pregnancy:
  defining the problem, 6
  high risk population, 9
  outcome variable, 149, 173, 256
  rates in Canada, 28
  recommendations for prevention programs, 270-271. *See also* Prevention programs
Age, for pregnancy prevention, 105, 270. *See also* Sexual intercourse, Age of onset
AIDS, 189-190, 197
Anonymity of self report, 176
Assertiveness skills, 133. *See also* Social Skills Training
Atlanta. *See* Postponing Sexual Involvement Program
Attitudes, 168
Attrition, 146, 161, 226
  differences between those who dropout and remain, 60-61, 244-246

ways of reducing, 60. *See also* Retention

Baltimore. *See* Johns Hopkins Adolescent Pregnancy Prevention Program
Behavioral outcomes, 69, 145, 275
Birth control pills, 206, 215

California. *See* Reducing the Risk Program
Canada. *See* McMaster Teen Program
Case management, 157
Clinic. *See* School-based clinic
Communication. *See* parent-child communication
Community service, 139-142
Comparison groups:
  chosen by participants "someone like you", 143
  cities, 274, 135
  equivalence, 89-90, 118, 272
  participants versus nonparticipants, 135
  random assignment, 272
  schools, 160, 163, 192-193, 196
  statistical adjustments for, 196
  test for selection bias, 147-148
  "usual program" approach, 231

About the Editors

Josefina J. Card received her Ph.D. in Social Psychology from Carne-gie-Mellon University in 1971. The first decade of her career was spent at the American Institutes for Research (AIR), where she directed over two dozen research projects on the antecedents and consequences of teenage pregnancy, military and war service, the international brain drain, and other social problems; and pursued implications of her findings for social policy and for personal decision making. Since founding Sociometrics in 1983, she has expanded on the work begun at AIR and pioneered in demonstrating the implications of emergent microcomputer technology for how social science research is conducted and disseminated. She has also worked to facilitate the scientific evaluation of social intervention programs. She serves frequently on federal advisory committees.

Brent C. Miller received his Ph.D. in Family Sociology from the University of Minnesota in 1975. Currently, he is Professor and Acting Head in the Department of Family and Human Development at Utah State University. He has been a member and chair of several national peer review and advisory panels for the National Institute of Child Health and Human Development and for the Office of Adolescent Pregnancy Programs. He has been the Publications Vice President and Program Chair for the National Council on Family Relations, and in 1991-1992 he became President of NCFR. He publishes widely about

289

marriage and family topics and about adolescent pregnancy-related issues.

Roberta L. Paikoff is Assistant Professor of Psychology in the Institute for Juvenile Research at the University of Illinios at Chicago. She received her B.S. from Cornell University in Human Development and Family Studies, and her Ph.D. in Child Psychology from the Institute of Child Development at the University of Minnesota. In addition, she has completed post-doctoral fellowships at the Hebrew University of Jerusalem and at the Educational Testing Service. Her major research interests are in the area of understanding the interplay among developmental processes during the transitions into and out of adolescence, and their implications for interventive and preventive programs working with youth and families.

James L. Peterson received his Ph.D. in Sociology from the University of Chicago in 1972. He served for 6 years as Study Director at the Institute for Survey Research at Temple University, where he directed over 20 studies including program evaluations involving data collection from the field. At the Social Science Research Council's Social Indicators Center he directed projects to assess the research potential of National Longitudinal Surveys of Labor Market Experience. He served for 10 years as Senior Research Associate and then Associate Director at Child Trends, Inc., a research firm devoted to improving the scope and quality of statistics on children's conditions. Since coming to Sociometrics in 1989, he has directed the Data Resources Program of the National Institute of Justice. He has particular expertise in computers and statistical software that are essential for the analysis of social science data.

About the Contributors

Joseph P. Allen is currently an Assistant Professor in the Department of Psychology at the University of Virginia. He received his Ph.D. from Yale University in Clinical/Community Psychology and worked as a Research Fellow at Harvard Medical School before moving to Virginia. His research focuses on factors influencing social development and the occurrence of serious problem behaviors in adolescence. In addition to evaluating programs serving at-risk adolescents, he is conducting basic research on the relationship of adolescent-parent interaction styles to the development of social competence and secure attachments in adolescence and beyond.

Richard P. Barth is Professor at the School of Social Welfare, University of California at Berkeley. He is the Associate Director of the Family Welfare Research Group and Principal Investigator of Berkeley's National Child Welfare Research Center funded by the United States DHHS. His research on adolescent pregnancy dates back to his development and evaluation of coping skills training for adolescent parents in the early 1980s and has included numerous investigations of services to adolescent parents. He is on the editorial board of *Journal of Adolescent Research, Social Work in Education,* and *Children and Youth Services Review.* He has been a Fulbright Scholar, a Lois and Samuel

292 About the Contributors

Silberman Senior Faculty Fellow, and winner of the Frank Bruel Prize of the University of Chicago for excellence in child welfare scholarship.

M. Corinne Devlin is currently a Professor of Obstetrics and Gynecology in the Faculty of Health Sciences at McMaster University, Hamilton, Ontario, Canada. Complementing clinical practices in Obstetrics and Gynecology are educational research interests focused in all aspects of women's health care. Special interests include sex education in the school systems, women in the middle years, and sex-related health care generally.

Marvin Eisen is Principal Research Scientist at Social Research Applications in Los Altos, California. His research interests are in adolescent sexuality decision making, children's mental health, and evaluation of primary prevention programs. He is currently directing a private foundation-funded evaluation network that provides technical assistance to teen pregnancy programs.

Joyce V. Fetro is the Health Education Curriculum Specialist for the San Francisco Unified School District. She received her doctoral degree in Health Education from Southern Illinois University with an emphasis on instrument development, research methods, and evalution. Her experience in health education spans 20 years, including 13 years as a middle school teacher, 2 years as a university instructor, and 3 years conducting research and evaluation studies related to pregnancy prevention, substance use prevention, and HIV/AIDS prevention programs. Currently, she is responsible for planning and implementing comprehensive school health education in the San Francisco Unified School District.

Charlie H. Goldsmith is currently a Professor of Biostatistics in the Department of Clinical Epidemiology and Biostatistics at McMaster University, Hamilton, Ontario, Canada. He has interests in experimental design and data analysis as applied to important health problems. He is involved in a variety of community-based studies, focusing on smoking cessation, teenage pregnancy, musculoskeletal problems, and evaluation of therapies. His interests extend to pharmacoepidemiology as it applies to therapeutic measures. These measures help evaluate drugs, devices, procedures, and legislation. He has been a statistical consultant for a variety of pharmaceutical companies, environmental pollution measurement companies, and a variety of academic colleagues in the university community.

Catherine G. Greeno received her Ph.D. in Psychology from Stanford University in 1989. Since graduating she has been a Fellow at the Stanford Center for Research in Disease Prevention and a Research Associate for NationalNet, a teen pregnancy impact evaluation technical assistance program. Her primary interests are in psychosocial predictors of health outcomes, especially as they affect women. She has presented research nationally and is the author of a number of reports and articles.

Marion Howard is a Professor in the Department of Gynecology and Obstetrics at the School of Medicine at Emory University in Atlanta, Georgia. She also directs the Emory University/Grady Hospital Teen Services Program, a family planning program for young teenagers at Grady Memorial Hospital. Previously she was Director of the Consortium on Early Childbearing and Childrearing in Washington, DC. She has also held appointments in the Department of Epidemiology and Public Health at Yale University and the Departments of Sociology and Health Care Administration at George Washington University.

Douglas Kirby Ph. D., is Director of Research at ETR Associates and formerly Director of Research at the Center for Population Options. He has directed nationwide studies of adolescent sexual behavior, sexuality education programs, direct mailings of STD/AIDS pamphlets to adolescent males, and school-based clinics. He has authored or coauthored numerous volumes, articles, and chapters both on these programs and on methods of evaluating them. Currently he is evaluating comprehensive aids and programs for teenage mothers.

Nancy Leland received her Ph.D. in 1990 at the University of California, Berkeley, in Social Welfare and her M.S.W. and M.P.H. in 1986 at the University of Minnesota. She is currently an Assistant Professor with the School of Public Health, Maternal and Child Health Major at the University of Minnesota. Her current research includes community interventions to reduce adolescent pregnancy in rural areas, childhood injuries, and birth outcomes and health care utilization among adolescent Native Americans.

Judith A. McCabe, M.P.H., is currently a Research Associate with the Colorado Trust, a philanthropic foundation in Denver, Colorado. She has worked in the public and private nonprofit health sector since 1978, focusing primarily on materal and child health and adolescent fertility related issues. Until 1989 she worked in the south eastern United States serving as a program and evaluation consultant. She is also completing a doctorate in medical anthropology through the University of North Carolina at Chapel Hill.

Alba Mitchell is an Associate Professor in the School of Nursing and an Associate Member of the Department of Clinical Epidemiology and Biostatistics at McMaster University in Hamilton, Ontario, Canada. She recently has received funding to study high-risk birth control clinic attenders. As part of her doctoral studies, she is planning to conduct a meta-analysis of evaluation of pregnancy prevention interventions. Her other research interests include development and evaluation of expanded nursing roles and development and validation of quality of life and patient/family satisfaction with care instruments.

Heather Johnston Nicholson is Director of the Girls Incorporated (formerly Girls Clubs of America) National Resource Center in Indianapolis, Indiana. She is principal investigator of that organization's Preventing Adolescent Pregnancy project and of a project to sustain girls' participation in math, science, and technology. She is the author of *Facts and Reflections on Female Adolescent Sexuality,* a review of the literature published by Girls Clubs of America in 1982, and of other monographs, articles, and curriculum materials on girls and young women. She holds a bachelor's degree with honors from Chatham College, a master's degree from the State University of New York at Buffalo, and a Ph.D. from the University of Iowa, all in political science.

Susan Philliber is currently a senior partner at Philliber Research Associates and a Research Professor at the State University of New York, College at New Paltz. Before assuming these positions she was Director of the Social Science Research Unit of the Center for Population and Family Health at Columbia University. She received her Ph.D. in Sociology/Demography from Florida State University. Her research has centered on reproductive health issues, including teen pregnancy, and she has had an extensive career in program evaluation.

Leticia T. Postrado is Research Associate at the Girls Incorporated National Resource Center in Indianapolis, Indiana. She holds a Ph.D. in Sociology from Purdue University and a master's degree in Statistics and Methods of Research. Her primary research interest is in female adolescent fertility and sexuality, and she has coauthored a monograph on this topic published by De La Salle University Research Center, Manila, Philippines. Her current research focuses on evaluation of the Girls Incorporated Preventing Adolescent Pregnancy Program.

Joel Singer is an Assistant Professor in the Department of Health Care and Epidemiology at the University of British Columbia, Canada. He also acts as the Co-Director of the Canadian HIV Trials Network Data and Analysis Center, which is responsible for the data management and analytical aspects of Canadian-based multicenter clinical trials of new treatments for HIV infection. He has spent more than 10 years collaborating on trials in diverse areas, including the evaluation of new cardiac and antithrombotic drugs, the construction and evaluation of disease-specific quality-of-life instruments, the assessment of diagnostic tools, and in the investigation of behavioral interventions for disease prevention and health promotion.

B. Helen Thomas is an Assistant Professor in the School of Nursing at McMaster University in Hamilton, Ontario, Canada. She is also a Clinical Nurse Consultant with the Hamilton-Wentworth Department of Public Health Services. She has recently completed a national survey of the knowledge and attitudes of health professionals toward childhood sexually transmitted diseases and its implications for child sexual abuse. Her current research activities and interests include adolescent health (including sexuality), emotional and behavioral disorders in children and youth, and measuring the effectiveness of interventions with abusive and neglecting families.

Cindy Waszak is Research Associate at Family Health International. Formerly she was the Research Director at the Center for Population Options (CPO). She is past Chair of the American Public Health Association Task Force on Adolescent Pregnancy. She has a Ph.D. in Social Psychology from the University of North Carolina at Chapel Hill.

Derek Watters was a Computer Data Manager at McMaster University, Hamiton, Ontario, Canada, in the Department of Clinical Epidemiology and Biostatistics while working on the McMaster Teen Project. He is currently a Research Associate in the School of Nursing at McMaster University, employed as the Research Coordinator for the McMaster-Aga Khan-CIDA Project.

Laurie Schwab Zabin is Associate Professor of Population Dynamics, Johns Hopkins School of Public Health. Her research focuses at the intersection of medicine and social sciences in reproductive health, including contraception, abortion, sterilization, and adolescent sexual behavior. She has been Chair of the Board of the Alan Guttmacher Institute and the Population and Family Planning Section of the American Public Health Association on whose Governing Council she serves. She served on the National Academy of Sciences Committee on the Behavioral Science of AIDS, is on the Technical Advisory Group of the Women and AIDS program, International Center for Research on Women, and is Consultant for Research to the Francis Scott Key Medical Center's Project on Addiction and Pregnancy. Her primary interest, however, has been exploring the reality of adolescent pregnancy, and its implications for policy and program.

Gail L. Zellman is a research psychologist at the RAND Corporation, Santa Monica, California, and practices clincial psychology in Los Angeles. Her research spans a broad range of youth policy issues, including education for teenage mothers, the prevention of teenage pregnancy, delinquency and drug abuse prevention, and child abuse. In her clinical work, she has treated victims of child abuse and their families and has worked with families and their teenage children on issues of adolescent sexual behavior.